FROM PORTLAND'S PALATE

A Collection of Recipes from the City of Roses

THE JUNIOR LEAGUE OF PORTLAND, OREGON

Illustration

JENNIFER WINSHIP MARK

Design

PATRICIA ZAHLER

Editors

JANE FISHER

LYNDA VULLES GEBHARDT

KAREN HENKHAUS

ANNE MANGAN

BRIDGET OTTO

KITTY WHEELER

Writers

MEGAN DAVIS

KAREN HENKHAUS

ANNE MANGAN

BECKY MOORE

KITTY WHEELER

Indexing

JULIE KAWABATA

The Junior League of Portland, Oregon is an organization of women committed to promoting voluntarism and to improving the community through the effective action and leadership of trained volunteers. Its purpose is exclusively educational and charitable.

Library of Congress Catalog Card Number 92-71488

ISBN 0-9632525-1-8

Printing: Graphic Arts Center

First printing, July 1992, 20,000

Second printing, October 1992, 20,000

Color Separations: Wy'East Color

Imagesetting: Burian Imagesetting

Portland, Oregon

To order additional copies of

FROM PORTLAND'S PALATE,

use the order blank provided in the back of the book.

Remember to follow proper procedures for health and safety in selecting, handling, preparing and storing your ingredients and prepared foods. Caution is particularly important when using raw ingredients (especially eggs) and foods susceptible to quick spoilage.

TABLE OF CONTENTS

Welcome to Portland's Palate, a collection of recipes carefully culled to present Portland's unique blend of cosmopolitan flair and small-city friendliness.

A river city, Portland is ideally situated to take advantage of the region's gourmet riches—Columbia River salmon, fruits and berries from the Willamette Valley, Dungeness crab caught in Pacific Ocean waters, Tillamook County cheese and crisp Hood River apples. The burgeoning wine and micro-brewery industries likewise enhance edible delicacies. All thrive within a wooden spoon's reach of the City of Roses, renowned for its spectacular parks and gardens.

Whether it's a festive holiday gathering, a private hilltop picnic or a backyard barbecue, Portlanders celebrate with warmth and verve. Seasoning Portland's palate are ethnic specialities and a richness of food traditions. Both reflect the essence of Portland living.

The Junior League of Portland proudly presents this recipe collection, highlighted by the commissioned illustrations of Portland artist Jennifer Winship Mark. Proceeds from the sale of this cookbook will benefit the community through the Junior League's many projects.

APPETIZERS & BEVERAGES

RED, WHITE AND BLUE

Is there anything finer than a summertime sail on the cool waters of the Willamette River? A blue sky, breezes, the soaring spans of Portland's eleven bridges, and the stunning white of snow-capped Mt. Hood (yes, even in summer!) can quench any boat lover's thirst for beauty.

Beauty is evident along the riverside as well, where Portland's nine-to-fivers trade in ties and heels for tennis shoes and picnic baskets at Tom McCall Waterfront Park. The creation of this park illustrates the true Portland spirit; the city replaced a four-lane expressway with a greenway. Scrambling to portside or starboard—or watching someone else do it—is appetite-whetting work. PESTO TORTE, PATÉ PRESTO and NORTHWEST SPREAD fill the bill. These delicacies can double as the main course.

Preserving Portland's landscape is a key element of Junior League projects. Marquam Hill Nature Park, the Oregon Preservation Resource Center and the Urban Tour Group are some of the League's past activities.

ROASTED RED PEPPER REVIEW

- *6 to 8 roasted red peppers (See note.)*
- *1 1/2 tablespoons garlic (5 cloves), minced and divided*
- *Freshly-ground pepper*
- *2 bunches fresh basil, chopped*
- *1/4 teaspoon dried oregano*
- *1 cup olive oil, divided*
- *2 tablespoons balsamic vinegar*
- *1 loaf Italian bread, sliced*

Cut peppers into lengthwise strips and then in half. Be sure to remove all seeds. Place in the bottom of a shallow dish.

In a large bowl, combine 1 tablespoon minced garlic, pepper, basil and oregano. Whisk in 1/2 cup of the olive oil and balsamic vinegar. Pour over sliced peppers and marinate for 3 to 4 hours or overnight.

Preheat oven to 500 degrees.

To make garlic toast, cut bread into thin slices. Add remaining garlic to remaining olive oil and brush over tops of bread. Place slices on baking sheet and broil until browned, approximately 3 to 4 minutes.

Serve peppers on top of toast. Garnish with fresh basil or flowers.

NOTHING CHANGES AS DRAMATICALLY AS A PEPPER AFTER IT'S ROASTED; THE FLAVOR IS RICH AND WONDERFUL.

MARINATE:
3 to 4 hours or overnight

TEMPERATURE:
Preheat 500 degrees

BAKE:
3 to 4 minutes

YIELD:
8 to 10 servings

NOTES:
To roast peppers, broil each side until charred. Remove from oven and place in a paper bag and close the bag. Allow peppers to steam in bag and cool. Charred skin will peel away easily .

BLACK OLIVE CANAPÉS

- *1 1/2 cups black olives, minced*
- *1/2 cup mayonnaise*
- *2 tablespoons onion, minced*
- *1/4 teaspoon curry powder*
- *1 cup sharp Cheddar cheese, grated*
- *1 baguette*

Preheat broiler to 500 degrees.

In a medium bowl, combine olives, mayonnaise, onion, curry powder and grated cheese. Cut baguette in half and spread mixture on top of both sides.

Place baguette under pre-heated broiler 2 inches from heat and broil for 3 to 4 minutes or until spread is bubbly and golden. Remove, cut baguette into serving-size pieces and serve.

TEMPERATURE:
Preheat 500 degrees

BAKE:
3 to 4 minutes

YIELD:
10 servings

HERBED MUSHROOM TERRINE

TEMPERATURE:
Preheat 400 degrees

BAKE:
1 hour and 30 minutes

YIELD:
12 to 15 servings

NOTES:
Can add 1/4 cup sherry to mushroom mixture just before stirring in breadcrumbs and herbs. Garnish serving plate with parsley or other leafy greens.

1/4 cup butter (1/2 cube)
1/3 cup onion, finely chopped
1/3 cup celery, finely chopped
1 pound fresh mushrooms, cleaned and finely chopped
2 eggs
1 (3-ounce) package cream cheese, room temperature
3/4 cup fine dried bread crumbs
1 teaspoon salt
1/2 teaspoon dried basil
1/4 teaspoon dried rosemary
1/4 teaspoon dried oregano
1/8 teaspoon freshly-ground black pepper
1/4 cup dry sherry (optional)

Preheat oven to 400 degrees.

Butter a 7 x 4 x 2-inch loaf pan. Cover long sides and bottom of pan with waxed paper, leaving a 1 1/2-inch strip of waxed paper overhanging the long sides of pan.

In a large saucepan over medium heat, melt butter. Add onion and celery and sauté until limp, about 5 minutes. Add chopped mushrooms and stir together. Set aside.

In a mixing bowl, beat eggs and cream cheese until smooth. Stir into mushroom mixture. Add bread crumbs, salt, basil, rosemary, oregano and black pepper.

Spoon mushroom mixture evenly into prepared pan. Cover with foil.

Bake in a 400-degree oven until firm, approximately 1 1/2 hours.

Remove from oven and cool in pan until lukewarm. Remove from pan, using waxed paper overhang to lift terrine out of pan. Place on serving plate and serve at room temperature with sliced bread or crackers.

BLUE CHEESE SPREAD

CAN BE SERVED AS A HOT DIP OR A COLD SPREAD.

- 1 *(8-ounce) package cream cheese, room temperature*
- 4 *ounces blue cheese*
- 1/3 *cup milk or half and half*
- 3 *tablespoons green onion, finely chopped*
- 1/4 *teaspoon dry mustard*
- *Dash of red pepper sauce*
- 8 to 9 *slices lean bacon, diced into 1/2 -inch pieces*
- 2 *large garlic cloves, minced*
- 1/4 *cup slivered almonds, toasted*
- *Sliced French bread, crackers or thinly-sliced green apples*

Preheat oven to 350 degrees.

In a medium bowl, combine cheeses. Pour in milk and blend thoroughly. Stir in green onion, mustard and red pepper sauce. Set aside.

In a sauté pan, brown bacon and garlic, being careful not to burn garlic. Drain well and add to cheese mixture. Pour into an ovenproof serving dish, sprinkle with almonds, and bake at 350 degrees for 25 minutes. Serve with green apples, French bread or crackers. Garnish with parsley sprigs.

TEMPERATURE:
Preheat 350 degrees

BAKE:
25 minutes

YIELD:
8 servings

NOTES:
If you are serving this as a cold spread, add almonds at the last minute.

PARMESAN PUFFS

- 1 *cup whole milk*
- 1/2 *cup unsalted butter (1 cube)*
- 1 *teaspoon salt*
- 1 *cup all-purpose flour*
- 5 *eggs, divided*
- 1 1/2 *cups freshly-grated Parmesan cheese, divided*

Preheat oven to 375 degrees. Grease 1 cookie sheet.

In a saucepan over high heat, combine milk, butter and salt, and bring to a boil. Remove pan from heat, add flour and whisk vigorously for a few minutes. Return pan to medium heat and stir constantly for approximately 5 minutes or until batter has thickened and begins to pull away from sides of pan.

Remove pan from heat again and whisk in 4 of the eggs, one at a time, incorporating each egg before adding the next. Stir in 1 cup of Parmesan cheese.

Drop the batter by teaspoonfuls onto a prepared baking sheet, spacing them at least 1 inch apart.

In a small bowl, beat remaining egg. Brush tops of puffs with beaten egg and sprinkle with remaining Parmesan cheese. Reduce heat to 350 degrees and bake 15 to 20 minutes or until puffy and well-browned.

TEMPERATURE:
Preheat 375 degrees/lower to 350 degrees

BAKE:
5 minutes/15 to 20 minutes

YIELD:
20 puffs

PESTO TORTE

A TERRIFIC MAKE-AHEAD HORS D'OEUVRE.

CHILL:
3 hours

YIELD:
10 to 12 servings

NOTES:
Sun-dried tomatoes, fresh parsley or basil leaves can be used as decorative garnishes.

2	*teaspoons garlic cloves, minced*
1/2	*cup pine nuts*
1	*cup fresh spinach, chopped*
1/4	*cup fresh basil, chopped or 1 tablespoon dried*
6	*tablespoons butter, room temperature*
1/2	*cup olive oil*
3/4	*cup freshly-grated Parmesan cheese*
1/4	*teaspoon salt*
1/8	*teaspoon freshly-ground pepper*
2	*cups unsalted butter (4 cubes), room temperature*
2	*(8-ounce) packages cream cheese, room temperature*
	Baguette

PESTO:

In a food processor, place garlic and process until finely minced. Add pine nuts and purée. Add spinach and basil. Process until finely chopped. Add butter and olive oil. Turn into medium bowl, add Parmesan cheese, salt and pepper, and stir well. This will yield 1 cup pesto.

TORTE:

Line a small terrine or bowl with damp cheesecloth. In a small bowl, cream butter and cheese until thoroughly mixed. Divide into 3 tennis ball-sized portions. Place 1 portion of cheese mixture between 2 sheets of plastic wrap and flatten into a 1/4 to 1/2-inch thickness which fits bottom of terrine.

Spread 1/8-inch layer of pesto on top of cheese mixture. Repeat the process making the following layers wider to follow shape of terrine.

Make at least three additional layers of pesto alternating with the cheese mixture, ending with a layer of the cheese mixture.

Wrap in a damp towel and cover with plastic wrap. Place in refrigerator and chill at least 3 hours.

When ready to serve, invert onto a plate, remove cheesecloth and serve with sliced baguette.

WINTERTIME BRIE

Either be prepared to share this recipe, or claim it's an "old family secret."

- 3/4 *cup pitted dates, chopped*
- 1 *small apple, peeled, cored and diced*
- 1 *small firm, ripe pear, peeled, cored and diced*
- 1/2 *cup currants (See note.)*
- 1/2 *cup pecans, chopped*
- 1/3 *cup rosé wine, apple juice or applejack*
- 1 *(2-pound) wheel ripe Brie, well-chilled*
- *Baguette, thinly sliced and toasted if desired*

Preheat oven to 350 degrees.

In a large bowl, combine dates, apple, pear, currants, pecans and wine, apple juice or applejack. Set mixture aside to allow fruit to marinate and soften for 2 hours.

Cut Brie wheel in half horizontally to make two layers. Place one layer, rind-side down, in a serving dish. Spread with 2 1/4 cups of the fruit mixture. Place remaining half of Brie on top of fruit with rind-side facing up to enclose the fruit. Spoon remaining fruit mixture onto center top of Brie wheel. Seal with plastic wrap and refrigerate up to 2 days. Bake Brie, uncovered, in 350-degree oven until it melts at the edges and the center is warm, approximately 25 to 30 minutes. Do not overcook as it will be runny and difficult to spread.

To serve, spread melted Brie onto sliced baguette.

Marinate:
2 hours

Chill:
Up to 2 days

Temperature:
Preheat 350 degrees

Bake:
25 to 30 minutes

Yield:
16 servings

Notes:
Substitute dried cranberries for currants.

BERRY PATCH CHEESE RING

Take advantage of the Northwest's finest berries and nuts.

- 2 *pounds sharp Cheddar cheese, coarsely-grated*
- 2 *cups Oregon walnuts or pecans, coarsely chopped*
- 1 1/2 *cups mayonnaise*
- 1 *medium onion, finely chopped*
- 1 to 2 *garlic cloves, crushed*
- 1 *teaspoon red pepper sauce*
- *Strawberry or raspberry preserves*

In a large bowl, mix together cheese, nuts, mayonnaise, onion, garlic and red pepper sauce. Do not use a food processor.

Spray a ring mold with vegetable spray. Gently pat mixture into mold and chill at least 1 hour.

Unmold cheese ring and place on serving platter. Spoon strawberry or raspberry preserves into small bowl. Place small bowl in center of cheese ring. Serve with mild crackers or breadsticks.

Chill:
1 hour

Yield:
15 to 20 servings

Notes:
Smoked cheddar cheese can be substituted and served with peach marmalade.

MOROCCAN EGGPLANT SALSA

A FOOD PROCESSOR STREAMLINES THIS DELICIOUS SALSA.

COOK:
25 minutes

YIELD:
3 cups

NOTES:
Good with PITA CRISPS, page 25 or as a relish with grilled seafood or meat.

- *1 large eggplant, trimmed and cubed*
- *1 large green pepper, seeded, deveined and sliced*
- *1 large yellow pepper, seeded, deveined and sliced*
- *1 large red pepper, seeded, deveined and sliced*
- *1 medium zucchini, quartered*
- *1/2 medium white onion, trimmed and sliced*
- *2 garlic cloves, minced*
- *1/4 cup fresh cilantro, chopped*
- *3 tablespoons olive oil*
- *1 tablespoon ground cumin*
- *1/4 teaspoon cayenne pepper*
- *2 teaspoons granulated sugar*
- *2 teaspoons salt*
- *1/4 cup rice vinegar*
- *1 (8-ounce) can tomato sauce*

In a food processor, dice eggplant, green pepper, red pepper, yellow pepper, zucchini, and onion. In a large saucepan, heat olive oil. Add eggplant, green, yellow and red peppers, zucchini, onion, garlic and cilantro and cook over medium heat for 5 minutes.

Stir in cumin, cayenne pepper, sugar, salt, rice vinegar and tomato sauce.

Cover and simmer ingredients for 20 minutes. Serve hot or cold.

"CAVOCADO" TERRINE

A holiday hors d'oeuvre with colorful red and green layers.

Chill:
4 to 24 hours

Yield:
15 servings

Notes:
Caviar makes this dish naturally salty. Serve with crackers or Lavosh Crackerbread.

- *2 envelopes unflavored gelatin*
- *4 large hard-boiled eggs, chopped*
- *1/2 cup plus 2 tablespoons mayonnaise, divided*
- *1/2 cup fresh parsley, chopped and divided*
- *1 green onion, chopped*
- *1/4 teaspoon red pepper sauce, divided*
- *2 avocados*
- *2 1/2 tablespoons freshly-squeezed lemon juice, divided*
- *2 shallots, minced*
- *Salt*
- *1 cup sour cream*
- *1/4 cup white onion, minced*
- *1/4 pound lumpfish roe caviar*

Grease bottom and sides of an 8-inch springform pan.

In a small saucepan, sprinkle gelatin over 1/2 cup cold water, and let it soften for 5 minutes. Heat the mixture over medium-low heat, stirring until the gelatin is dissolved.

In a bowl, combine the eggs, 1/2 cup mayonnaise, 1/4 cup parsley, green onion, 1/8 teaspoon red pepper sauce and 1 1/2 tablespoons gelatin mixture. Spread mixture evenly in pan and chill for 10 minutes.

In a medium bowl, thoroughly mash avocados. Add shallots, 2 tablespoons lemon juice, remaining 2 tablespoons mayonnaise, 1/8 teaspoon red pepper sauce, salt, and 1 1/2 tablespoons of remaining gelatin mixture and combine thoroughly.

Spread this mixture evenly over egg layer to form a second layer.

In a small bowl, combine sour cream, onion and remaining gelatin mixture. Spread this mixture evenly over avocado layer. Cover mold and chill for at least 4 hours or to a maximum of 24 hours.

To serve, place pan on top of serving plate and run a thin knife around inside edge of pan. Remove side of the pan and release the terrine. Complete final layer of the terrine by spreading caviar on the top. Sprinkle with the remaining 1/2 tablespoon lemon juice and garnish with the remaining 1/4 cup parsley.

SHRIMP DIP

CHILL:
2 to 4 hours

YIELD:
2 cups

NOTES:
For variation, serve as a spread on top of cucumber rounds.

1/4 cup sour cream
1 (8-ounce) package cream cheese, room temperature
1 tablespoon freshly-squeezed lemon juice
Dash of Worcestershire sauce (optional)
3 tablespoons green onion, thinly sliced
1/4 teaspoon crushed red pepper flakes
1 tablespoon milk
1/2 pound small shrimp, cooked
Salt
1 to 2 tablespoons almonds, toasted

In a large bowl, beat sour cream and cream cheese together until smooth and fluffy. Stir in lemon juice, Worcestershire sauce (if desired), green onion, red pepper flakes, milk and shrimp (reserving a few shrimp for garnish). Season with salt. Cover dip and chill for 2 to 4 hours.

Just prior to serving, stir dip gently and pour into serving dish. Top with reserved shrimp and toasted almonds. Serve with crackers.

KNOCK-YOUR-SOCKS-OFF HOT CRAB DIP

Don't forget to leave room for dinner!

Temperature:
Preheat 350 degrees

Bake:
30 minutes

Yield:
10 to 12 servings

- 1/2 *cup dry white wine*
- 4 *ounces cream cheese, room temperature*
- 1 *(16-ounce) can water-packed artichoke hearts, drained and finely chopped*
- 1 *cup mayonnaise*
- 1 *egg*
- 1 *pound fresh crab or 2 (8-ounce) cans crab meat*
- 2 *ounces blue cheese, finely crumbled*
- *Sliced black olives for garnish (optional)*

Preheat oven to 350 degrees.

In a saucepan over low heat, combine white wine and cream cheese and simmer until cheese is creamy. Remove from heat and blend thoroughly with wire whisk.

Stir in artichoke hearts, mayonnaise, egg, crab meat and blue cheese. Pour into 8 x 8-inch ovenproof baking dish and bake for 30 minutes at 350 degrees. Garnish with black olives if desired.

Serve with crackers.

NORTHWEST SPREAD

A mellow salmon spread.

Yield:
2 cups

- 1 *(8-ounce) package cream cheese, room temperature*
- 1/4 *cup whipping cream*
- 1 *green onion, thinly sliced*
- 2 *teaspoons freshly-squeezed lemon juice*
- *Dash of red pepper sauce*
- 4 *ounces smoked salmon, gently shredded*
- 1 *ripe avocado, mashed*

In a large mixing bowl, combine cream cheese and whipping cream together until smooth and creamy. Stir in green onion, lemon juice and red pepper sauce. Gently fold in smoked salmon and mashed avocado, being careful not to overmix. Serve with crackers.

SHRIMP CAPER MYSTERY

THERE'S REALLY NO MYSTERY; IT'S SHRIMPLY DELICIOUS.

MARINATE:
24 HOURS

YIELD:
8 servings

NOTES:
Drain thoroughly to prevent dripping. Be careful; it doesn't take much curry to do the trick.

- 1/4 *cup white vinegar*
- *Curry powder*
- *Salt*
- *Freshly-ground pepper*
- 3/4 *cup vegetable oil*
- 1 *pound freshly-cooked large shrimp, peeled and deveined*
- 1/2 *cup green onions, sliced*
- 4 *tablespoons capers*

In a medium bowl, whisk together vinegar, curry, salt and pepper. Slowly incorporate oil into mixture. Continue to whisk until mixture thickens.

Place shrimp into a glass bowl and sprinkle with green onions and capers. Pour in dressing and toss to coat shrimp. Cover with foil and marinate in refrigerator for 24 hours.

To serve, drain off excess oil and serve with toothpicks.

PATÉ PRESTO

YIELD:
10 to 20 first course servings

NOTES:
Serve accompanied by sourdough bread, Swiss cheese slices and Gherkin pickles.

- 2 *tablespoons onion, chopped*
- 1 *(6 1/8-ounce) can tuna, drained*
- 1/2 *cup butter (1 cube), room temperature*
- 1/8 *teaspoon cayenne pepper*
- 1/4 *teaspoon dry mustard*
- 1/8 *teaspoon ground cloves*
- *Dried dill weed*

In a food processor, chop onion, then add tuna and process until mixture reaches a smooth consistency. Add butter, cayenne pepper, mustard and cloves and process until thoroughly combined. Place in a serving dish and sprinkle with dill weed.

EMBASSY PATÉ

1 1/2	*cups cooked chicken, finely ground*
1	*cup toasted almonds, finely chopped*
1/4	*cup green onions or chives, chopped*
3	*tablespoons preserved or crystallized ginger, finely chopped*
1 1/2	*tablespoons garlic-flavored wine vinegar*
1/2 to 1	*teaspoon Worcestershire sauce*
1/2	*cup mayonnaise*
	Salt
	Freshly-ground pepper
1 to 1 1/2	*cups sour cream*
	Parsley sprigs for garnish
	Almonds, whole for garnish

In a food processor, combine chicken, almonds, onions, ginger, vinegar, Worcestershire sauce, mayonnaise, salt and pepper and purée thoroughly. Cover and refrigerate for 24 hours.

Place in a pastry bag, and using a large tip, squeeze conical shapes that are 1/2-inch high domes onto a baking sheet. Freeze 2 to 4 hours. Remove and frost with sour cream and garnish with parsley and an almond. Serve each canapé on a cracker.

ACCOMPANY THIS APPETIZER WITH A DRY CHAMPAGNE.

CHILL:
24 hours

YIELD:
12 servings

NOTES:
This can be made in advance, chilled for 24 hours and frozen unfrosted for 2 to 3 weeks.

CURRY PATÉ

A fast and easy variation which will delight cheese and cracker lovers.

Yield:
10 to 15 appetizers

Notes:
Try our Peach Chutney, this page.
1/3 cup sliced toasted almonds can be substituted for green onions.

- 2 *(3-ounce) packages cream cheese, room temperature*
- 1 *cup sharp Cheddar cheese, grated*
- 2 *tablespoons dry sherry*
- 1/2 to 1 *teaspoon curry powder*
- 1/4 *teaspoon salt*
- 1/2 *pint peach chutney (See note.)*
- 1/3 *cup green onions with tops, finely sliced (See note.)*

In a medium bowl, combine cream cheese, Cheddar cheese, sherry, curry and salt, and mix well. Mold or shape into desired form and refrigerate until serving time.

When ready to serve, spread chutney over top and garnish with green onions. Serve with melba toast rounds or crisp crackers.

PEACH CHUTNEY

Don't miss this opportunity if you haven't tried making homemade chutney.

Yield:
6 half-pints

Notes:
Can be used in chicken salad, spread on a turkey sandwich or on top of Curry Paté. Try it on our Pork Chops with Chutney, page 152.

- 5 *pounds fresh peaches, blanched, peeled and coarsely chopped*
- 1 *lemon, including peel, chopped*
- 1 1/4 *cups apple cider vinegar*
- 1/4 *cup freshly-squeezed lime juice*
- 2 1/2 *cups granulated sugar*
- 1/3 *cup crystallized ginger, chopped*
- 1 *cup dates, chopped*
- 1 *cup golden raisins*

In a large saucepan, combine peaches, lemon, vinegar, lime juice and sugar.

Cook mixture over low heat for 1 to 1 1/2 hours, stirring frequently until chutney thickens. Do not allow mixture to become too stiff. Add ginger, dates and raisins. Cook a few more minutes to incorporate these ingredients, allowing some of the liquid to be absorbed. Remove from heat and cool.

Distribute among 6 half-pint canning jars. Process 10 to 15 minutes in a boiling water bath.

CRISPY CHICKEN WONTONS WITH MUSTARD SAUCE

MUSTARD SAUCE:

- 1/3 cup dry mustard (See note.)
- 1/2 cup white vinegar
- 1/2 cup granulated sugar
- 1 egg yolk

WONTON FILLING:

- 1 (8-ounce) package cream cheese, room temperature
- 2 cups cooked chicken (1 whole breast), drained and diced
- 3 tablespoons mild green chile peppers, diced
- 1 tablespoon jalapeño pepper, diced
- 1/8 cup seasoned bread crumbs
- 1/2 teaspoon salt (optional)
- 1/4 teaspoon garlic powder or 1 garlic clove, minced
- 1 (16-ounce) package wonton wrappers
- Egg white to brush wontons
- Vegetable oil for frying

YIELD:
20 wontons
1 1/2 cups sauce

NOTES:
Adjust the amount of mustard used in sauce from 1/3 to 1/2 cup for degree of spiciness you desire. Sauce must be made ahead. Wontons can be prepared in advance and frozen prior to frying. To serve, fry as directed.

MUSTARD:

In a small bowl, combine dry mustard and vinegar. Cover and let stand at room temperature overnight.

In a small saucepan, combine mustard/vinegar mixture with sugar and egg yolk. Simmer over low heat until slightly thickened. Cover and store in refrigerator up to 1 month.

FILLING:

In a large bowl, combine cream cheese, chicken, peppers, bread crumbs, salt and garlic and mix thoroughly.

Place a teaspoon of filling in center of wonton. Moisten one side of wonton wrapper with egg white and fold over to look like a crescent. Press edges together and seal.

In a deep sauté pan or wok over high heat (approximately 350 degrees), heat vegetable oil and fry filled wontons until golden, approximately 2 minutes. Drain and serve with spicy mustard.

PITA CRISPS

An easy addition to any lunch or supper menu.

Temperature:
Preheat 400 degrees

Yield:
6 servings

Notes:
Serve with slices of red pepper.

- *1/2 cup butter (1 cube), room temperature*
- *1 to 2 garlic cloves , minced*
- *1/4 cup freshly-grated Parmesan cheese*
- *1 to 2 green onions, finely chopped*
- *1 1/2 tablespoons freshly-squeezed lemon juice*
- *Salt*
- *Lemon pepper*
- *1 (16-ounce) package pita pocket bread*
- *1 red pepper, seeded, deveined and sliced*

In a small bowl, combine butter, garlic, Parmesan cheese, green onions, lemon juice, salt and lemon pepper to taste. Split pita bread in half around seams. (Looks like a tortilla.)

Spread mixture on inside surface of pita halves and slice pita bread into strips or triangles.

Place on baking sheet and toast in a 400-degree oven until surface turns crispy and brown. Watch carefully. Remove crisps from oven as they begin to brown and allow to cool and harden.

WALNUT ROQUEFORT SHORTBREAD

Pair this appetizer with a robust Oregon Pinot Noir.

Chill:
4 hours

Temperature:
Preheat 425 degrees

Bake:
10 minutes

Yield:
3 dozen

Notes:
If using frozen dough, bring to room temperature before baking.

- *1 1/2 cups unbleached all-purpose flour*
- *1 cup walnut pieces*
- *1/2 pound Roquefort cheese, chilled and crumbled*
- *1/2 cup unsalted butter (1 cube), chilled and cut into small pieces*
- *2 egg yolks*
- *2 teaspoons freshly-ground pepper*

In a food processor, combine flour, walnuts, cheese, butter, yolks and pepper. Process until ball of dough forms. Divide dough in half. On a lightly floured surface, form each piece into a 1 1/2-inch diameter cylinder. Wrap cylinders in waxed paper and chill until firm, at least 4 hours. (Can be made ahead and refrigerated up to 3 days or frozen for 1 month.)

Preheat oven to 425 degrees.

Remove dough from refrigerator and cut into 1/2-inch rounds. Place on ungreased baking sheets and bake at 425 degrees for about 10 minutes or until edges are golden brown. Turn baking sheet once halfway through baking time.

When done, place rounds on paper towels to cool. Serve warm or at room temperature.

CAFÉ MOCHA PUNCH

- 8 *cups freshly-brewed espresso or good-quality, freshly-ground strong coffee*
- 1 *cup granulated sugar*
- 5 *sticks cinnamon*
- 1 *pint whipping cream, whipped until stiff, and divided*
- 4 *teaspoons vanilla extract*
- 3 *cups brandy or rum (one fifth)*
- 1 *quart coffee ice cream*
- *Crushed ice*
- ½ *teaspoon ground cinnamon (optional)*

In a container with a tight lid, pour eight cups coffee, add sugar and cinnamon sticks. Set aside to cool, cover and refrigerate until ready to assemble punch .

At serving time, whip cream until stiff. Place half of whipped cream into large punch bowl. Reserve other half to garnish punch. To the whipped cream in punch bowl, add cold cinnamon-coffee mixture, vanilla and brandy or rum. Stir gently.

Add large spoonfuls of coffee ice cream to punch bowl. Stir gently. Float remainder of whipped cream on top of punch.

Serve from punch bowl in tall, chilled glasses partially filled with ice. If desired, sprinkle ground cinnamon over top of drinks.

THE TRICK TO THIS DELICIOUS PUNCH IS FRESHLY-BREWED, STRONG COFFEE.

YIELD:
10 to 12 servings

NOTES:
Omit brandy or rum to make a non-alcoholic punch.

BRUNCH PUNCH

A family tradition.

Chill:
10 hours

Yield:
8 to 10 servings

Notes:
As an alternative, try 2 cups brandy with 1 cup Kahlua.

5 quarts milk
1 quart half and half
3 cups brandy (one fifth)
2 cups light rum
Granulated sugar
Ground nutmeg for garnish

In a large container with tight lid, mix milk, half and half, brandy and rum. Add sugar, stirring well, until reaching desired sweetness. Cover and refrigerate at least ten hours. Serve in a decorative punch bowl over ice or in a pitcher. Garnish with nutmeg.

IMPOSTOR PUNCH

A cocktail the entire family can enjoy.

Yield:
15 servings

1 (6-ounce) can frozen lemonade concentrate
1 (6-ounce) can frozen pineapple juice concentrate
2 cups cold water
1 (32-ounce) bottle sparkling water
1 (32-ounce) bottle sparkling grape juice (or white grape juice)
1 (32-ounce) bottle ginger ale
Ice mold
Fresh mint for garnish
Orange and lemon slices for garnish

In a large punch bowl, combine lemonade and pineapple juice concentrates. Add cold water and sparkling water. Slowly add grape juice and ginger ale, pouring along the inside surface of bowl. Gently place ice mold into punch bowl.

Garnish with mint leaves, orange and lemon slices.

PINEAPPLE PERCOLATOR PUNCH

A perfect "hands-off" recipe.

Yield:
4 to 6 servings

- 2 1/2 *cups pineapple juice*
- 1 3/4 *cups water*
- 2 *cups cranberry juice*
- 1/2 *cup firmly-packed brown sugar*
- 1 *tablespoon whole cloves*
- 1 *tablespoon whole allspice*
- 3 *sticks cinnamon, broken into pieces*

In an 8-cup percolator or large stockpot, combine pineapple juice, water and cranberry juice. Add brown sugar. Place cloves, allspice and cinnamon in percolator basket and percolate for 10 minutes, or place whole spices in a cheesecloth bag, tie closed and bring to a boil for 10 minutes. Remove spices and serve hot in mugs.

RUM CALYPSO

A summer cocktail.

Yield:
1 serving

- *Crushed ice*
- 2 *ounces light or dark rum*
- 2 *ounces freshly-squeezed orange juice*
- *Ginger ale or ginger beer*
- *Orange or lemon slices to garnish*

Fill a tall highball glass with ice. Pour in rum and orange juice. Fill glass with ginger ale or ginger beer. Stir and serve garnished with fruit slices.

RED SUNSET SANGRIA

CHILL:
Several hours

YIELD:
10 servings

3	*cups dry red wine*
4 to 6	*tablespoons granulated sugar*
3	*tablespoons freshly-squeezed lime juice*
3	*tablespoons freshly-squeezed lemon juice*
1	*lemon, thinly sliced*
1	*orange, thinly sliced*
1/4	*cup brandy*
6	*ounces club soda*

In a large pitcher or punch bowl, combine wine, sugar, fruit juice, fruit slices and brandy. Chill several hours, stirring occasionally. Add club soda just before serving.

NIGHT BEFORE FROZEN DAIQUIRIS

RELAX, PUT YOUR BLENDER AWAY AND ENJOY YOUR GUESTS!

YIELD:
24 servings

NOTES:
Keeps in the freezer up to three weeks!

2	*(12-ounce) cans frozen lemonade concentrate*
3	*(12-ounce) cans water*
1/2	*(6-ounce) can frozen limeade concentrate*
1	*quart lemon-lime carbonated soda*
6	*cups strawberry purée*
3	*cups light rum (one fifth)*

In a large bowl, combine lemonade, water, limeade, lemon-lime soda, strawberry purée and rum. Pour into 4 to 5 freezer containers and freeze overnight, or until ready to serve. Remove just before serving, thaw slightly and scoop daiquiri into glasses.

MARGARITAS

The fresh taste of the Southwest cools off any Northwest summer.

- 1 *egg white, beaten*
- 1 *cup tequila*
- 1 *(6-ounce) can frozen limeade concentrate*
- 1/4 *cup triple sec*
- 3 *tablespoons freshly-squeezed lemon juice*
- 3 *cups crushed ice*
- 1 *lemon or lime for garnish*
- *Coarsely ground salt for rims of glasses*

In a blender, whip egg white until double in volume. Add tequila, limeade, triple sec, lemon juice, and crushed ice. Add more ice to fill container, if desired. Blend until slushy.

To garnish drinks, slice lemon or lime and rub rims of glass. Roll dampened rim in salt to coat, pour in margarita and serve with a lemon or lime wedge.

Yield:
4 to 6 servings

Notes:
Egg white keeps drinks from separating.

SUMMER SIPPER

When you uncover the barbecue, pull out this recipe.

- 4 *limes, halved*
- 4 *lemons, halved*
- 1 1/2 *cups Curaçao (orange liqueur)*
- 3 *liters dry white wine*
- 2 *(2-liter) bottles tonic water, chilled*

Place limes and lemons into a punch bowl. Pour Curaçao over and chill for 4 hours.

Chill wine and tonic water in refrigerator. Just prior to serving, pour wine and tonic water over marinated fruit in punch bowl.

Chill:
4 hours

Yield:
30 servings

Notes:
Pour over crushed ice in tall chilled glasses. If using a large punch bowl, a molded ice ring will keep punch well chilled.

GINGER'S EGGNOG

Absolutely the best eggnog we've ever tasted!

Yield:
6 to 8 servings

- *8 eggs, separated*
- *1 cup plus 3 to 5 tablespoons granulated sugar*
- *1 pint half and half*
- *1 pint whole milk*
- *1 pint rum*
- *1 pint heavy whipping cream*
- *Nutmeg, freshly ground*
- *Ground cinnamon*

Beat egg whites until frothy and set aside.

In a large punch bowl, vigorously whisk egg yolks and granulated sugar until mixture reaches a pale yellow color. Pour in half and half, whole milk and rum.

Whip heavy cream to form soft peaks, and gently fold into mixture in punch bowl. Fold in beaten egg whites.

Sprinkle with nutmeg and cinnamon. Thin with additional milk, if necessary. Serve in glasses sprinkled with additional nutmeg, if desired.

CHILLY CRANBERRY COCKTAIL

A colorful holiday beverage.

Chill:
24 hours

Yield:
8 servings

- *1 (6-ounce) can frozen orange juice concentrate*
- *1 (6-ounce) can frozen lemonade concentrate*
- *4 cups cranberry juice*
- *2 cups vodka*

Thaw orange juice and lemonade. Pour into a two-quart plastic container. Add cranberry juice and vodka.

Chill in freezer for six hours. Remove from freezer and stir with meat fork or potato masher to break up any chunks or large crystals.

Return to freezer for an additional 18 hours. Must be frozen a total of 24 hours to complete process.

Scoop into glasses and serve.

ESKIMO LATTÉ

Yield: 2 servings

Notes: Kahlua can be blended in for variation.

- 1 cup freshly-brewed espresso or good-quality, freshly-ground strong coffee, chilled
- 1 cup cold milk
- 1 cup crushed ice
- 1 teaspoon granulated sugar
- Whipped cream
- Ground cinnamon

In a blender, mix coffee, milk, ice and sugar. Pour into glasses. Top with whipped cream and sprinkle with ground cinnamon.

COZY RUM COCOA

Yield: 4 servings

Notes: Chocolate shavings can be used as garnish.

- 3/4 cup dark rum
- 1/4 cup dark crême de cocoa
- 2 1/2 cups hot chocolate
- 1 1/2 cups heavy cream

Pour rum, crême de cocoa and hot chocolate into heat-resistant glass mugs and stir. Pour cream into glasses by slowly letting cream pour off back side of teaspoon in order to float cream on top of drink.

HOT SPICED CRANBERRY CIDER

Spice up your next holiday party with this favorite!

Yield: 12 servings

Notes: Strain spices before serving. Garnish with cinnamon sticks.

- 8 cups apple cider
- 8 cups cranberry juice
- 2 tablespoons brown sugar
- 4 cinnamon sticks
- 8 whole allspice
- 8 whole cloves
- 1 orange, quartered

In a large kettle, combine apple cider and cranberry juice. Stir in brown sugar and add cinnamon sticks, allspice, cloves and orange. Heat mixture to just below boiling point, reduce heat to simmering and serve warm.

SALADS & DRESSINGS

Caesar, Spinach and Citrus

This Sunday afternoon, a father and his young daughter are the only ones at a city community garden site. Usually they have company on either side of them...fellow gardeners weeding, tending, or gathering vegetables for next week's meals. Today, everyone else has already come and gone.

Talking quietly between themselves, their hushed tones broken occasionally by giggles from the little girl, they weed their rows, then select vegetables and flowers to bring home. The child asks whether a tomato is ready to be picked. She places a bunch of carrots in their wire basket.

Shadows grow long; dusk approaches. The father's and daughter's baskets are full of red leaf lettuce, cabbages, cucumbers and radishes...several salads in the making. Pink, red and blue flowers gaily grow in between the vegetable rows. "Time to go," the father says.

Children love to dig in gardens. But some do not have the chance. Junior League volunteers have reached out to children through Kids on the Block, a disability awareness project, as Court Appointed Special Advocates, and with Waverly Children's Home.

WILLAMETTE VALLEY SALAD

- 2 *heads mixed salad greens, torn into pieces*
- 2 to 3 *avocados, peeled and sliced*
- 1/3 *pound blue cheese (See note.)*
- 1 *cup Oregon hazelnuts, toasted and chopped (See note.)*

DRESSING:

- 1/3 *cup red wine vinegar*
- 2/3 *cup olive oil*
- 2 *tablespoons Dijon mustard*
- *Sea salt*
- *Freshly-ground pepper*

Prepare salad greens and chill.

DRESSING:

In a small bowl, whisk vinegar, oil, mustard, salt and pepper. Set aside.

Just before serving, arrange greens in a bowl. Arrange avocado slices on greens. Add dressing and toss lightly. Crumble cheese over top. Sprinkle with nuts and serve.

YIELD :
6 TO 8 servings

NOTES:
To roast nuts: Place hazelnuts in single layer on a cookie sheet in a 350-degree oven. Toast for 5 to 10 minutes watching closely. Shake cookie sheet occasionally. As nuts begin to brown they cook very quickly. Allow to cool and chop nuts by hand.
Use a good quality blue cheese.

COLORWHEEL WALNUT SALAD

ORANGES, RED ONION AND AVOCADO FILL THIS SALAD WITH FLAVOR AND VIBRANT COLOR.

YIELD:
6 servings

NOTES:
For a Mediterranean twist, use Greek olives and crumbled feta cheese.

3/4 cup walnuts, toasted and halved
3 medium oranges, peeled
1 medium red onion, thinly sliced
1 large avocado, peeled and sliced
24 pitted black olives (See note.)
2 heads butter lettuce, torn into pieces

DRESSING:

1/4 cup freshly-squeezed lemon juice
1/2 teaspoon Dijon mustard
Salt and pepper
3/4 cup walnut oil

Preheat oven to 325 degrees.

Place walnuts in a single layer on a baking sheet and roast 5 to 7 minutes.

Peel oranges, removing as much of bitter white rind as possible. Slice into rounds.

Set aside oranges, onion, avocado and olives.

DRESSING:

In a small bowl, whisk lemon juice, mustard, salt and pepper. Slowly whisk in walnut oil. Toss lettuce with a small amount of dressing and distribute lettuce among six plates.

Arrange orange slices, red onion slices, avocado slices and olives on lettuce.

Sprinkle with walnuts and drizzle a small amount of dressing over each serving.

SPINACH-RASPBERRY SALAD

A REFRESHING NORTHWEST VARIATION OF AN OLD FAVORITE.

YIELD:
6 to 8 servings

- *6 cups spinach leaves, separated*
- *1 cup fresh raspberries, divided*
- *1 small Bermuda onion, thinly sliced*
- *1 cup macadamia nuts, chopped and divided*
- *1 avocado, peeled and sliced*
- *1/2 cup cilantro leaves, chopped*

DRESSING:

- *1/2 cup sesame oil*
- *1/4 cup raspberry vinegar*
- *1 tablespoon seedless raspberry jam*
- *Salt and pepper*

In a large bowl, combine spinach, raspberries, onion, nuts, avocado and cilantro. Reserve a few raspberries and nuts for garnish.

DRESSING:

In a small bowl, mix oil, vinegar, jam, salt and pepper. Pour dressing over salad and toss gently. Garnish with reserved raspberries and nuts. Serve immediately.

SPINACH SALAD WITH BASIL DRESSING

FOR FETA CHEESE LOVERS EVERYWHERE!

YIELD:
6 to 8 servings

NOTES:
A mixture of spinach and red leaf lettuce adds festive color. Consider jicama root as an addition to this salad.

- *1 bunch spinach, torn into pieces (See note.)*
- *1 small avocado, cubed*
- *1/2 small red onion, thinly sliced*
- *4 ounces feta cheese (1/2 cup), crumbled*
- *1/2 cup walnuts or pecans, coarsely chopped*

DRESSING:

- *2 large garlic cloves, minced*
- *1/4 cup fresh basil leaves (packed) or 2 tablespoons dried basil*
- *1/4 cup red wine vinegar*
- *2 teaspoons granulated sugar*
- *1/2 cup olive oil*
- *1/2 teaspoon freshly-ground black pepper*

In a large bowl, combine spinach, avocado, onion, feta and nuts.

DRESSING:

In a food processor or blender, add garlic and pulse 4 to 5 times. Add basil, pulse to combine, then add vinegar and sugar. With processor running, drizzle in olive oil until emulsified. Season with pepper.

Pour dressing over salad and toss well. Serve immediately.

MINTED FRUIT SALAD

Chill:
2 to 3 hours

Yield:
10 to 12 servings

Notes:
Mint has a very strong flavor. The amount of mint used depends on personal taste.

- *3¼ cup (1 pint) whole strawberries*
- *3 kiwi fruits*
- *1 medium cantaloupe*
- *1 medium honeydew melon*
- *Handful of fresh mint leaves, finely chopped and divided (See note.)*

DRESSING:

- *¼ cup freshly-squeezed orange juice*
- *¼ cup freshly-squeezed lemon juice*
- *3 tablespoons granulated sugar*

Wash, drain and hull strawberries. Peel kiwis and slice. Reserve some slices for garnish. Peel and cut melons into pieces, or use a melon baller.

In a large bowl, mix fruit together. Finely chop mint and sprinkle over fruit, reserving a few sprigs for garnish.

DRESSING:

In a small bowl, whisk orange and lemon juices with sugar and pour over fruit. Toss salad gently and thoroughly. Arrange kiwi and mint leaves on top as garnish. Refrigerate for 2 to 3 hours.

CLASSIC FRUIT SALAD

Take advantage of the bounty of fresh fruits available in the Northwest during spring and summer.

- 2 *tart green apples, such as Granny Smiths, peeled and diced*
- 1/2 *cup golden raisins*
- 1/4 *cup walnuts, toasted and chopped*
- 1/2 *cup fresh blueberries or 1 dozen fresh strawberries, sliced*
- 1 *(11-ounce) can mandarin oranges, drained*
- 1 *cup red seedless grapes, halved*
- 6 *iceberg lettuce leaves, washed*

DRESSING:

- 1 *cup plain yogurt (See note.)*
- 2 *tablespoons frozen orange juice concentrate*
- 1 *tablespoon granulated sugar*
- 1/2 *teaspoon ground nutmeg*
- 1 *teaspoon grated orange peel*

In a large mixing bowl, combine apples, raisins, walnuts, blueberries, oranges and grapes. Set aside.

DRESSING:

In a small bowl, combine yogurt, orange juice concentrate, sugar, nutmeg and orange peel.

Slowly drizzle dressing over salad and toss well. Chill for 30 minutes. Line 6 salad plates with lettuce and distribute salad on each.

Chill:
30 minutes

Yield:
6 servings

Notes:
Mayonnaise may be substituted for plain yogurt.

CELESTIAL SALAD

Chill:
Several hours

Yield:
6 servings

½ cup almonds, sliced
2 tablespoons granulated sugar
1 cup celery (2 stalks), sliced diagonally
2 green onions, sliced
2 navel oranges, sectioned and cut into 1-inch pieces
1 avocado, peeled, pitted and cubed
1 cucumber, peeled and diced
Romaine and leaf lettuce, torn into pieces

DRESSING:

½ teaspoon salt
Dash of pepper
¼ cup olive oil
1 tablespoon granulated sugar
2 tablespoons white vinegar
½ teaspoon red wine vinegar
Dash of red pepper sauce

In a small pan over medium heat, cook almonds and sugar, stirring occasionally to coat nuts with melted sugar. Watch carefully as they will burn easily. Cool and store in an air-tight container.

In a large salad bowl, combine almonds, celery, onions, oranges, avocado, cucumber and lettuce.

DRESSING:

In a small bowl, whisk salt, pepper, oil, sugar, vinegars and red pepper sauce. Chill.

To serve, pour dressing over salad and toss well.

CANLIS SALAD

THIS SIGNATURE SALAD HAS FOUND ITS WAY ONTO DOZENS OF MENUS AROUND AMERICA.

1 to 2 tomatoes, peeled and sliced into 8 wedges
1 large head romaine lettuce, sliced in 1-inch squares
1/4 cup green onions, chopped
1 cup freshly-grated Romano cheese
1 cup bacon, cooked and crumbled
2 tablespoons fresh mint, chopped
1/4 teaspoon dried oregano

DRESSING:
1/2 teaspoon freshly-ground pepper
1/4 cup freshly-squeezed lemon juice
1 egg, coddled (See note.)
1/2 cup olive oil
1/3 cup prepared croutons
Romano cheese for garnish

In a large bowl, place tomato wedges and lettuce. Add green onions, cheese, bacon, mint and oregano.

DRESSING:

In a small bowl, combine pepper, lemon juice and coddled egg and whisk vigorously. Slowly drizzle in oil, whisking constantly until it reaches a thick consistency. Pour over salad and toss thoroughly. Add croutons and a sprinkle of Romano cheese to garnish.

YIELD:
4 to 6 servings

NOTES:
To coddle an egg: Let egg warm to room temperature. Bring a pan of water to a boil and set egg in pan. Remove from heat, cover pan and let stand one minute. Remove egg from pan and break into bowl. The egg will be quite runny.

GREEN PEA SALAD

ROAST RACK OF LAMB OR GRILLED SALMON WORKS WELL WITH THIS SIMPLE SALAD.

CHILL:
Several hours

YIELD:
6 to 8 servings

NOTES:
Cashew nuts may be added.

1 (10-ounce) package frozen green peas, thawed
1 (8-ounce) can sliced water chestnuts
1/3 cup green onions, sliced
2 hard-boiled eggs, chopped
1 (2-ounce) jar pimientos, diced
1/2 cup celery (1 stalk), sliced

DRESSING:

1/3 cup light mayonnaise
1 tablespoon Dijon mustard
1/2 teaspoon garlic salt
1/4 teaspoon pepper

Butter lettuce leaves

In a large bowl, combine green peas, water chestnuts, green onions, eggs, pimientos and celery.

DRESSING:

In a small bowl, whisk mayonnaise, mustard, garlic salt and pepper. Pour dressing over pea salad mixture and toss well. Cover and refrigerate several hours.

To serve, line individual salad plates with butter lettuce and distribute pea salad on each.

CRUNCHY CURRIED COLE SLAW

CHILL:
2 to 3 hours or overnight

YIELD:
8 servings

- *1 (10-ounce) package frozen peas*
- *1 1/2 cups red cabbage, shredded*
- *1 1/2 cups green cabbage, shredded*
- *1/4 cup green onions, sliced*

DRESSING:

- *1/4 cup sour cream*
- *1/4 cup mayonnaise*
- *1 teaspoon curry powder*
- *1/4 teaspoon salt*
- *Dash of pepper*
- *1 teaspoon Dijon mustard*
- *1 teaspoon red wine vinegar*
- *3/4 cup Spanish peanuts*

In a large bowl, combine peas, cabbages and onions.

DRESSING:

In a separate bowl, whisk sour cream, mayonnaise, curry, salt, pepper, mustard and vinegar. Combine with vegetables, toss well and chill at least 2 to 3 hours, or overnight.

Garnish with peanuts prior to serving.

BROCCOLI SALAD

A pretty addition to your serving table.

Yield:
6 to 8 servings

- 2 *bunches broccoli florets*
- 1 *pound bacon, divided*
- 1 *cup currants or golden raisins, divided*
- 1 *cup unsalted sunflower seeds, divided*
- 1 *red onion, chopped, divided*
- 1/2 *cup candied orange peel, divided*

DRESSING:

- 1 *cup mayonnaise*
- 1/3 *cup granulated sugar*
- 2 *tablespoons red wine vinegar*

In a sauté pan over high heat, cook bacon until crisp. Remove from pan, drain and coarsely chop.

In a large bowl, combine broccoli, bacon, currants, sunflower seeds, onion and orange peel. Reserve some bacon, currants, sunflower seeds, onion and orange peel for garnish.

DRESSING:

In a small bowl, whisk mayonnaise, sugar and vinegar. Pour over salad approximately 1/2 hour before serving and toss well.

To serve, spread broccoli salad in rectangular serving dish and place garnishes in long rows down center.

MEXICAN BLACK BEAN AND CORN SALAD

CHILL:
Several hours

YIELD:
6 to 8 servings

NOTES:
May be served over leaf lettuce with slices of avocado and garnished with fresh cilantro sprigs.

- *2 ears of corn*
- *4 cups cooked black beans, or 3 (14-ounce) cans, drained*
- *2 cups cooked rice*
- *1/2 red bell pepper, seeded, deveined and chopped*
- *1/2 small red onion, chopped*

DRESSING:

- *1/2 cup tarragon vinegar*
- *1/3 cup vegetable oil*
- *3/4 teaspoon ground cumin*
- *3/4 teaspoon chili powder*
- *1 garlic clove, minced*
- *1 teaspoon honey*

Steam corn until tender but still crisp. Remove kernels from cob.

In a large bowl, combine corn, black beans, rice, bell pepper and onion.

DRESSING:

In a small bowl, whisk vinegar, oil, cumin, chili powder, garlic and honey. Pour over bean salad mixture. Toss well and chill.

MEDITERRANEAN POTATO SALAD

CHILL:
2 hours

YIELD:
6 to 8 servings

NOTES:
Red onion and/or crumbled feta cheese can also be added.

- *2 cups green beans (1/2 pound)*
- *5 cups red potatoes (10 medium), cubed*
- *1 (2 1/4-ounce) can black olives, sliced*
- *1/3 cup capers, drained*
- *3 tablespoons fresh parsley, chopped*
- *2 to 3 tablespoons fresh dill, chopped*
- *2 to 3 teaspoons freshly-ground pepper*
- *1 teaspoon salt*
- *2 tablespoons freshly-squeezed lemon juice or balsamic vinegar*
- *1/4 cup olive oil*

Clean beans, snap off ends and break into 1-inch pieces. In a saucepan over high heat, blanch beans for 5 minutes, until bright green. Drain, rinse under cold water and set aside.

In a large stockpot over high heat, boil potatoes in lightly salted water for 10 to 15 minutes until tender (do not peel). Cool and cut into cubes.

In a large bowl, combine beans, potatoes, olives, capers, parsley, dill, pepper, salt, lemon juice and olive oil and toss. Chill for at least 2 hours. Remove from refrigerator 1/2 hour before serving to allow the flavors to blend.

TOMATOES ORIENTAL

THERE IS NOTHING LIKE A SALAD WITH LOCAL TOMATOES FRESH OFF THE VINE.

- 6 *medium tomatoes, cut into thin wedges*
- 1 *cup fresh asparagus tips, blanched (See note.)*
- 1 *(8-ounce) can sliced water chestnuts, drained*

DRESSING:

- 1 *garlic clove, minced*
- 1 *teaspoon salt*
- 1 *teaspoon granulated sugar*
- 1/2 *teaspoon freshly-ground black pepper*
- 2 *teaspoons Dijon mustard*
- 2 *tablespoons tarragon vinegar*
- 1/2 *cup olive oil*

In a medium bowl, combine tomatoes, asparagus tips and water chestnuts.

In a small bowl, whisk together garlic, salt, sugar, pepper, mustard, vinegar and oil. Toss gently with tomato mixture.

Let stand at room temperature for 1 hour to allow flavors to blend. Toss again lightly, then return to refrigerator to chill at least 4 hours.

CHILL:
4 hours

YIELD:
6 servings

NOTES:
To blanch asparagus tips: bring water to a boil and drop tips in. Let water return to a boil and cook for approximately 3 to 4 minutes.

SPICY SESAME SALAD

Add crusty Italian bread and you've got a terrific summertime supper.

Chill:
2 to 3 hours or overnight

Yield:
6 to 8 servings

1 pound thin spaghetti

DRESSING:

1/2 cup vegetable oil, divided
1/2 cup sesame oil
1/3 cup red wine vinegar
1/2 teaspoon red pepper flakes
1/2 teaspoon ground ginger
3 tablespoons creamy peanut butter
1/3 cup soy sauce
1 garlic clove, minced

1 carrot, shredded
1/2 cup green onions (4 to 6), chopped
1 1/2 tablespoons sesame seeds, toasted
1/4 pound pea pods
1/3 cup broccoli florets

Cook noodles according to package directions. Drain, place in serving bowl and toss with 1 tablespoon vegetable oil.

DRESSING:

In a blender or food processor, combine oils, vinegar, red pepper flakes, ginger, peanut butter, soy sauce and garlic and blend thoroughly.

Pour dressing over noodles and toss while noodles are still warm. Cool, add carrots, green onions, sesame seeds, pea pods and broccoli and toss. Refrigerate several hours or overnight.

MIXED GREENS WITH WALNUTS

Yield:
6 to 8 servings.

- 1/2 *head red lettuce, torn into pieces*
- 1/2 *head romaine lettuce, torn into pieces*
- 1/2 *head butter lettuce, torn into pieces*
- 1 *green apple, cored and chopped*
- 1/2 *cup walnut pieces*
- 1 *hard-boiled egg, cut into thin wedges*
- 1/2 *pound freshly-grated Gruyere or Swiss cheese*

DRESSING:

- 3/4 *teaspoon Dijon mustard*
- 1 *garlic clove, crushed*
- 1/2 *teaspoon salt*
- 1 1/2 *tablespoons freshly-squeezed lemon juice*
- 1 *cup walnut oil*

In a large bowl, combine red, romaine and butter lettuces, apple, walnuts, egg and cheese.

DRESSING:

In a small bowl, whisk mustard, garlic, salt, lemon juice and oil.

Pour dressing over salad and toss well.

PRIME-TIME PESTO PRIMAVERA

CHILL:
Overnight

YIELD:
8 to 10 servings

NOTES:
For best results, use extra virgin olive oil. Flavored vinegars will add another twist to this recipe. Shrimp, scallops or crab meat make this a great main course salad.

1 pound fusilli pasta
1 cup frozen peas, thawed
1/2 cup green onions, thinly sliced
1 cup carrots (1 carrot), steamed and sliced
1/4 cup broccoli florets, blanched

MARINADE:
1/2 cup olive oil (See note.)
1/4 cup white wine vinegar (See note.)
Salt and pepper

CREAM SAUCE:
1/4 cup mayonnaise
1/4 cup sour cream
2 tablespoons pesto
1 teaspoon Dijon mustard
2 tablespoons freshly-grated Parmesan cheese

Cook pasta according to package directions, rinse in cold water and drain well.

MARINADE:

In a small bowl, whisk oil, vinegar, salt and pepper together. In a large bowl, combine pasta with marinade and chill overnight.

CREAM SAUCE:

In a small bowl, mix together mayonnaise, sour cream, pesto, mustard and cheese. Toss together with pasta mixture. Refrigerate until ready to serve.

When ready to serve, add peas, onions, carrots and broccoli to pasta.

GOURMET CHINESE CHICKEN SALAD

THIS IS THE VERY BEST VERSION WE'VE FOUND.

MARINATE: *Overnight*

YIELD: *6 servings*

NOTES: *This salad wilts very quickly. Do not add dressing until just before serving.*

MARINADE:

- *1 cup soy sauce*
- *1 cup dry sherry*
- *1 tablespoon ginger, freshly grated*
- *1 garlic clove, minced*

CHICKEN & NOODLES:

- *2 pounds chicken breasts, boneless and skinless, cubed*
- *1/4 cup cornstarch*
- *1/4 cup all-purpose flour*
- *4 ounces saifan noodles (rice sticks)*
- *1 cup wonton skins, sliced*
- *1/4 cup oil plus oil to fry wontons*

DRESSING:

- *1/2 cup granulated sugar*
- *2 garlic cloves, minced*
- *2 tablespoons soy sauce*
- *1/4 teaspoon cayenne pepper*
- *1/2 cup sesame oil*
- *2/3 cup rice vinegar*

SALAD:

- *16 green onions, diced or cut lengthwise*
- *8 tablespoons slivered almonds, toasted*
- *8 tablespoons sesame seeds*
- *2 small heads butter lettuce, torn into pieces*
- *1/2 cup radishes, sliced*
- *1/2 cup bean sprouts*
- *1/2 cup fresh cilantro, chopped*

MARINADE:

In a large bowl, whisk together soy sauce, sherry, ginger and garlic. Add chicken pieces and marinate overnight in the refrigerator.

CHICKEN & NOODLES:

In a separate bowl, mix together cornstarch, flour and salt. Drain marinated chicken and dredge in flour mixture.

In a large sauté pan over medium-high heat, fry chicken in 1/4 cup oil until browned. Place cooked chicken on paper towels to absorb excess oil. Set aside.

In a large sauté pan, heat oil until very hot, but not smoking. Drop the saifan noodles into the oil. They will puff up instantly. Remove and drain on paper towel. Repeat process with wonton skins; fry quickly until golden. Remove and drain on paper towel.

DRESSING:

In a small bowl, whisk together sugar, garlic, soy sauce, pepper, sesame oil and vinegar and set aside.

In a large serving bowl, combine green onions, almonds, sesame seeds, lettuce, radishes, sprouts and cilantro. Add chicken, saifan noodles and wonton skins. Toss entire mixture with dressing. Serve immediately.

CURRIED CHICKEN SALAD

This makes a great filling for pita bread pocket sandwiches, too.

Yield:
6 servings

Notes:
To poach chicken: In a large sauté pan, place chicken in a single layer. Add only enough water to cover 2/3 of the chicken breasts. Cover pan, but not tightly, allowing for steam to escape. Bring water to a low boil, over medium-high heat. Poach chicken breasts for approximately 20 minutes, or until no longer pink in middle of thickest part of breast.

3 cups chicken breasts, boneless, poached and cubed (See note.)
1 cup raisins
1 cup celery (2 stalks), sliced
1/2 cup red onions, sliced
1/3 cup slivered almonds
1/4 cup toasted coconut
1/2 cup tart apple, such as Granny Smith, chopped

DRESSING:

2/3 cup mayonnaise
3 tablespoons freshly-squeezed lemon juice
1 teaspoon curry powder
1 teaspoon fennel seeds
1 teaspoon honey
1/8 teaspoon ground cinnamon

In a large bowl, combine chicken, raisins, celery, onions, almonds, coconut and apples.

DRESSING:

In a small bowl, whisk mayonnaise, lemon juice, curry, fennel, honey and cinnamon. Pour over chicken mixture and toss well. Serve on a bed of romaine lettuce.

FLANK STEAK SHUFFLE

This salad is truly a meal and is perfect for hot summer nights.

- 2 *pounds flank steak*
- 1 *red onion, thinly sliced and separated into rings*
- 1 *red bell pepper, seeded, deveined and cut into thin strips*
- 1 *green bell pepper, seeded, deveined and cut into thin strips*
- 1 *cup celery (2 stalks), thinly sliced diagonally*
- *Mixed greens, torn into pieces*

DRESSING:

- 1 *garlic clove, crushed*
- 1/4 *cup rice vinegar*
- 2 *tablespoons Dijon mustard*
- 1 *tablespoon lemon juice*
- 3/4 *cup olive oil*
- 1 *teaspoon salt*
- 1/2 *teaspoon freshly-ground pepper*
- *Fresh parsley*

Temperature:
Preheat 500 degrees

Broil:
5 to 7 minutes

Marinate:
1 hour

Yield:
4 to 6 servings

Notes:
May be marinated up to 24 hours before serving.

Preheat oven broiler to 500 degrees. Place steak on a broiler pan and broil for 5 to 7 minutes per side. Refrigerate steak. Thinly slice cold steak diagonally, then cut each slice in half.

In a large bowl, combine steak, onion, peppers and celery.

DRESSING:

In a blender or food processor, place garlic, vinegar, mustard and lemon juice. With processor running, drizzle in oil until emulsified. Season with salt and pepper and add parsley. Pour dressing over steak and toss well. Marinate at room temperature for 1 hour before serving.

Serve over a bed of mixed greens.

DESCHUTES-STYLE SALMON SALAD

Deschutes river rafters turn to this hearty sandwich filling as an alternative to a main course.

Temperature:
Preheat 450 degrees

Bake:
10 to 12 minutes

Yield:
5 to 6 servings

2 to 3	*pounds salmon fillet*
5	*garlic cloves, minced and divided*
1 1/2	*tablespoons dried dill weed*
1	*teaspoon dried tarragon*
	Seasoning salt
5	*bay leaves*
1/2	*medium red onion, minced*
1/2	*green bell pepper, seeded, deveined and diced*
1/2	*red bell pepper, seeded, deveined and diced*
1	*medium carrot, grated*
1 1/2	*cups celery (3 stalks), thinly sliced*
1	*tablespoon mayonnaise, or to taste*
1	*tablespoon Dijon mustard*
	Red leaf lettuce

Prepare salmon fillet by mincing 4 garlic cloves and spreading over fish. Sprinkle top of fish with 1 tablespoon dill, tarragon and seasoning salt. Cover fish with bay leaves and grill on barbecue with skin-side down until flaky, yet moist. (If baking in the oven, allow 10 minutes for each 1-inch thickness of fish at 450 degrees.)

Chill fish in refrigerator until cool. Remove bay leaves and discard.

In a large bowl, flake salmon with fork into small pieces. Add onions, peppers, carrot, celery and remaining garlic. Stir in mayonnaise and Dijon mustard.

Serve on salad plates lined with lettuce leaves.

CREAMY NUTMEG DRESSING

Nutmeg brings a unique flavor to this dressing.

- 1/3 *cup heavy cream*
- 2 *tablespoons honey (See note.)*
- 2 *tablespoons cider vinegar*
- 1/2 *teaspoon salt*
- *Dash nutmeg*

In a jar with a tight lid, combine cream, honey, vinegar, salt and nutmeg. Chill 1 to 2 hours. Serve over salad greens.

Chill:
1 to 2 hours

Yield:
1 cup

Notes:
Sugar may be substituted for honey.

MOCK CAESAR DRESSING

- 1/2 *cup olive oil*
- 1 *garlic clove, minced*
- 1 *egg, coddled and beaten (See note.)*
- 1 *dash Worcestershire sauce*
- 1/4 *cup freshly-squeezed lemon juice*
- 1/2 *cup freshly-grated Parmesan cheese*
- *Freshly-ground pepper*
- 1/4 *teaspoon Dijon mustard*

In a jar with a tight lid, combine oil and minced garlic. Shake well. Set aside.

In a bowl, combine egg and Worcestershire and mix well. Add lemon juice, Parmesan cheese, mustard and pepper and whisk thoroughly.

Add egg mixture to jar with oil and garlic and shake vigorously.

Yield:
1 cup

Notes:
Toss with romaine lettuce and serve with cheesy bread sticks. Keeps in refrigerator for 1 week.
To coddle an egg: refer to notes for *Canlis Salad, page 42.*

CREAMY TARRAGON VINAIGRETTE

Prepare this dressing in elegant bottles for a holiday gift.

Chill:
1 hour

Yield:
1 1/2 cups

Notes:
To coddle an egg: refer to notes for Canlis Salad, page 42.

1	*egg yolk, coddled (See note.)*
1	*tablespoon tarragon vinegar*
1/2	*teaspoon onion salt*
1	*cup olive oil*
1	*tablespoon dried tarragon*
1/2	*cup half and half*
1	*tablespoon freshly-squeezed lemon juice*
2	*tablespoons green onion, finely chopped*

In a food processor with a metal blade, lightly pulse together egg yolk, vinegar and onion salt. With machine running, gradually add oil. Add dried tarragon, half and half, lemon juice and green onion and pulse several times to blend well.

Refrigerate for at least 1 hour to allow ingredients to blend.

TANGY CELERY SEED DRESSING

Yield:
1 cup

Notes:
Serve over Bibb lettuce, with mushrooms and sliced Bermuda onions. Also works well mixed with cooked, cubed chicken and served as a sandwich filling.

1/4	*cup granulated sugar*
1	*teaspoon dry mustard*
1	*teaspoon salt*
1	*tablespoon onion, finely chopped*
1/3	*cup white wine vinegar*
2/3	*cup olive oil*
1	*teaspoon celery seed*
1	*teaspoon paprika*

In a jar with a tight lid, combine sugar, mustard, salt, onion, vinegar, oil, celery seed and paprika. Shake well and store in refrigerator until ready to serve.

TANGY POPPY SEED DRESSING

- 1/3 *cup honey*
- 1 *teaspoon salt*
- 2 *tablespoons vinegar*
- 1 *tablespoon Dijon mustard*
- 3/4 *cup oil*
- 1 *tablespoon onion, finely chopped*
- 2/3 *teaspoon poppy seeds*

In a jar with a tight lid, blend honey, salt, vinegar and mustard. Gradually add oil, stirring to blend thoroughly. Stir in onion and poppy seed.

Cover and chill for several hours to blend flavors. Shake well before using.

A LUNCHEON FAVORITE.

CHILL:
Several hours

YIELD:
1 1/4 cups

HERBED GARLIC AND PARMESAN CROUTONS

- 2 *large garlic cloves, thinly sliced*
- 1 *teaspoon dried oregano*
- 1 *teaspoon dried basil*
- 1 *teaspoon dried thyme*
- 1/2 *teaspoon salt*
- 1/2 *teaspoon pepper*
- 1/2 *cup olive oil*
- 6 *slices firm, thick white or French bread, cubed*
- 1/4 *cup freshly-grated Parmesan cheese*

Preheat oven to 350 degrees.

In a small saucepan over medium heat, combine garlic, oregano, basil, thyme, salt, pepper and oil. Simmer mixture for 5 minutes. Remove pan from heat and let stand for 15 minutes. Remove garlic slices and discard.

In a bowl, toss bread cubes with oil mixture and spread them on a baking sheet. Bake in the middle of a 350-degree oven for 8 minutes. Sprinkle the croutons with Parmesan and bake an additional 7 minutes or until golden brown.

Remove from oven, sprinkle with additional salt and let them cool.

THESE EASY-TO-MAKE CROUTONS ARE FABULOUS WITH OUR MOCK CAESAR DRESSING!

COOK:
5 minutes

TEMPERATURE:
Preheat 350 degrees

BAKE:
15 minutes

YIELD:
5 cups

NOTES:
Croutons can be kept in an air-tight container up to one week.

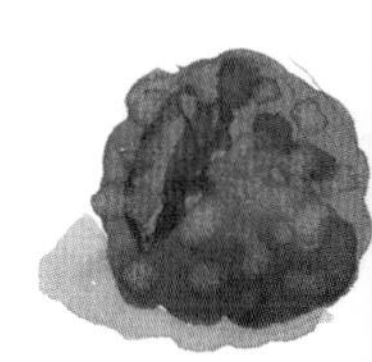

Breads & Muffins

BREADS AND MUFFINS

On a city stroll, croissants and cappuccino become a tasty tradition. Choose a favorite bistro and sit outside on a sunny Saturday for people-watching. Or stake out an indoor table during damper weather, share the newspaper with a friend and feel very European. Sip coffees from around the world. Portlanders delight in java—in fact, we're the second highest imbibers in the country.

Portland bread lovers yearning for crusty loaves of sourdough and warm baguettes are living in the right place. Good breads are easy to find here, along with wonderful cafés to enjoy freshly baked rolls or a *pain au chocolat* right on the spot. Choose a savory sampling of Italian peasant breads, Russian rye or sweet muffin bread to nibble later. Or use recipes like PEAR-NUT BREAD, BUTTERMILK SCONES and HONEY-WHEAT BREAD.

Meticulously restored to its 1872 cast iron splendor, the New Market Theater now serves as a stage for people-watching, shopping, street performers and the Saturday Market. The League's own involvement with historic preservation began in 1954 with financial assistance to the Oregon Historical Society.

SOUR CREAM CRESCENT ROLLS

1	*package dry yeast*
1/4	*cup warm water*
1/4	*cup plus 1 tablespoon butter, divided*
1/4	*cup granulated sugar*
1/2	*cup sour cream*
1	*egg*
2	*cups unbleached flour*
1	*teaspoon salt*

In a large bowl, sprinkle yeast over warm water and stir. Let stand for 5 minutes.

In a saucepan over medium heat, melt 1/4 cup butter. Mix in sugar and sour cream. Cool slightly and add to yeast. Beat in 1 egg.

In a separate bowl, combine flour and salt. Add to yeast mixture. Mix until soft dough forms. Cover with plastic wrap and refrigerate overnight. Remove from refrigerator and let stand for 1 hour or until softened and ready to knead.

Preheat oven to 375 degrees.

Lightly grease 2 baking sheets.

Punch dough down and knead until smooth. Divide into 2 pieces.

On lightly floured surface, roll out one piece into a 10-inch round. Brush with 1 tablespoon melted butter. Cut into 8 wedges. Roll up each wedge, beginning at the wide end. Shape into crescents. Repeat process with second round of dough.

Place crescent rolls on prepared sheets. Cover rolls and let rise in warm area until doubled, about 1 hour.

Bake rolls in a 375-degree oven for 15 to 20 minutes. Serve warm.

CHILL:
Overnight

TEMPERATURE:
Preheat 375 degrees

BAKE:
15 to 20 minutes

YIELD:
16 rolls

NOTES:
The dough can be prepared up to 2 days in advance.

FRENCH BREAD

FILL YOUR HOME WITH THE WONDERFUL AROMA OF BREAD BAKING IN THE OVEN!

RISING TIME:
2 to 3 hours

TEMPERATURE:
Preheat 400 degrees

BAKE:
60 minutes

YIELD:
3 loaves

NOTES:
Brushing loaves every 15 to 20 minutes with cold water during baking will make the crust crisp and hard.

1 1/2	*tablespoons butter*
1 1/2	*tablespoons salt*
1 1/2	*tablespoons granulated sugar*
2	*cups boiling water*
1	*package dry yeast*
2/3	*cup warm water*
6	*cups unbleached flour*

Preheat oven to 400 degrees.

Prepare baking sheet by buttering it and sprinkling cornmeal lightly on top.

In a large bowl, combine butter, salt, sugar and boiling water, stirring until all ingredients have dissolved.

In a small bowl, sprinkle yeast over 2/3 cup lukewarm water and let yeast dissolve. Add yeast to butter mixture and stir well.

Stir in flour a small amount at a time. After adding 4 cups of flour, mix vigorously with a wooden spoon for about 1 minute. Add remaining flour until dough is too stiff to mix with spoon.

Turn dough out onto a large, floured board and knead, adding flour until it is satiny smooth and very elastic. Form into a ball and place in a well-oiled bowl. Cover and let rise in a warm place for 1 1/2 hours, or until dough is double in size. Punch down and let rise again until doubled, about 1 hour.

Divide dough into 3 balls and shape each into a very long slender loaf. Place loaves onto prepared pan.

Cover shaped loaves with a tea towel and let rise until almost doubled in size. Brush tops with cold water and make 3 or 4 diagonal slashes across the top of each loaf. Bake approximately 1 hour.

HONEY WHOLE-WHEAT BREAD

- 2 *cups milk*
- 3 *tablespoons vegetable oil*
- 1 *tablespoon salt*
- 1/2 *cup honey (See note.)*
- 2 *tablespoons active dry yeast*
- 1/3 *cup warm water*
- 5 1/2 *cups unsifted whole-wheat flour, divided*

Preheat oven to 375 degrees.

In a saucepan over low heat, warm milk.

In a mixing bowl, combine oil, salt and honey. Add lukewarm milk and combine. Dissolve yeast in warm water. Let stand 4 to 5 minutes and add to mixture.

Add 3 cups flour. Stir 8 minutes with mixer at low speed. Add 2 cups flour and mix well. Knead until dough is smooth and elastic. If necessary, add 1/2 cup more flour.

Oil a large bowl. Place dough in bowl, cover with a towel and let rise in a warm place until dough has doubled in size, about 1 hour.

Punch dough down to original size. Cover and let rise again. Punch dough down again.

Divide dough in half. Shape into 2 loaves and place in two 9 x 5-inch loaf pans. Cover with towels and let rise until dough begins to lift towel. Bake in a 375-degree oven for 45 minutes.

TEMPERATURE:
Preheat 375 degrees

BAKE:
45 minutes

YIELD:
2 loaves

NOTES:
Try using clover honey for a mild flavor.

DILL BREAD

TRY THIS BREAD FOR HAM SANDWICHES.

TEMPERATURE:
Preheat 350 degrees

BAKE:
40 to 50 minutes

YIELD:
8 to 10 servings

NOTES:
Adjust flour quantity to achieve stiff ball.

1	*package dry yeast*
1/4	*cup warm water*
1	*cup creamed cottage cheese, room temperature*
2	*tablespoons granulated sugar*
1	*tablespoon minced onions*
1	*tablespoon butter, melted*
2	*tablespoons dried dill*
1	*teaspoon salt*
1/4	*teaspoon baking soda*
1	*egg*
2 1/4	*cups all-purpose flour (See note.)*
	Melted butter
	Coarse salt

Preheat oven to 350 degrees.

In a small bowl, pour yeast over warm water. Let stand for 5 minutes.

In a large mixing bowl, combine cottage cheese, sugar, onions, butter, dill, salt, baking soda, egg and yeast. Add flour in portions, beating after each addition, to form a stiff ball. Cover and let rise until doubled in size, about 1 hour.

Punch dough down and turn into well-greased 1 1/2 to 2-quart ovenproof dish. Let dough rise another 30 to 40 minutes until light. Bake in a 350-degree oven for 40 to 50 minutes, until golden brown. Brush with butter and sprinkle with salt.

CHEDDAR-PEPPER BREAD

Temperature:
Preheat 350 degrees

Bake:
30 to 35 minutes

Yield:
6 to 8 servings

- 1 *package yeast*
- 1/4 *cup warm water*
- 3 *cups all-purpose flour*
- 1 *tablespoon granulated sugar*
- 2 *teaspoons freshly-ground black pepper*
- 1/2 *cup warm milk*
- 2 *tablespoons butter, melted*
- 1 *large egg*
- 1 *cup sharp Cheddar cheese, grated*

In a small bowl, combine yeast and lukewarm water, stirring with a fork until dissolved. Let stand 5 to 10 minutes.

In a food processor with a metal blade, combine flour, sugar and pepper. Pulse the processor several times to mix the dry ingredients.

In a separate bowl, combine milk, butter and egg and stir well.

With processor running, pour yeast mixture and then milk mixture through feed tube. When dough has formed a ball around the center, stop and add cheese. Pulse again for approximately 14 seconds until cheese is mixed into dough.

Turn dough out on a lightly floured surface and knead until smooth, about 1 minute. Place dough in a warm, buttered bowl, rotating to coat all sides. Cover loosely with plastic wrap and a towel. Let rise 30 minutes.

Punch down, form into a loaf and place in an 8 x 4 1/2-inch lightly greased loaf pan, or make a free-form loaf and place it on a greased baking sheet. Cover and let rise 30 minutes. During the last 10 minutes of rising time, preheat oven to 350 degrees. Bake in preheated oven for 30 to 35 minutes.

DOUBLE CINNAMON ROLLS

TAKE A THERMOS OF HOT COCOA AND A PAN OF THESE CINNAMON ROLLS TO THE ROSE PARADE!

RISING TIME:
2 hours

TEMPERATURE:
Preheat 375 degrees

BAKE:
25 minutes

YIELD:
30 1-inch rolls

NOTES:
On a nice, warm summer day, the rising time will shorten. Check dough during rising time and allow more time on cool days.

DOUGH:

- *1 cup boiling water*
- *1 cup butter (2 cubes) plus 2 tablespoons melted butter, divided*
- *3/4 cup granulated sugar*
- *1 cup raisins*
- *2 eggs, beaten*
- *2 tablespoons dry yeast (2 packages), dissolved in 1 cup lukewarm water*
- *7 cups all-purpose flour*
- *Dash of salt*

FILLING:

- *7 tablespoons cinnamon*
- *9 tablespoons granulated sugar*
- *3 tablespoons brown sugar, firmly packed*

GLAZE:

- *1 1/2 cups powdered sugar*
- *1/4 cup butter (1/2 cube), room temperature*
- *1 to 2 tablespoons milk*
- *1 tablespoon vanilla extract*
- *3 tablespoons cinnamon*

DOUGH:

In a large mixing bowl, pour boiling water over butter and sugar. Add raisins and eggs.

Dissolve yeast in a cup of warm water and add to above mixture.

Stir in flour and begin kneading when dough becomes difficult to stir with a spoon. Knead dough until it no longer feels sticky on your fingertips.

Cover bowl with plastic wrap and set aside to rise in a warm, draft-free place, about 1 hour. Meanwhile, mix cinnamon and sugars together for filling and set aside. When dough doubles in size, divide dough in half.

Roll out each half to approximately 6 x 12 inches. Brush dough with 2 tablespoons of melted butter. Then evenly sprinkle filling over dough and roll in a jellyroll fashion. Slice 1-inch thick and place in a deep-dish pan.

Cover and let rise again until double in size.

Bake in a preheated oven at 375 degrees for 25 minutes.

While rolls are baking, prepare glaze by creaming butter and powdered sugar, then add milk, vanilla and cinnamon, blending until smooth.

Remove rolls from oven and spread glaze mixture over hot cinnamon rolls.

PUMPKIN BREAD

Welcome autumn with this warm, spiced bread.

Temperature:
Preheat 350 degrees

Bake:
1 hour and 15 minutes

Yield:
10 servings

- 1 *cup dark brown sugar, firmly packed*
- 1/2 *cup granulated sugar*
- 1 *cup canned pumpkin*
- 1/2 *cup vegetable oil*
- 2 *eggs*
- 2 *cups all-purpose flour, sifted*
- 1 *teaspoon baking soda*
- 1/2 *teaspoon salt*
- 1/2 *teaspoon nutmeg*
- 1/2 *teaspoon cinnamon*
- 1/4 *teaspoon ground ginger*
- 1/4 *cup water*
- 1 *cup raisins*
- 1 *cup walnuts or pecans (optional)*

Preheat oven to 350 degrees.

Grease a 9 x 5-inch loaf pan.

In a large bowl, combine sugars, pumpkin, oil and eggs. Beat until well blended.

In a separate large bowl, sift together flour, soda, salt and spices. Add pumpkin mixture and mix well. Stir in water, raisins and nuts and blend together.

Turn into prepared pan. Bake in a 350-degree oven for 1 hour and 15 minutes or until done. Turn out on rack to cool.

FRESH STRAWBERRY BREAD

Remember this recipe when strawberry season arrives.

- 1 1/2 *cups all-purpose flour*
- 1 *cup granulated sugar*
- 1 1/2 *teaspoons ground cinnamon*
- 1/2 *teaspoon salt*
- 1/2 *teaspoon baking soda*
- 2 *eggs, beaten*
- 1/2 *cup vegetable oil*
- 1 1/2 *cups fresh strawberries, chopped*
- 1/2 *cup chopped walnuts or pecans*

Temperature:
Preheat 350 degrees

Bake:
50 to 60 minutes

Yield:
10 to 12 servings

Preheat oven to 350 degrees.

Grease and flour a 9 x 5-inch loaf pan.

In a large bowl, combine flour, sugar, cinnamon, salt and soda. In a separate bowl, combine eggs, oil, strawberries and nuts. Add to flour mixture.

Pour into prepared pan and bake in a 350-degree oven for 50 to 60 minutes.

PEAR-NUT BREAD

This moist bread is a nice switch from banana bread.

Temperature:
Preheat 350 degrees

Bake:
30 minutes

Yield:
Approximately 16 slices

Notes:
Make in mini-loaf pans for gifts during the holidays. Adjust cooking time as loaves will cook quicker.

- *1/2 cup vegetable oil*
- *1 cup granulated sugar*
- *2 eggs, beaten*
- *2 ripe pears, peeled and mashed, or 1 (15-ounce) can unsweetened pears, drained and mashed*
- *2 cups all-purpose flour, sifted*
- *1 teaspoon baking powder*
- *1/2 teaspoon salt*
- *1/2 teaspoon cinnamon*
- *1/4 teaspoon allspice*
- *1/4 teaspoon nutmeg, freshly grated*
- *1/8 teaspoon ground cloves*
- *1/8 teaspoon ground ginger*
- *3 tablespoons milk*
- *1/2 teaspoon vanilla*
- *1/2 cup walnuts, chopped*

Preheat oven to 350 degrees.

In a large food processor, mix oil, sugar, eggs and mashed pears, pulsing well after each addition.

In a separate bowl, sift flour, baking powder, salt, cinnamon, allspice, nutmeg, cloves, and ginger. Add to sugar mixture and blend well. Add milk, vanilla, nuts and mix thoroughly.

Turn into a Bundt pan or an 8 x 4 1/2-inch loaf pan. Bake in a 350-degree oven for 30 minutes or until a toothpick inserted into center of loaf comes out clean.

Let cool and slice.

BUTTERSCOTCH PECAN ROLLS

- 1 *(3-pound) loaf frozen bread dough (See note.)*
- 1/4 *cup plus 2 tablespoons butter, divided*
- 1 *cup brown sugar, firmly packed*
- 1/2 *cup dark corn syrup*
- 2/3 *cup pecans, chopped and divided*
- 1/2 *cup granulated sugar*
- 1 1/2 *teaspoons ground cinnamon*

Preheat oven to 375 degrees.

Thaw frozen bread dough and let rise according to package directions. This takes 5 to 7 hours. Grease two 9-inch round cake pans.

In a saucepan over medium heat, melt butter and add brown sugar. Add corn syrup and stir until blended. Pour into prepared pans. Sprinkle 1/3 cup pecans into each pan.

On a lightly floured surface, roll out dough into a 12 x 24-inch rectangle. Spread with 2 tablespoons soft butter.

In a small bowl, combine sugar and cinnamon. Sprinkle mixture over dough. Beginning at the long end, roll up dough jelly-roll style. Cut into 24 slices. Place cut-side down in pans prepared with syrup. Let rise for about 40 minutes.

Bake in a 375-degree oven for 20 to 25 minutes.

THESE SPECTACULAR ROLLS ARE A GUARANTEED HIT FOR BREAKFAST, BRUNCH OR LUNCH.

TEMPERATURE:
Preheat 375 degrees

BAKE:
20 to 25 minutes

YIELD:
24 servings

NOTES:
We suggest taking frozen dough out of freezer and refrigerating overnight as it takes several hours to thaw.

CRANBERRY UPSIDE-DOWN COFFEE CAKE

TEMPERATURE:
Preheat 350 degrees

BAKE:
1 hour

YIELD:
6 to 8 servings

NOTES:
Serve garnished with a dollop of whipped cream flavored with sugar and vanilla.

- 9 *tablespoons butter (1 cube plus 1 tablespoon), room temperature, divided*
- 1 *cup granulated sugar, divided*
- 2 *cups cranberries*
- 1 *egg*
- 1 *teaspoon vanilla*
- 1 *teaspoon orange rind, grated*
- 1 1/4 *cups all-purpose flour*
- 1 1/2 *teaspoons baking powder*
- 1/4 *teaspoon salt*
- 1/2 *cup milk*
- 1/3 *cup currant jelly*

Preheat oven to 350 degrees.

Butter the bottom and sides of a 9-inch cake pan with 3 tablespoons of butter.

Sprinkle with 1/2 cup of sugar. Arrange cranberries evenly in pan.

In a large bowl, cream remaining butter and sugar. Add egg, vanilla and orange rind and beat until well combined. In another bowl, sift flour, baking powder and salt. Sift this flour mixture again into the butter mixture, alternating 1/2 cup of flour at a time with 1/2 cup of milk. Stir until just combined.

Spoon batter over berries and spread evenly. Place prepared pan on a baking sheet. Bake in a 350-degree oven for 1 hour or until well-browned.

Cool in pan for 20 minutes. Run a knife around edges of pan and invert cake onto a serving plate. Melt jelly over low heat, stirring, or heat in the microwave for 1 to 2 minutes on high. Brush over the cranberries. Serve warm or at room temperature.

RASPBERRY CREAM CHEESE COFFEE CAKE

PASTRY:

- 2 1/4 *cups all-purpose flour*
- 1 *cup granulated sugar, divided*
- 3/4 *cup butter, chilled*
- 1/2 *teaspoon baking powder*
- 1/2 *teaspoon baking soda*
- 3/4 *cup sour cream*
- 2 *eggs, divided*
- 1 *teaspoon almond extract*

FILLING:

- 1 *(8-ounce) package cream cheese, room temperature*
- 3/4 *cup raspberry preserves*
- 1/2 *cup sliced almonds*

TEMPERATURE:
Preheat 350 degrees

BAKE:
45 to 55 minutes

YIELD:
10 to 12 servings

NOTES:
If you have leftovers, be sure to refrigerate!

Preheat oven to 350 degrees.

Grease and flour bottom and sides of a 9-inch springform pan.

In a large bowl, combine flour and 3/4 cup sugar. Cut in butter using a pastry blender or fork and work into coarse crumbs. Set aside 1 cup of crumb mixture.

Into remaining crumb mixture, add baking powder, soda, salt, sour cream, 1 egg and almond extract. Blend well.

Spread batter over bottom and 2 inches up sides of pan. Batter should be about 1/4-inch thick on sides.

In a small bowl, combine cream cheese, remaining sugar and 1 egg and blend well. Pour over batter in pan. Carefully spoon preserves evenly over cheese filling.

In a small bowl, combine the 1 cup reserved crumb mixture and sliced almonds. Sprinkle over the top.

Bake in a 350-degree oven for 45 to 55 minutes, or until cream cheese filling is set and crust is golden brown. Cool 15 minutes. Remove sides of pan. Serve warm or cool, cut into wedges.

PEACH COFFEE CAKE

MAKE THIS IN ADVANCE. IT IS EVEN MORE DELICIOUS THE SECOND DAY!

TEMPERATURE:
Preheat 350 degrees

BAKE:
55 minutes

YIELD:
6 to 8 servings

NOTES:
Serve with yogurt or dollops of whipped cream.

4 cups fresh peaches, sliced
1 3/4 cups granulated sugar, divided
3/4 cup all-purpose flour
1 pinch salt
2 teaspoons baking powder
1/2 cup milk
1/4 teaspoon almond extract
1/2 cup butter (1 cube)

Preheat oven to 350 degrees.

In a large bowl, combine peaches with 3/4 cup sugar. Let stand 30 minutes.

In a separate bowl, sift together flour, salt, baking powder and remaining sugar. Stir in milk and almond extract and mix well.

Melt butter in a 9 x 13-inch baking dish and pour batter over top of butter. Do not stir. Pour peach mixture over top of batter. Bake in a 350-degree oven for 55 minutes. Top should be golden brown.

CRUNCHY GRANOLA

Your kitchen will smell heavenly while it's baking.

Temperature: *Preheat 275 degrees*

Bake: *25 to 40 minutes*

Yield: *Approximately 10 cups*

Notes: *You may add 1 cup pitted dates and 1 cup of millet for a refreshing change.*

- 6 *cups rolled oats*
- 2 *cups coconut*
- 1 1/2 *cups wheat germ*
- 1 *cup raw sunflower seeds*
- 1/2 *cup pecans or hazelnuts, finely chopped*
- 3/4 *cup sesame seeds*
- 3/4 *cup bran*
- 1 1/2 *cups raisins (optional)*
- 3/4 *cup honey*
- 3/4 *cup vegetable oil*
- 1 *teaspoon vanilla*

Preheat oven to 275 degrees.

In a large bowl, combine oats, coconut, wheat germ, sunflower seeds, nuts, sesame seeds, bran and raisins and mix well. Stir in honey, oil and vanilla.

Spread granola mix onto foil-lined baking sheet. Bake in a 275-degree oven for 25 to 40 minutes, stirring occasionally.

BUTTERMILK SCONES

These are delicious served with fresh Oregon berry preserves.

Temperature: *Preheat 425 degrees*

Bake: *15 minutes*

Yield: *12 scones*

- 2 *cups all-purpose flour*
- 2 *teaspoons baking powder*
- 1 *tablespoon granulated sugar*
- 1/2 *teaspoon salt*
- 4 *tablespoons butter*
- 2 *eggs, well beaten*
- 1/2 *cup buttermilk*
- 1/2 *cup raisins*

Preheat oven to 425 degrees.

Lightly butter a baking sheet.

In a large bowl, mix flour, baking powder, sugar and salt. Cut in butter with fingers or a pastry blender until mixture resembles coarse meal. Add eggs and buttermilk and stir until well blended.

Turn out onto a lightly-floured board and knead for about 1 minute. Pat or roll the dough about 3/4-inch thick and cut into wedges. Place on prepared baking sheet. Bake in a 425-degree oven for 15 minutes. Serve warm with Oregon berry preserves.

CINNAMON COFFEE BARS

CAREFUL! YOUR CO-WORKERS IN THE BREAKFAST POOL WILL WANT THESE EVERY WEEK.

TEMPERATURE:
Preheat 350 degrees

BAKE:
20 minutes

YIELD:
12 to 15 servings

NOTES:
Use golden raisins for a milder flavor.

1/4 cup shortening
1 cup brown sugar, firmly-packed
1/2 cup strong, good-quality hot coffee
1 1/2 cups all-purpose flour, sifted
1 teaspoon baking powder
1/4 teaspoon baking soda
1/2 teaspoon salt
1 1/4 teaspoons cinnamon
1/2 cup raisins (See note.)
1/2 cup almonds or hazelnuts, chopped

FROSTING:
1 cup powdered sugar, sifted
1/4 teaspoon salt
1/2 teaspoon vanilla extract
2 tablespoons milk

Preheat oven to 350 degrees.

Grease a 9 x 13-inch baking pan.

In a large bowl, cream together shortening and brown sugar. Stir in coffee. In a separate bowl, sift together flour, baking powder, soda, salt and cinnamon. Stir into sugar mixture. Blend in raisins and nuts.

Spread into prepared pan. Bake in a 350-degree oven for 20 minutes. Cut into bars.

FROSTING:

Blend together powdered sugar and salt. Mix in vanilla and milk. Spread frosting over cooled bars.

MINIATURE ORANGE-PINEAPPLE MUFFINS

THESE MUFFINS ARE LIGHT AND FLAVORFUL, AND NOT TOO SWEET.

TEMPERATURE:
Preheat 375 degrees

BAKE:
15 to 20 minutes

YIELD:
Approximately 42 muffins

TOPPING:

- *1 cup granulated sugar*
- *1/2 cup orange juice*

MUFFINS:

- *1/2 cup butter (1 cube), room temperature*
- *1 cup granulated sugar*
- *1 egg*
- *3/4 cup sour cream*
- *1 teaspoon orange extract*
- *2 cups all-purpose flour*
- *1 teaspoon salt*
- *1 teaspoon baking soda*
- *1 tablespoon orange rind, grated*
- *1 (8-ounce) can crushed pineapple, thoroughly drained*
- *1/2 cup walnuts, chopped*

Preheat oven to 375 degrees.

Grease miniature muffin tins.

In a medium bowl, combine sugar and orange juice. Mix together and set aside for dipping after muffins are baked.

In a large bowl, cream together butter and sugar. Add egg, sour cream and orange extract. Beat until well mixed. Sift together flour, salt, baking soda and add to mixture. Batter will be stiff. Fold in orange rind, pineapple and walnuts.

Pour mixture into prepared tins, 3/4 full.

Bake in a 375-degree oven for 15 to 20 minutes. Remove from pan and dip into orange juice-sugar mixture while muffins are still warm.

BLUEBERRY-YOGURT MUFFINS

NUTRITIOUS INGREDIENTS MAKE THE DIFFERENCE.

TEMPERATURE:
Preheat 350 degrees

BAKE:
20 to 30 minutes

YIELD:
12 muffins

1/4 cup butter (1/2 cube), room temperature
1/2 cup granulated sugar
1 egg
1/4 teaspoon ground cinnamon
1/8 teaspoon ground nutmeg
1/2 teaspoon vanilla
2/3 cup whole-wheat flour
2/3 cup all-purpose flour
2 teaspoons baking powder
1/2 teaspoon salt
1/2 cup milk
1/2 cup plain yogurt
1 cup blueberries, fresh or frozen, thawed and drained

Preheat oven to 350 degrees.

Line muffin tins with paper cups.

In a large bowl, cream butter and sugar. Add egg, cinnamon, nutmeg and vanilla. Add flour, baking powder and salt alternately with milk and yogurt. Do not over mix. Carefully fold in blueberries.

Spoon into paper-lined muffin tin. Bake in a 350-degree oven for 20 to 30 minutes.

CARAWAY-CHEESE MUFFINS

A SAVORY MUFFIN TO SERVE WITH HAM OR ROAST BEEF.

TEMPERATURE:
Preheat 425 degrees

BAKE:
20 minutes

YIELD:
12 muffins

- 2 *cups all-purpose flour*
- 3 *teaspoons baking powder*
- 1/2 *teaspoon salt*
- 1/2 *teaspoon freshly-ground pepper*
- 2 *eggs, beaten*
- 1 *cup milk*
- 1/4 *cup butter (1/2 cube), melted*
- 2 *tablespoons Dijon mustard*
- 1/2 *cup grated Cheddar cheese*
- 1/2 *teaspoon caraway seeds*

Preheat oven to 425 degrees.

Prepare 12 muffin tins with melted butter or vegetable spray.

In a large mixing bowl, combine flour, baking powder, salt and pepper and blend well. In a separate bowl, mix eggs, milk and butter. Add Dijon mustard to milk mixture and whisk with a fork until smooth.

Make a well in flour mixture and add Dijon mixture. Stir rapidly with a rubber spatula until dry ingredients are just moistened. Fold in cheese and caraway seeds.

Fill muffin cups and bake in a 425-degree oven for 20 minutes.

Soups & Sandwiches

A Square Meal

The Square's downtown. Pioneer Courthouse Square, that is.

It's the heart of the city.

Sometimes people crowd the place, reading the named bricks under their feet. Portlanders paid for the bricks to help the Square get its start–and in return had their names engraved on them. There's the 80-foot Douglas fir tree-lighting ceremony in the winter, the Festival of Flowers and brownbag concerts in the summer, and the weather machine stands guard year-round.

Sometimes the Square's almost empty.

We like it both ways.

A school stood there first, then the stately Portland Hotel. Its wrought-iron gate still graces the Square.

In the summer a super sandwich is the ticket. Try LE PAIN FLORENTINE.

In the winter, a warming soup seems right. How about ITALIAN SAUSAGE SOUP?

Fall and spring? Anything goes.

Sooner or later, everyone experiences the Square.

Junior League volunteers have enlivened urban Portland in many ways. They have written GUIDE TO DOWNTOWN ART GALLERIES and CIRCLING THE CITY, a booklet on handicapped access to Portland buildings. The South Park Blocks now have attractive wooden benches donated by the Junior League of Portland to commemorate its 75th anniversary.

BARBECUED CRAB SOUP

THIS SOUP IS WONDERFUL SERVED IN CLEAR GLASS BOWLS.

YIELD:
4 servings

NOTES:
Canned crab meat, which has been rinsed and drained, can be substituted for fresh crab meat.

- 2 *(10 1/2-ounce) cans beef consommé*
- 2 *tablespoons soy sauce*
- 2 *tablespoons Worcestershire sauce*
- 1 *cup ketchup*
- 1/4 *teaspoon whole peppercorns*
- 1 *tablespoon onion, finely chopped*
- 2 *garlic cloves, minced*
- 1/2 *cup celery (1 stalk), chopped*
- 1/2 *cup fresh parsley, chopped*
- 1 *whole bay leaf*
- 1/2 *cup butter (1 cube)*
- 1 *pound fresh crab meat, cleaned and rinsed (See note.)*

In a large saucepan over medium heat, combine consommé, soy sauce, Worcestershire sauce, ketchup, peppercorns, onion, garlic, celery, parsley, bay leaf and butter. Simmer over medium heat until vegetables are tender. (Soup can be prepared ahead to this point and refrigerated or frozen until ready to serve.) Add crab meat to simmering mixture and gently heat through.

RIVER CITY CLAM CHOWDER

USE THIS RECIPE WHEN CLAM SEASON HITS THE NORTHWEST.

YIELD:
8 servings

- 8 *slices pepper bacon, diced*
- 1/2 *cup butter (1 cube)*
- 1/2 *large onion, chopped*
- 1 *cup celery (2 large stalks), chopped*
- 1/2 *cup all-purpose flour*
- 4 *(6-ounce) cans chopped clams or 2 cups fresh clams, shucked*
- 3 *large potatoes, peeled and cubed*
- 3 *cups milk*
- 1/2 *cup half and half*
- *Salt and white pepper*

In a large stockpot over medium-high heat, cook bacon until browned. Drain grease. Add butter, onions, and celery to stockpot and cook over medium heat until softened and onions are translucent. Add flour and cook 3 minutes, stirring constantly.

Drain clams and reserve liquid in a 1-pint measuring cup. Add enough water to clam liquid to equal 2 cups.

Add this liquid slowly to mixture in stockpot, stirring constantly. Add potatoes and bring mixture to boil. Reduce heat and simmer about 20 minutes or until potatoes are tender. Add clams, milk and half and half. Heat until thickened, being careful not to boil. Add salt and pepper and serve.

CIOPPINO

A West Coast favorite and a complete meal when served with our Crusty French Bread, page 63.

Yield:
6 to 8 servings

Notes:
To prepare shellfish: Scrub mussels and clams with stiff brush and rinse under cool water. Beard mussels just prior to cooking. Place mussels and clams in a large stockpot with enough water to cover. Cover and cook over medium heat until shells open. Discard any of the mussels and/or clams that do not open.

- 1 *large onion, sliced*
- 1 *bunch green onions (4 to 5 stalks), sliced*
- 1 *garlic clove, minced*
- 1 *green bell pepper, seeded, deveined and diced*
- 1/3 *cup olive oil*
- 1/3 *cup fresh parsley, chopped*
- 2 *cups tomato juice*
- 1 *(8-ounce) can tomato sauce*
- 1 *cup dry white wine*
- 2 *cups water*
- 1 *bay leaf*
- 1/2 *teaspoon freshly-ground black pepper*
- 1/2 *teaspoon rosemary, crumbled*
- 1/2 *teaspoon thyme*
- 1 *pound white fish (halibut, cod, snapper) cut into one-inch pieces*
- 1/2 *pound cooked medium shrimp*
- 1 *pound fresh clams or mussels in shells (See note.)*

In a large stockpot over medium-high heat, sauté onions, green onions, garlic and bell pepper in olive oil for 5 minutes or until softened. Add parsley, tomato juice, tomato sauce, white wine, bay leaf, water, pepper, rosemary and thyme and bring to a boil.

Reduce heat, cover and simmer for 1 hour. (Soup broth can be made ahead to this point and refrigerated.)

Add fish and simmer gently until fish is done. Add cooked shellfish, simmer briefly to heat through, and serve.

TANGY BAY SHRIMP CHOWDER

- *1/2 cup butter (1 cube)*
- *1 large onion, coarsely chopped*
- *2 cups celery (4 stalks), finely chopped*
- *3 cups mashed potatoes (3 potatoes, peeled, cut into thirds, boiled and mashed. Do not whip.)*
- *2 1/2 cups half and half*
- *1 cup dry white wine*
- *1 1/2 pounds cooked bay shrimp, divided*
- *Salt and white pepper*
- *Shrimp, parsley and chopped green onion for garnish*

In a large stockpot over medium heat, melt butter. Add onion and celery. Sauté until softened (about 8 minutes). Add potatoes and half and half and stir. Stir in wine and pepper. Reduce heat to medium low. Heat 10 minutes, stirring frequently. (Soup base may be made ahead.)

Just before serving, stir in 1 pound shrimp and simmer 5 minutes. If soup is too thick, thin with 1/2 cup of half and half. Garnish and serve with remaining shrimp, parsley and green onion.

A TANGY TREAT WHEN MADE WITH GOOD-QUALITY DRY WHITE WINE.

YIELD:
4 to 6 servings

NOTES:
May substitute 2 cans cream of potato soup for mashed potatoes.

ITALIAN SAUSAGE SOUP

- *1 pound hot Italian sausage (mild can be substituted), sliced and casings removed*
- *2 cups carrots (4 carrots), chopped*
- *1 medium onion, chopped*
- *1/2 cup celery (1 stalk celery), chopped*
- *1 cup fresh mushrooms, sliced*
- *2 tablespoons butter*
- *1/2 cup fresh parsley, chopped*
- *3 cups chicken broth*
- *1 (15 1/2-ounce) can garbanzo beans with liquid*
- *1 teaspoon dried sage*
- *Salt and pepper*
- *1 cup freshly-grated Parmesan cheese*

In a large saucepan over medium-high heat, sauté sausage until browned. Remove and set aside. Drain off excess grease. Add carrots, onion, celery, mushrooms and sauté in butter over medium-low heat for 5 to 10 minutes or until vegetables are softened.

Return sausage to pan and add parsley, chicken broth, garbanzo beans with liquid, sage, salt and pepper. Simmer 30 to 40 minutes.

To serve, sprinkle individual servings with Parmesan cheese.

THIS BEAUTIFULLY SIMPLE SOUP BRINGS THE FLAVOR OF ITALY TO YOUR TABLE.

YIELD:
6 servings

NOTES:
Serve this soup with French bread, sliced, buttered, sprinkled with Parmesan cheese, and broiled until lightly browned and crisp.

ZUCCHINI SOUP

This is a quick and easy microwave recipe!

Yield:
4 to 6 servings

Notes:
Make a triple batch and freeze when zucchini is in season.

- 3 *cups fresh zucchini, peeled and diced (See note.)*
- 1 1/3 *cups water*
- 2/3 *cup chicken broth*
- 1/4 *cup onion, chopped*
- 2 *slices bacon, cooked, drained and crumbled*
- 1 *garlic clove, minced*
- 2 *tablespoons fresh parsley, chopped*
- 1/2 *teaspoon dried basil*
- 1/2 *teaspoon salt*
- *Freshly-ground black pepper*
- *Freshly-grated Parmesan cheese*

Place zucchini in a 2-quart microwave-safe casserole. Gradually blend in water, broth, onion, bacon, garlic, parsley, basil and salt. Cover and cook in microwave 15 minutes on high. Stir casserole every five minutes. Zucchini should be tender after 15 minutes.

Remove casserole from microwave and cool slightly. Pour mixture into blender or food processor and purée until smooth. Return to casserole and reheat slowly in microwave for 2 to 3 minutes on high heat, stirring occasionally. Add pepper. Pour into serving bowls and garnish with Parmesan cheese.

GREEN CHILI CORN SOUP

A pretty, colorful soup with a Mexican flair.

Yield:
6 servings

Notes:
If using frozen corn kernels, thaw before puréeing.

- 6 *cups corn kernels, fresh or frozen, divided (See note.)*
- 1 *cup chicken broth*
- 4 *tablespoons butter (1/2 cube)*
- 2 *cups milk*
- 1 *garlic clove, minced*
- 1 *teaspoon dried oregano*
- *Salt and pepper*
- 1 *(4-ounce) can diced green chilies*
- 2 *cups Monterey Jack cheese, cubed*
- 2 *cups fresh tomatoes (3 medium tomatoes), peeled, seeded and diced*

In a food processor or blender, purée 4 cups corn and chicken broth. In a medium saucepan over medium heat, melt butter. Reduce heat to low and stir in puréed corn mixture and remaining 2 cups corn kernels. Add milk, garlic, oregano, salt and pepper to saucepan .

Add chilies and bring soup to boil. Reduce heat to medium-low and stir in cheese. Continue stirring until cheese is melted and blended into soup, being careful not to boil. When cheese is melted, soup is done.

To serve, place 3 tablespoons diced tomatoes in bottom of soup bowls and ladle soup over the top.

TOMATO-BASIL SOUP

YIELD:
8 to 10 servings

NOTES:
To substitute dried basil, use 2½ tablespoons. Fresh tomatoes can be substituted for canned whole tomatoes. Use 5 cups fresh tomatoes (7 to 8 medium tomatoes) peeled, seeded and chopped.

¼ cup butter (½ cube), plus 2 tablespoons, divided
5 tablespoons fresh basil, chopped and divided (See note.)
1 large yellow onion, coarsely chopped
6 garlic cloves, minced and divided
1 (35-ounce) can Italian plum tomatoes
1 (35-ounce) can whole tomatoes (See note.)
Salt and pepper
1½ teaspoons Italian seasoning
2 cups chicken broth
Fontina cheese, grated

In a large saucepan over medium heat, melt ¼ cup butter. Add 3 tablespoons basil, chopped onion and 4 cloves garlic. Cook until tender, about 15 minutes. Pour in tomatoes and their liquid. Simmer uncovered for 30 minutes. Season with salt and pepper.

In a food processor or blender, purée tomato mixture in small batches. Return mixture to saucepan. (Soup can be stored in refrigerator up to one day ahead at this point.)

In a small saucepan over medium heat, melt remaining 2 tablespoons butter. Add remaining 2 tablespoons basil, garlic and Italian seasoning and sauté for 5 minutes. Combine sautéed herbs with chicken broth and tomato mixture. Simmer until heated through. Serve immediately and garnish with grated Fontina cheese.

ARTICHOKE SOUP

A SPECIAL TREAT FOR ARTICHOKE LOVERS.

YIELD:
6 servings

NOTES:
This is a favorite from NO REGRETS, an earlier Junior League of Portland cookbook. Try serving it with a lemon twist.

4 (10-ounce) packages frozen artichoke hearts, divided
3 cups chicken broth
2 cups milk
1 tablespoon butter
2 garlic cloves, minced
Salt and pepper
Freshly-grated Parmesan cheese (optional)

Cook artichoke hearts as package directs. Drain. Reserve 1 cup artichoke hearts for garnish. Purée the remainder in a blender or food processor. Add chicken broth and blend until smooth.

Add milk, butter, garlic, salt and pepper. Blend until smooth. Pour mixture into a medium saucepan. Heat soup, stirring constantly, being careful not to boil.

Divide reserved artichokes evenly into 6 bowls. Ladle soup over top, sprinkle with Parmesan cheese and serve.

LEMON-MUSHROOM BISQUE

This very unusual mushroom soup gets its distinctive flavor from the lemon juice.

Yield:
4 to 6 servings

- 1 *pound firm white mushrooms (20-24 mushrooms), divided*
- 1/2 *cup freshly-squeezed lemon juice (2 lemons), divided*
- 1 *tablespoon unsalted butter*
- 2 *tablespoons shallots (4 shallots), minced*
- 1/2 *teaspoon dried thyme*
- 1 *teaspoon salt*
- 1/2 *bay leaf*
- 1/2 *teaspoon white pepper*
- 2 *cups half and half*
- 2 *cups chicken broth*
- 1 *teaspoon cornstarch dissolved in one tablespoon cold water*
- 1 *tablespoon parsley, minced*

In a food processor, place half of mushrooms and half of the lemon juice. Process mushrooms until finely chopped. Do not overprocess. Repeat with remaining mushrooms and remaining juice.

In a heavy saucepan over medium heat, melt butter. Add shallots and lightly sauté until softened, about 5 minutes. Pour in mushrooms, thyme, salt and bay leaf. Sauté over moderate heat until all liquid evaporates, approximately 10 minutes.

Add pepper, half and half and chicken broth to saucepan and bring mixture to a boil. Reduce heat and simmer 20 minutes. Add cornstarch mixture and simmer an additional 10 minutes, stirring constantly.

Serve in warmed bowls with a garnish of minced parsley and crusty French bread.

RED POTATO STEW

BEEF BROTH GIVES THIS WINTRY STEW AN UNUSUAL FLAVOR. SERVE THIS WITH GREEN SALAD AND CRUSTY BREAD FOR A SUNDAY NIGHT SUPPER.

YIELD:
6 servings

- *12 small red potatoes*
- *6 slices pepper bacon, diced*
- *1/2 medium red onion, chopped*
- *1/2 green or purple bell pepper, seeded, deveined and chopped*
- *3 tablespoons all-purpose flour*
- *3 cups beef bouillon or beef broth*
- *1 cup dry white wine (See note.)*
- *2 teaspoons dried thyme*
- *Freshly-ground pepper*
- *2 tablespoons fresh parsley, chopped*
- *1 cup half and half*

In a large stockpot over high heat, boil potatoes until tender. Drain and cool. Chop potatoes into quarters and set aside. In the same stockpot, sauté bacon until slightly browned. Remove bacon and set aside. Add onion and pepper to bacon drippings and sauté until softened. Add flour and stir until smooth.

Add beef bouillon or broth and bring to a boil. Reduce heat to low and add potatoes and bacon. Pour in white wine. Add thyme, pepper and parsley. Then add half and half. Heat through and serve.

NOTES:
Be sure to use a dry white wine.

CURRIED PUMPKIN SOUP

WARD OFF THE FIRST CHILL OF AUTUMN WITH THIS SEASONAL SOUP.

YIELD:
8 servings

- *1 large onion, diced*
- *1/4 cup butter (1/2 cube)*
- *1 teaspoon curry powder*
- *2 1/2 cups chicken broth*
- *3 cups canned pumpkin*
- *1/2 teaspoon salt*
- *2 cups half and half*
- *Sour cream*
- *Fresh parsley, coarsely chopped*

In a large saucepan over medium heat, sauté diced onions in butter until softened. Sprinkle in curry powder. Pour mixture into blender or food processor and purée until smooth. Return to saucepan and add chicken broth, canned pumpkin, salt and half and half. Heat through over medium heat. Do not bring to boil or soup will curdle. Garnish with a dollop of sour cream and chopped parsley flakes.

GINGER-PEA SOUP

THIS COLORFUL SOUP IS A WONDERFUL SPRING OR SUMMER DISH AND CAN BE SERVED HOT OR COLD.

YIELD:
6 to 8 servings

NOTES:
May be refrigerated and served chilled.

- *3 tablespoons butter*
- *3 inches fresh ginger, peeled and thinly sliced*
- *1 large potato, peeled and thinly sliced*
- *1 large onion, thinly sliced*
- *1 (14 1/2-ounce) can chicken broth, divided*
- *3 (10-ounce) packages frozen green peas, thawed and divided*
- *Milk or half and half to thin soup as desired*
- *1 tablespoon fresh parsley, finely chopped*

In a medium saucepan over medium heat, melt butter. Add ginger slices to butter and sauté over low heat until ginger is limp, but not browned. Remove 1/3 of ginger slices and set aside. Add potato, onion and 1/3 of chicken broth. Simmer until vegetables have softened.

Turn off heat and add all but one cup of peas. Purée mixture in blender or food processor. Add reserved chicken broth and ginger to puréed mixture and strain. Add reserved peas. Thin to desired consistency with milk or half and half. Return to saucepan, heat through and serve immediately. Garnish with fresh parsley.

CREAMY BRIE SOUP

SERVED IN CLEAR GLASS BOWLS, THIS SOUP IS VERY ATTRACTIVE.

YIELD:
4 to 6 servings

NOTES:
Serve this with PITA CRISPS, page 25.

- *4 tablespoons butter (1/2 cube)*
- *3/4 cup onion (1 medium onion), chopped*
- *3/4 cup celery (1 stalk celery), sliced*
- *1/4 cup all-purpose flour, sifted*
- *2 cups chicken broth*
- *2 cups milk or half and half*
- *1 (15-ounce) wheel Brie, rind removed and cut into 1-inch cubes*
- *Salt and pepper*
- *1 tablespoon freshly-grated Parmesan cheese*
- *2 tablespoons green onions, thinly sliced*

In a heavy saucepan over medium-low heat, melt butter. Add onions and celery and sauté 5 to 10 minutes or until softened. Add flour and cook 1 minute.

Gradually add liquids, stirring constantly until slightly thickened. (Soup can be made in advance to this point and stored in refrigerator until serving time.)

Over low heat, add cubes of Brie cheese. Use a heat-proof rubber spatula and stir constantly until all of cheese has completely melted. Add salt and pepper as desired.

Garnish with Parmesan cheese and thinly sliced green onions.

GAZPACHO

- 4 *medium tomatoes, peeled, seeded and diced, juice reserved*
- 1 *large red onion, diced*
- 2 *green onions, finely chopped*
- 1 *large cucumber, peeled, seeded and diced*
- 1/2 *green bell pepper, seeded, deveined and finely chopped*
- 1/2 *red bell pepper, seeded, deveined and finely chopped*
- 1 *large garlic clove, minced*
- 2 *cups tomato juice*
- 1/2 *cup beef broth*
- 1/4 *cup red wine vinegar*
- 3 *tablespoons olive oil*
- 3 *tablespoons fresh parsley, finely chopped*
- 2 *tablespoons freshly-squeezed lemon juice*
- 1/2 *teaspoon paprika*
- 1 *teaspoon salt*
- 1/4 *teaspoon pepper*
- 1/4 *teaspoon Worcestershire sauce*
- *Red pepper sauce (3 to 4 dashes)*
- *Sour cream*
- *Fresh parsley*

In a large bowl, combine tomatoes, red onion, green onions, cucumber, bell peppers and garlic. In a separate bowl, combine tomato juice, beef broth, vinegar, oil, parsley, lemon juice, paprika, salt, pepper, Worcestershire sauce and red pepper sauce and blend well. Pour over tomato mixture and blend together. Refrigerate at least 3 hours. Stir occasionally.

To serve, garnish individual bowls with a dollop of sour cream and parsley sprigs.

COOL OFF DURING HOT SUMMER DAYS WITH THIS CLASSIC COLD SOUP. TRY SERVING THIS IN TALL MARGARITA GLASSES WITH LIME WEDGES ON THE SIDE.

CHILL:
3 hours

YIELD:
4 to 6 servings

NOTES:
Lime wedges served as garnish add a piquant flavor when squeezed over the top of the soup. For a different taste, try cilantro instead of parsley.

CHILLED AVOCADO SOUP

TAKE ADVANTAGE OF FRESH RIPE AVOCADOS FOR THIS DELICIOUSLY RICH SOUP.

CHILL:
2 hours

YIELD:
6 servings

NOTES:
This is a favorite from NO REGRETS, an earlier Junior League of Portland cookbook.

- 4 *tablespoons all-purpose flour*
- 1/4 *teaspoon white pepper*
- 4 *cups plus 4 tablespoons chicken broth, divided*
- 3 *ripe avocados, peeled*
- 1/2 *cup half and half, chilled*
- *Salt and pepper*
- 1 *tablespoon fresh dill, chopped to garnish*
- 1 *tablespoon fresh chives, chopped to garnish*
- 1 *teaspoon dried oregano*
- *Freshly-ground black pepper*

In a large saucepan over medium heat, whisk together flour, white pepper and 4 tablespoons chicken broth. Add remaining 4 cups of broth, raise heat and bring to boil, stirring constantly. Remove from heat.

In the meantime, in a food processor or blender, purée the avocados. Add avocado to the chicken broth and cool. Pour into storage container and chill for at least 2 hours.

When ready to serve, stir in half and half and season with salt and pepper. Garnish with dill, chives, oregano and freshly-ground pepper.

ANNABANANA SOUP

THIS RECIPE SOUNDS UNUSUAL, BUT IT'S WONDERFUL AND IT'S FUN TO GUESS WHAT INGREDIENTS ARE USED!

CHILL:
1 hour

YIELD:
4 to 6 servings

- 2 *cups chicken broth*
- 1 *onion, thinly sliced*
- 1 *potato, peeled and thinly sliced*
- 1 *tart green apple, peeled and chopped*
- 1 *banana, sliced*
- 2 to 3 *teaspoons mild curry powder*
- 2 *cups half and half*
- *Sour cream*
- *Fresh chives, minced*

In a saucepan over medium heat, slowly heat chicken broth. Add onion, potato, apple and banana to stock and simmer until vegetables are tender.

Remove from heat and add curry powder. Purée mixture in blender or food processor. Pour into large bowl. Stir in half and half and chill at least 1 hour. To serve, pour into individual bowls and garnish with a dollop of sour cream and fresh chives.

TAILGATE SANDWICH

1	*loaf focaccia*
	Olive oil
	Salt and other desired dried herbs
6 to 8	*tablespoons butter, room temperature*
4 to 6	*tablespoons mayonnaise*
4 to 6	*tablespoons Dijon mustard*
1/4	*pound turkey, sliced*
1/4	*pound prosciutto, sliced*
1	*red onion, thinly sliced*
1/4	*pound provolone cheese, sliced*
1	*small tomato, thinly sliced*
1	*cup fresh spinach, shredded*

Preheat oven to 300 degrees.

Season bread by brushing top of loaf with olive oil and sprinkling with salt and other seasonings. Place on lightly greased cookie sheet and bake for 15 to 20 minutes in a 300-degree oven. Remove and cool.

Slice cooled focaccia in half horizontally and spread both halves with butter, mayonnaise and mustard. Layer ingredients on bottom half of bread in the following order: turkey, prosciutto, onion, provolone, tomato slices and spinach. Place second half on top of layered half. Wrap sandwich tightly with plastic wrap, then wrap in aluminum foil.

Refrigerate at least 8 hours, or overnight.

Cut into wedges to serve.

INSPIRED BY THE ANNUAL "CIVIL WAR" FOOTBALL GAME BETWEEN THE UNIVERSITY OF OREGON AND OREGON STATE UNIVERSITY.

TEMPERATURE:
Preheat 300 degrees

BAKE:
15 to 20 minutes

CHILL:
8 hours or overnight

YIELD:
4 to 6 servings

LE PAIN FLORENTINE

A favorite from the Pittock Mansion Gate Lodge.

Chill:
Several hours

Yield:
6 to 8 servings

Notes:
To serve warm, brush outside of loaf with olive oil, wrap in foil and bake at 325 degrees for 30 minutes. For a variation, substitute capers for pimiento and add tomato slices.

- 1 *(10-inch) round loaf French or sourdough bread*
- 1 *(3-ounce) package cream cheese, softened and whipped*
- 1/2 *pound ham, thinly sliced*
- 1 *cup frozen spinach, thawed, well-drained and chopped*

CHEESE MIXTURE:

- 1 *cup Cheddar cheese, grated*
- 1 *cup mozzarella cheese, grated*
- 1/2 *cup mayonnaise*
- 2 *tablespoons pimiento, chopped*

Cut a 1-inch slice off top of round loaf of bread and set aside. Hollow out inside of loaf, leaving approximately 1/2 to 3/4-inch thickness of bread on sides and bottom. Spread cavity with whipped cream cheese. Layer ham inside bread so it overlaps and hangs about 3 inches over the outside of bread round.

Spread 1/2 of cheese mixture over layered ham slices, in bottom of loaf.

Spread chopped spinach on top of cheese layer. Top with remaining cheese mixture. Fold overhanging edges of ham over top of cheese layer to seal. Replace top slice of bread. Chill for several hours.

To serve, cut into wedges.

TURKEY WITH CHEESE IN PUFF PASTRY

- 2 *(10-inch) squares frozen puff pastry, partially thawed*
- 2 *tablespoons Dijon mustard*
- 1/2 *pound turkey, thinly sliced*
- 1 1/2 *cups Swiss cheese, grated*
- 1 *egg, beaten*

Preheat oven to 350 degrees.

Spread top of one pastry sheet with mustard. Layer turkey slices followed by a layer of grated cheese. Place other pastry sheet on top. Crimp edges together using a fork dipped in cold water. Make sure edges are well-sealed.

Brush top with beaten egg. Cut vent holes in top of pastry dough. Place on lightly greased cookie sheet and bake in a 350-degree oven for approximately 35 minutes or until pastry is puffy and golden brown. Serve hot or at room temperature.

Another treat from the Pittock Mansion Gate Lodge. A perfect brunch item when served with Gazpacho, page 90.

Temperature:
Preheat 350 degrees

Bake:
35 to 40 minutes

Yield:
6 to 8 servings or 16 hors d'oeuvre squares

Notes:
Ham and honey mustard can be substituted for turkey and Dijon mustard.

CHUTNEY ROAST BEEF SANDWICH

- 2 *(10-inch) sheets frozen puff pastry, thawed*
- 1 1/2 *pounds lean roast beef, thinly sliced*
- 1 1/2 *cups mango chutney*
- 1 *egg, beaten*

Preheat oven to 350 degrees.

Join edges of puff pastry to form a rectangle. Layer roast beef on top of pastry. Spread chutney over roast beef and roll the pastry in a jelly-roll fashion. Place seam-side down on cookie sheet and brush with beaten egg. Place in a 350-degree oven and bake for about 30 minutes or until pastry is golden.

Remove from oven, cool slightly, cut into one-inch slices and serve.

Temperature:
Preheat 350 degrees

Bake:
30 minutes

Yield:
6 servings

CUCUMBER TEA SANDWICHES

An elegant classic for any luncheon.

Chill:
Several hours

Yield:
6 to 8 servings

Notes:
If made the night before, place a layer of damp paper towels over the sandwiches before wrapping in plastic wrap to prevent bread from drying out.

- 3/4 *cup fresh parsley, chopped*
- 1/2 *cup green onions, chopped*
- 1 *(8-ounce) package cream cheese, room temperature*
- 1 *cup mayonnaise*
- 1 1/2 *loaves soft white thin-sliced sandwich bread*
- 2 *long, narrow cucumbers*

In a food processor, combine parsley and green onions and pulse 3 to 4 times, until mixture is finely chopped.

In a small bowl, combine cream cheese and mayonnaise. Add parsley mixture and mix well. Set aside.

Using a 1 3/4-inch round cookie cutter, cut 2 rounds out of each slice of bread.

Score the sides of the cucumbers with a fork or an orange grinder. Slice the cucumbers into thin slices.

Spread cream cheese mixture on bread rounds. Top with a slice of cucumber and place each sandwich on a tray lined with wax paper. Cover the tray tightly with plastic wrap and refrigerate until ready to serve.

LAMB GYROS (LAMB MEATLOAF SANDWICH)

1 1/2 to 2 pounds ground lamb
1 (8-ounce) can tomato sauce
1 cup onion (1 large onion), finely chopped
1 cup green bell pepper (2 medium peppers), seeded, deveined and finely chopped
1/2 cup bread crumbs
2 eggs, lightly beaten
1/4 cup fresh mint, chopped (See note.)
1/2 teaspoon freshly-ground pepper
1/2 teaspoon dried basil
1/2 teaspoon dried oregano
2 large garlic cloves, minced
2 Roma tomatoes, thinly sliced
1 large cucumber, thinly sliced
1 red onion, thinly sliced
8 pita pocket breads

TZATZIKI SAUCE:

8 ounces plain yogurt
1/2 teaspoon ground cumin
1 medium garlic clove, minced
1/2 cup freshly-squeezed lemon juice
Dash of red wine vinegar
Salt and pepper

Preheat oven to 350 degrees.

In a large bowl, combine lamb, tomato sauce, onion, bell pepper, bread crumbs, eggs, mint, pepper, basil, oregano and garlic. Mix well and pour into large loaf pan. Bake in a 350-degree oven for approximately 1 1/2 hours, or until top is browned and loaf is cooked through.

In a small bowl, prepare sauce by combining yogurt, cumin, garlic, lemon juice, wine vinegar, salt and pepper. Set aside.

Cool meatloaf and cut into 1-inch thick slices. Slice pocket breads in half and spread inside of pockets with tzatziki sauce. Place a few slices of tomato, cucumber and onion inside of pocket. Place slice of meatloaf into each pocket and serve immediately. Serve with sauce on the side.

HOMEMADE FRENCH FRIES WOULD MAKE THIS A GREAT SUNDAY NIGHT MEAL.

TEMPERATURE:
Preheat 350 degrees

BAKE:
1 1/2 hours

YIELD:
6 to 8 servings

NOTES:
Mint is optional; use only if fresh mint is available. Feta cheese and lettuce leaves can be added to sandwiches for variation.

DILLED REUBEN SANDWICH

A WELCOME LUNCH AFTER GOLF.

TEMPERATURE:
Preheat 500 degrees

BROIL:
4 to 6 minutes

YIELD:
6 servings

NOTES:
Serve with horseradish, and dill pickles.

- 1 *cup mayonnaise*
- 1/4 *cup Dijon mustard*
- 1 *teaspoon dried dill*
- 3 *tablespoons butter*
- 12 *slices rye bread*
- 1/2 *pound corned beef, thinly sliced, room temperature*
- 1 1/2 *cups sauerkraut, rinsed, drained, room temperature*
- 1/2 *pound Jarlsberg Swiss cheese (6 slices)*

In a small bowl, combine mayonnaise, mustard and dill. Mix well and set aside.

Butter one side of each of 6 slices of bread and place buttered-side down on an ungreased baking sheet. Spread top sides with mayonnaise mixture. Place one layer each of corned beef, sauerkraut and cheese on slices of bread. Place remaining slices on top of layered slices with buttered side up. Broil for 2 to 3 minutes on each side. Serve immediately.

CURRIED CHICKEN POCKET SANDWICHES

YIELD:
4 to 5 servings

- 2 *cups cooked chicken, chopped*
- 4 *ounces water chestnuts, diced*
- 1 *cup celery (2 stalks), diced*
- 1/2 *cup slivered almonds, toasted*
- 1/2 *cup seedless grapes*
- 1 *cup mayonnaise*
- 1/2 *teaspoon curry powder*
- 1 *teaspoon soy sauce*
- 4 *pita pocket breads*

In a large bowl, combine chicken, water chestnuts, celery, almonds, and grapes. In a small bowl, mix together mayonnaise, curry and soy sauce. Pour over top of chicken mixture and toss until all ingredients are well coated.

Slice pita pocket breads in half to form two pockets. Fill each half with chicken mixture and serve.

FRENCH DIP SANDWICHES

Delicious!

Cook:
4 hours

Yield:
8 servings

1/4	*cup olive oil*
1	*5-pound chuck roast, fat trimmed*
2	*large garlic cloves, minced*
	Salt and pepper
1	*cup beef broth*
1	*cup good quality, freshly-brewed strong coffee*
1	*cup red wine*
1	*package dry onion soup mix*
1	*cup water*
8	*sandwich-sized French rolls*

In a large stockpot, warm oil over medium-high heat. Rub roast with minced garlic and sprinkle with salt and pepper. Place roast into stockpot and brown on all sides.

Drain oil and add beef broth, coffee, red wine, soup mix and water. Bring to a boil. Reduce heat, cover stockpot and simmer approximately 4 hours. Turn roast over once, midway through cooking.

Remove from heat, lift roast from broth and set aside at least 15 minutes to cool before slicing.

Reheat broth and skim off any excess grease. Place rolls in a 250-degree oven and warm.

While rolls are in oven, slice roast.

Remove rolls from oven. Slice in half horizontally. Place sliced roast beef on half of each roll. Top with second half and slice sandwiches in half on the diagonal. Serve with a cup of warm broth for dipping.

Vegetables & Side Dishes

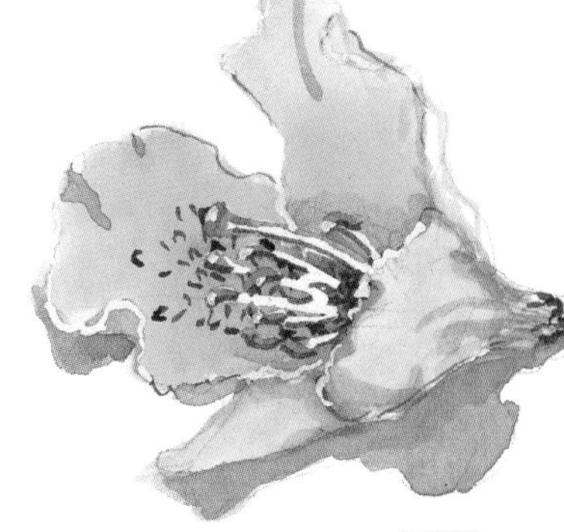

W. Mark

Gardens and Garnishes

What mother wouldn't treasure a stroll with her children along the serene pathways of a Portland park, glorying in a spectacular mass of color from rhododendrons and azaleas bursting into spring bloom?

Each May such strolls are a tradition in the Crystal Springs Rhododendron Gardens, where the Mother's Day Rhododendron Show draws families and friends to feed the ducks, explore the garden and watch the sun set over Portland's West Hills.

Crystal Springs' floral magnificence will inspire a Mother's Day menu to enjoy afterwards, a menu filled with the flavor of fresh vegetables which signal spring. Invite New Potato Francaise and tender Sesame Asparagus to grace the table. A spray of cherry blossoms cut from a private garden provides the finishing touch.

Junior League volunteers feel a strong connection to gardens and the outdoors, digging energetically into such past projects as the Leach Botanical Garden Outdoor Classroom and the World Forestry Center's Tropical Rainforest exhibit.

MARINATED GARLIC TOMATOES

- *3 large beefsteak tomatoes, peeled and sliced into 1/2-inch pieces*
- *1/2 cup vegetable or olive oil*
- *2 tablespoons lemon juice or vinegar*
- *2 garlic cloves, minced*
- *1/2 teaspoon salt*
- *1/2 teaspoon freshly-ground pepper*
- *1/2 teaspoon dried oregano (See note.)*
- *1/2 teaspoon dried thyme or lemon thyme (See note.)*
- *1 teaspoon granulated sugar*

Place sliced tomatoes in a serving bowl. In a separate mixing bowl, combine oil, lemon juice, garlic, salt, pepper, oregano, thyme and sugar. Pour over tomatoes and marinate in refrigerator for a minimum of 2 hours. Serve at room temperature.

THIS IS EXCELLENT WITH BARBECUED HAMBURGERS.

MARINATE:
2 hours

YIELD:
4 servings

NOTES:
1 tablespoon of fresh oregano and 1 tablespoon of fresh thyme can be substituted.

STUFFED ITALIAN TOMATOES

ALMONDS ADD A CRUNCHY TEXTURE TO THESE TOMATOES.

SAUTÉ:
20 minutes

TEMPERATURE:
Preheat 350 degrees

BAKE:
20 minutes

YIELD:
8 to 10 servings

- *8 large tomatoes*
- *3 tablespoons olive oil*
- *1 cup onions (1 large onion), chopped*
- *1 (10-ounce) package frozen chopped spinach, thawed and drained*
- *1 cup ricotta cheese*
- *2 egg yolks, beaten*
- *1/2 cup parsley, chopped*
- *1/2 cup mozzarella cheese, grated*
- *2/3 cup freshly-grated Parmesan cheese*
- *1/2 cup almonds, toasted and slivered*
- *Salt and pepper*

Preheat oven to 350 degrees.

Wash tomatoes, remove tops and scrape out pulp. Salt cavity of tomatoes and turn upside down to drain for 30 minutes.

In a sauté pan over medium heat, cook onions in oil for 20 minutes or until softened. Add spinach to onions and stir until heated through. Remove from heat and set aside.

In a mixing bowl, beat together ricotta cheese and egg yolks. Add parsley, mozzarella cheese, Parmesan cheese and slivered almonds. Season with salt and pepper.

Stir in sautéed onion and spinach mixture and blend until all ingredients are well combined. Fill tomatoes with mixture and place stuffed tomatoes in a shallow, greased baking dish.

Sprinkle tops of stuffing with additional Parmesan cheese and place in 350-degree oven. Bake for 20 minutes or until tops are brown.

FRESH TOMATO TART

CRUST:

- 2 *cups all-purpose flour*
- 1/2 *teaspoon salt*
- 2 *tablespoons granulated sugar*
- 4 *teaspoons baking powder*
- 1/3 *cup butter, chilled*
- 3/4 *cup buttermilk or milk*

FILLING:

- 5 *medium tomatoes*
- 3/4 *teaspoon salt*
- 1/2 *teaspoon dried basil*
- 1/4 *teaspoon dried oregano*
- 1/4 *teaspoon dried thyme*
- 1/4 *teaspoon savory or mixed Italian herbs*
- 1/4 *teaspoon freshly-ground black pepper*

TOPPING:

- 1 *cup mayonnaise*
- 1 *cup Swiss cheese, grated*
- 1 *cup Cheddar cheese, grated*

TEMPERATURE:
Preheat 450 degrees/lower 400 degrees

BAKE:
8 minutes/15 minutes

YIELD:
6 servings

NOTES:
One large tart can be made using a deep 9-inch round baking or soufflé dish. Follow instructions as shown, placing entire baked crust and all of filling into baking dish. Increase assembled tart baking time by 10 minutes.

CRUST:

Preheat oven to 450 degrees.

In a medium bowl or food processor, sift flour, salt, sugar and baking powder. Add butter and cut with two knives or process until a coarse crumb mixture forms. Add buttermilk (or milk) and combine mixture until a soft dough forms. Cover dough and place in a draft-free area for 30 minutes to allow dough to rise slightly.

FILLING:

In a large saucepan over high heat, bring water to a boil. Add tomatoes and leave in boiling water for 10 to 15 seconds. Drain tomatoes and rinse immediately with cold water.

When tomatoes are cool enough to handle, remove and discard skins. Cut tomatoes into 1-inch pieces and sprinkle with herbs. Toss gently and adjust seasoning as necessary. Set aside.

TOPPING:

In a mixing bowl, combine mayonnaise, Swiss and Cheddar cheeses.

TO ASSEMBLE TART:

Prepare six 10-ounce baking cups, soufflé dishes or ramekins by lightly greasing the inside surface with butter. Divide dough into 6 pieces.

Line baking dishes with dough, pressing dough evenly into bottom and up sides of dishes being used. Place into oven and bake crust approximately 8 minutes or until crust just begins to brown.

The crust will become puffy and slightly pull away from top rim of baking dish. Remove from oven and fill each crust with about 1/2 cup of filling and 1/2 cup of topping. Turn oven down to 400 degrees and return tarts to oven. Bake 15 minutes longer, until crust is browned and topping is lightly browned and puffy. Serve warm or cold.

GREEN BEANS WITH PEANUT SAUCE

Blanch:
1 minute

Sauté:
2 to 4 minutes

Yield:
4 servings

Notes:
Substitute 1 tablespoon freshly-grated ginger for ground ginger. If peanut or sesame oil is unavailable, butter can be substituted.

1 1/2 pounds fresh green beans, cleaned and trimmed
2 tablespoons creamy peanut butter
1/2 cup water
1 teaspoon ground ginger (See note.)
1/4 teaspoon cayenne pepper
1 teaspoon peanut or sesame oil (See note.)
1 to 2 garlic cloves, minced
1/2 teaspoon salt

In a medium saucepan, bring salted water to a boil. Add beans and blanch until just tender and bright green, approximately 1 minute. Drain and rinse under cold water to stop beans from cooking any further. Set aside.

In a small mixing bowl, combine peanut butter, water, ginger and cayenne pepper. Set aside.

In a large sauté pan over medium-high heat, add oil and sauté garlic until softened. Add salt, pour in peanut butter mixture and combine well. Add green beans, sauté for 2 to 4 minutes and serve immediately.

FRESH GREEN BEANS ITALIANO

- 1 *pound fresh green beans, cleaned with ends snapped off (See note.)*
- 2 *tablespoons olive oil*
- 2 *garlic cloves, minced*
- *Salt and pepper*

In a medium saucepan over high heat, bring salted water to a boil. Add green beans. Blanch until beans are bright green, approximately 5 minutes.

In a serving bowl, combine olive oil and garlic. Set aside.

When beans are done, remove from heat and rinse with cold water to stop beans from cooking any further. Drain. Pour into serving bowl and toss thoroughly with olive oil and garlic. Season with salt and pepper. Set aside to allow flavors to blend and serve at room temperature.

This is a great summer vegetable dish that can be prepared in advance.

Blanch:
5 minutes

Yield:
4 servings

Notes:
Adding salt to boiling water keeps beans a bright green color.

TOSSED ZUCCHINI

- 6 *medium zucchinis, sliced into 1/3-inch strips or julienned*
- 1 *tablespoon olive oil*
- 1/2 *teaspoon onion salt*
- 3/4 *cup freshly-grated Parmesan cheese*
- 2 *tablespoons pine nuts, toasted*
- *Salt and pepper*
- *Parmesan cheese for garnish*

Preheat oven to 350 degrees.

Warm olive oil in a large saucepan over medium heat. Sauté zucchini for 5 to 10 minutes or until tender. Add onion salt, Parmesan cheese, pine nuts, salt and pepper. Remove from heat. Place zucchini mixture in a shallow casserole dish. Sprinkle additional Parmesan cheese over top and place in a 350-degree oven for approximately 10 minutes or until cheese browns.

Sauté:
5 to 10 minutes

Temperature:
Preheat 350 degrees

Bake:
10 minutes

Yield:
6 servings

ZUCCHINI RELLENOS

This main course dish makes good use of bumper zucchini crops!

Sauté:
15 minutes

Temperature:
Preheat 350 degrees

Bake:
30 minutes

Yield:
4 to 6 servings

- 6 medium whole zucchini
- 1 1/2 cups fresh corn kernels or frozen corn kernels, thawed and drained
- 2 eggs
- 2 tablespoons milk
- 1/4 teaspoon salt
- 2 tablespoons mild green chilies, diced
- 2 cups mozzarella cheese, grated and divided
- 2 tablespoons butter, room temperature

TOMATO SAUCE:

- 4 large fresh tomatoes, chopped
- 1/3 cup red onion, chopped
- 2 garlic cloves, minced
- 1 teaspoon ground cumin
- 1/4 teaspoon salt
- 2 tablespoons olive oil
- 1/3 cup fresh cilantro, chopped

Preheat oven to 350 degrees.

Cut zucchini in half lengthwise and scoop out flesh. (Discard flesh or save for another use.) Place hollowed-out zucchini in a greased baking dish.

In a blender or food processor, combine corn kernels, eggs, milk and salt. Pulse until ingredients form a coarse purée. Pour into a bowl and stir in green chilies and 1 1/2 cups mozzarella cheese, reserving remaining 1/2 cup cheese for topping.

Fill zucchini shells with corn mixture. Sprinkle with remaining cheese and dot with butter. Cover baking dish with foil and bake approximately 30 minutes or until zucchini is tender, being careful not to overbake.

TOMATO SAUCE:

In a blender or food processor, combine tomatoes, onion, garlic, cumin and salt until coarsely chopped. In a sauté pan, heat olive oil and pour in tomato mixture. Cook for approximately 15 minutes or until mixture thickens. Stir in cilantro. Serve with zucchini.

ENCORE CAULIFLOWER

GUARANTEED TO MAKE A CAULIFLOWER LOVER OUT OF YOU!

TEMPERATURE:
Preheat 350 degrees

BAKE:
30 minutes

YIELD:
6 to 8 servings

- 1 *lemon, halved*
- 1 *medium cauliflower, broken into bite-sized pieces*
- 4 *tablespoons butter, divided*
- 1/2 *cup onion, chopped*
- 3 *tablespoons all-purpose flour*
- 1 1/2 *cups milk*
- 1/4 *teaspoon dried thyme*
- 1/4 *teaspoon dried basil*
- 1/4 *teaspoon curry powder*
- 1 *teaspoon salt*
- 1/2 *cup Cheddar cheese, grated*
- 1/4 *cup parsley, chopped*
- 1/2 *cup bread crumbs*

Preheat oven to 350 degrees.

Fill a saucepan with 1 inch of water. Squeeze one lemon half into water and add salt. Place cauliflower in saucepan, add squeezed lemon half and bring to a boil. Boil until cauliflower is just tender. Drain and set aside.

In a medium saucepan, melt 1 tablespoon butter and sauté onion until it is softened. Add flour and stir into mixture until smooth, approximately 1 minute. Gradually pour in milk, seasonings and grated cheese. Squeeze juice from remaining lemon half and add to sauce. While stirring, add parsley and remove from heat.

Place cauliflower in a buttered 1 1/2-quart baking dish. Pour sauce over cauliflower. Sprinkle with bread crumbs and dot with butter. Bake uncovered at 350 degrees for 30 minutes.

SESAME ASPARAGUS

STEAM:
8 to 10 minutes

SAUTÉ:
5 minutes

YIELD:
4 to 6 servings

- 2 *pounds fresh asparagus, trimmed*
- 2 *tablespoons butter*
- 1/4 *cup sesame seeds*
- 1/4 *cup freshly-squeezed lemon juice*
- *Salt*

In a medium saucepan, steam asparagus 8 to 10 minutes or until just tender. In a separate sauté pan over medium heat, melt butter. Add sesame seeds and sauté until golden, approximately 5 minutes. Add lemon juice and heat thoroughly.

Transfer asparagus to heated serving platter and pour sauce over the top. Season lightly with salt and serve.

DEVILED ASPARAGUS

A GOOD WAY TO USE LEFTOVER HARD-BOILED EASTER EGGS.

STEAM:
4 to 5 minutes

YIELD:
4 to 6 servings

NOTES:
The asparagus can be placed in a glass pie pan, with a small amount of water, covered with plastic wrap and microwaved for 3 to 4 minutes.

- *2 hard-boiled eggs, coarsely chopped*
- *2 tablespoons parsley, finely chopped*
- *1/2 teaspoon salt*
- *1/8 teaspoon pepper*
- *2 to 4 dashes red pepper sauce*
- *3/4 cup butter, melted and cooled*
- *2 to 3 pounds fresh asparagus, trimmed and stalks peeled (See note.)*

In a small bowl, whisk together eggs, parsley, salt, pepper and red pepper sauce. Continue to stir and pour melted butter into mixture in a steady stream. Cover bowl tightly and set aside.

In a tall stockpot, steam asparagus until just tender, being careful not to overcook. Transfer asparagus to a heated plate and arrange spears in a decorative pattern. Pour half of sauce over the asparagus and serve. Pour remainder of sauce in a bowl to serve with asparagus.

DOUBLE ORANGE CARROTS

BLANCH :
5 to 6 minutes

COOK
2 to 3 minutes

YIELD:
4 servings

- *4 cups water*
- *10 medium carrots, peeled and sliced diagonally*
- *2 tablespoons granulated sugar*
- *2 teaspoons cornstarch*
- *1/2 teaspoon salt*
- *1/2 teaspoon ground ginger*
- *1/2 cup orange juice*
- *4 tablespoons butter (1/2 cube)*

In a saucepan, bring water to a boil. Add carrots and cook until just tender. Drain, set aside and cover to keep warm.

In a small saucepan over medium heat, combine sugar, cornstarch, salt, ginger and orange juice. Stir constantly until mixture thickens. Raise heat and boil 1 minute longer. Stir in butter, pour over hot carrots, toss thoroughly and serve.

OREGON WALNUT BROCCOLI

- 4 *cups (1 1/2 bunches) fresh broccoli, blanched and cut into florets*
- 1/2 *cup plus 3 tablespoons butter, divided*
- 4 *tablespoons all-purpose flour*
- 4 *cups chicken broth*
- 1/3 *package dry stuffing mix*
- 1/3 *cup Oregon walnuts, chopped*

Preheat oven to 350 degrees.

Cook broccoli until just tender. Drain and place in a greased 9 x 13-inch casserole. Set aside.

In a saucepan over medium heat, melt 1/2 cup butter. Stir in flour until blended and add broth. Pour over broccoli.

In a small saucepan, melt remaining 3 tablespoons of butter and pour over stuffing mix. Toss to coat and layer stuffing over top of broccoli. Sprinkle with walnuts.

Place in a 350-degree oven and bake 30 minutes.

TEMPERATURE:
Preheat 350 degrees

COOK:
5 to 7 minutes

BAKE:
30 minutes

YIELD:
6 to 8 servings

NOTES:
Two (8-ounce) packages of frozen broccoli can be substituted for fresh broccoli.

EGGPLANT CASSEROLE

Broil:
4 minutes per side, per batch

Sauté:
10 minutes

Temperature:
Preheat 500 degrees/lower 350 degrees

Bake:
30 minutes

3	*medium eggplants, sliced into 1/4-inch slices*
	Salt
1/2	*cup canola or olive oil*
1/2	*cup onion (1 medium), coarsely chopped*
1	*pound ground beef*
1	*garlic clove, minced*
1/2	*teaspoon dried oregano*
1	*teaspoon dried basil*
1/2	*teaspoon cinnamon*
1	*teaspoon salt*
	Dash of freshly-ground pepper
1	*(8-ounce) can tomato sauce*
10	*slices mozzarella cheese*
1/4	*cup freshly-grated Parmesan cheese*

Preheat broiler to 500 degrees.

Place sliced eggplant into a colander, sprinkle well with salt and set aside for at least 30 minutes to allow salt to draw excess liquid from eggplant. Pat eggplant slices dry with a paper towel. Place on a greased or non-stick baking sheet and brush with oil using a pastry brush. Broil for approximately 4 minutes or until slices are just browned. Turn slices over and repeat process for remaining side.

Layer broiled eggplant slices in a 9 x 13-inch greased baking dish. Set aside.

In a sauté pan over medium-high heat, combine onion and ground beef and sauté until meat is browned. Stir in garlic, oregano, basil, cinnamon, salt and pepper. Add tomato sauce, remove from heat and cool.

Preheat oven to 350 degrees.

Place large tablespoons of beef mixture on top of eggplant slices in baking dish. Place slices of mozzarella cheese over top to completely cover beef layer. Sprinkle with Parmesan cheese and bake at 350 degrees for 30 minutes.

Sprinkle with additional Parmesan cheese just prior to serving.

GINGER PEAS WITH SUMMER SQUASH

- 2 *tablespoons olive oil*
- 3 *tablespoons green onions, thinly sliced*
- 2 *teaspoons freshly-grated ginger*
- 1 *garlic clove, minced*
- 1 *pound snow peas, stems and tips removed and thinly sliced*
- 3/4 *pound yellow summer squash, thinly sliced*
- 1 *yellow bell pepper, seeded, deveined and chopped*
- 1 *tablespoon fresh cilantro, chopped (See note.)*
- *Salt and pepper*

In a sauté pan, heat oil and sauté green onions, ginger and garlic for about 1 minute.

Add peas, squash and pepper and sauté an additional 4 to 5 minutes or until vegetables are just tender. Remove from heat, sprinkle with cilantro and season with salt and pepper. Serve immediately.

AN OUTSTANDING VEGETABLE MEDLEY. THE GINGER ADDS AN UNEXPECTED TWIST.

SAUTÉ:
6 minutes

YIELD:
4 servings

NOTES:
Substitute chopped parsley for cilantro.

JULIENNED PEPPER MEDLEY

- 3 *tablespoons freshly-squeezed lemon juice*
- 2 *tablespoons fresh cilantro, chopped (See note.)*
- 1/2 *teaspoon ground cumin*
- 1 *teaspoon granulated sugar*
- 1/3 *cup olive oil*
- 2 *red or purple bell peppers, seeded, deveined and sliced into thin strips*
- 2 *green or yellow bell peppers, seeded, deveined and sliced into thin strips*
- *Salt and freshly-ground black pepper*

In a mixing bowl, combine lemon juice, cilantro, cumin and sugar. Gradually pour in oil, whisking constantly until thoroughly blended. Place sliced peppers into a serving bowl, pour oil over them and toss until coated with dressing. Add salt and pepper. Cover and chill for at least 1 hour prior to serving to allow flavors to blend.

THIS COLORFUL BELL PEPPER COMBINATION GOES WELL WITH BARBEQUED MEATS.

CHILL:
1 hour

YIELD:
4 servings

NOTES:
Substitute chopped parsley for cilantro.

WALLA WALLA ONION CASSEROLE

Walla Walla onions are available in late summer. Don't miss an opportunity to showcase these deliciously sweet onions from the Northwest.

Temperature:
Preheat 350 degrees

Bake:
30 minutes

Yield:
6 servings

Notes:
Two dozen soda crackers, crushed, can be substituted for bread crumbs. If using soda crackers, add 1 teaspoon Accent or similar seasoning to milk and egg mixture.

- *3 large or 6 small Walla Walla sweet onions, sliced*
- *1/2 cup butter (1 cube)*
- *1 cup seasoned bread crumbs (See note.)*
- *2 cups milk*
- *3 eggs, lightly beaten*
- *Salt and pepper*
- *2 cups Cheddar cheese, grated*

Preheat oven to 350 degrees.

In a sauté pan over medium heat, melt butter. Sauté sliced onions in butter until softened. Grease a 9 x 13-inch pan with butter or margarine. Line bottom of baking pan with bread crumbs. Place onions on top of bread crumbs.

In a mixing bowl, combine milk, eggs, salt and pepper together and pour over onions. Sprinkle Cheddar cheese over mixture and place in oven. Bake at 350 degrees for 30 minutes. Remove from oven, cover with a dish towel and let stand for 15 minutes prior to serving.

LEPRECHAUN POTATOES

KIDS WILL LOVE THIS RECIPE!

- 4 *large baking potatoes, baked (See note.)*
- 1/2 *cup butter (1 cube), room temperature*
- 1/2 *teaspoon salt*
- 1 *teaspoon granulated sugar*
- 1/4 *cup fresh chives, chopped*
- 1/2 *teaspoon dried dill*
- 1/2 *teaspoon garlic powder*
- *Dash of ground nutmeg*
- 1 *(10-ounce) package frozen chopped spinach, cooked and drained*
- 2 *tablespoons sour cream*
- 1/4 *cup freshly-grated Parmesan cheese*

Preheat oven to 350 degrees.

Slice cooled potatoes in half lengthwise and scoop out flesh.

In a large bowl, combine potato pulp, butter, salt, sugar, chives, dill, garlic powder, nutmeg, cooked spinach and sour cream. Mix together thoroughly.

Fill potato skins with mixture and place in a baking dish. Bake uncovered at 350 degrees for 30 minutes. Remove from oven and sprinkle with Parmesan cheese. Return to oven and broil at 500 degrees for approximately 3 minutes, or until tops are golden brown.

TEMPERATURE:
Preheat 350 degrees/raise to 500 degrees

BAKE:
30 minutes

BROIL:
3 minutes

YIELD:
6 to 8 servings

NOTES:
Potatoes can be baked in the microwave oven to save time.

GARLIC-ROASTED POTATOES

- 3 *tablespoons olive oil*
- 12 *small red potatoes, washed and cut into 1/2-inch slices*
- 1 *head garlic, separated into cloves and peeled*
- 5 *sprigs fresh rosemary, thyme or basil*

Preheat oven to 400 degrees.

Pour olive oil into bottom of a 9 x 13-inch glass baking dish. Add potatoes and garlic cloves and toss until thoroughly coated with oil. After tossing, spread potatoes and garlic to form a single layer on bottom of dish. Place fresh herbs on top and cover pan with foil.

Place in oven and bake for 20 minutes. Remove from oven, uncover, return to oven and continue baking an additional 15 to 20 minutes or until potatoes are tender and beginning to brown. Remove sprigs of herbs before serving.

TEMPERATURE:
Preheat 400 degrees

BAKE:
35 to 40 minutes

YIELD:
4 to 6 servings

NOTES:
For variation, drain an 8-ounce jar of marinated artichoke hearts and toss with garlic and potatoes.

NEW POTATOES FRANCAIS

TEMPERATURE:
Preheat 350 degrees

BAKE:
1 hour and 20 minutes

YIELD:
8 servings

NOTES:
For milder flavor, use Swiss cheese instead of Gruyere.

10	*new red potatoes, thinly sliced*
1 1/4	*cups Swiss or Gruyere cheese, grated and divided (See note.)*
1/2	*teaspoon dried basil*
	Salt and pepper
1	*cup half and half*

Preheat oven to 350 degrees.

Grease a 7 x 11-inch glass baking dish. Cover bottom of dish with one layer of potatoes. Sprinkle with 1/4 cup of cheese, a sprinkle of basil and salt and pepper. Repeat this process for two additional layers. Pour half and half into dish after completing the final layer.

Place in oven and bake at 350 degrees, uncovered for 1 hour. Remove from oven, add remaining 1/2 cup cheese and bake an additional 20 minutes. Do not overcook.

BAKED POTATO DUET

TEMPERATURE:
Preheat 350 degrees

BOIL:
20 minutes

BAKE:
15 minutes

YIELD:
8 to 10 servings

NOTES:
Sprinkle with paprika just before serving to accent the pale orange color of the finished dish.

2	*large sweet potatoes, peeled and cubed*
5	*large russet potatoes, peeled and cubed*
1/4	*cup milk*
4	*tablespoons butter (1/2 cube)*
	Salt and pepper
2	*eggs*

Preheat oven to 350 degrees.

In 2 large stockpots, cook sweet potatoes and russet potatoes separately. Potatoes are done when easily pierced with a fork. Drain and set aside. (The sweet potatoes will take slightly longer than the russet.)

In a large bowl, combine potatoes, milk, butter and salt and pepper and thoroughly mash. Taste and adjust seasonings as necessary. Continue to whip potato mixture, adding eggs one at a time, until all ingredients are thoroughly incorporated.

Pour into a 9 x 13-inch greased baking dish. Cover and bake at 350 degrees for 15 minutes.

CAJUN POTATOES

10 small red potatoes, unpeeled and thinly sliced
1 cup half and half
1 1/2 cups Cheddar cheese, grated and divided (See note.)
1 teaspoon chili powder
1/4 teaspoon dried red pepper flakes
Salt and freshly-ground black pepper

Preheat oven to 350 degrees.

In the bottom of a 9 x 13-inch baking dish, place a layer of sliced potatoes. Sprinkle with 1/3 of cheese, chili powder and red pepper flakes. Season first layer with salt and pepper.

Repeat layering process twice more, leaving grated cheese off top layer. Pour the half and half over layered potatoes. Place uncovered dish in oven and bake at 350 degrees for 1 hour. Remove from oven. Sprinkle reserved 1/2 cup of Cheddar cheese over mixture and return to oven. Bake for an additional 20 minutes.

SERVE WITH BLACKENED SEAFOODS AND STEAKS.

TEMPERATURE:
Preheat 350 degrees

BAKE:
1 hour and 20 minutes

YIELD:
4 to 6 servings

NOTES:
To add a little more zing, substitute jalapeño Monterey Jack cheese.

BAKED MUSHROOM RICE

1 cup rice, uncooked
1/2 cup green onions, sliced, including tops
1 tablespoon butter
1/2 pound fresh mushrooms, thinly sliced
1 1/2 cups chicken broth or stock
1/2 cup dry sherry
1 teaspoon salt
1/2 teaspoon freshly-ground black pepper

Preheat oven to 375 degrees.

Butter a 7 x 11-inch baking dish and pour in uncooked rice. In a medium saucepan, sauté green onions in butter until softened. Add mushrooms and continue to sauté until mushrooms are softened. Pour in chicken broth, sherry, salt and pepper. Bring to a boil, remove from heat and pour over rice in baking dish.

Cover baking dish, and bake in a 375-degree oven for 25 to 30 minutes or until rice is done.

THIS IS A FAVORITE FROM NO REGRETS, AN EARLIER JUNIOR LEAGUE OF PORTLAND COOKBOOK.

SAUTÉ:
5 to 10 minutes

TEMPERATURE:
Preheat 375 degrees

BAKE:
25 to 30 minutes

YIELD:
6 servings

NOTES:
The sherry adds a special flavor to this dish. Garnish with additional sautéed mushrooms over top of finished dish.

WILD HERBED RICE

COOK:
1 hour and 10 minutes

YIELD:
6 to 8 servings

NOTES:
Cooked chicken, turkey or ground beef can be added just before serving to make this a main dish casserole.

- *1/4 cup butter (1/2 cube)*
- *1 cup brown rice*
- *1 cup wild rice*
- *1 cup onions, chopped*
- *1 cup celery (2 stalks), chopped*
- *1 pound fresh mushrooms, sliced*
- *3 3/4 cups chicken broth*
- *1/4 cup fresh parsley, chopped*
- *1/2 teaspoon salt*
- *1/4 teaspoon dried thyme*
- *Freshly-ground pepper*
- *1/4 cup pecans, chopped (optional)*

In a large saucepan, melt butter over medium heat. Add brown rice, wild rice, onion, and celery and sauté for approximately 5 minutes or until onion and celery are tender. Add mushrooms, chicken broth, parsley, salt, thyme and pepper. (Add pecans to mixture if desired.) Bring to a boil, reduce heat to low and simmer for 1 hour or until liquid has evaporated.

FAR EAST NOODLES

- 1 *tablespoon garlic (2 cloves), finely minced*
- 1 *tablespoon fresh ginger, minced*
- 2 *tablespoons olive oil*
- 1/4 *cup dry sherry*
- 2 *tablespoons oyster sauce*
- 2 *tablespoons rice vinegar*
- 1 *tablespoon sesame oil*
- 1 *teaspoon granulated sugar*
- 3 to 4 *dashes red pepper sauce*
- 1/2 *cup green onions, chopped*
- *Salt*
- 4 *quarts water*
- 1/2 *pound spaghetti noodles, preferably Chinese-style*

In a small bowl, combine garlic, ginger and olive oil. Set aside. In another small bowl, combine sherry, oyster sauce, rice vinegar, sesame oil, sugar, red pepper sauce and green onions. Set aside. (These two sauces can be made in advance.)

To cook noodles, bring at least 4 quarts of salted water to a boil. Add noodles and cook al dente, approximately 5 minutes. Pour into colander and toss noodles with a small amount of oil to prevent sticking. Drain and transfer to a large serving bowl.

While water is coming to a boil, place garlic, ginger and olive oil mixture in a small sauté pan and cook over medium-high heat. After 30 seconds, add second mixture of sauce ingredients. Bring entire mixture to a low boil and remove from heat.

Add sauce to cooked noodles, toss well and serve on a heated serving platter.

THIS SIDE DISH, SERVED HOT OR COLD, COMPLEMENTS A VARIETY OF ENTRÉES.

COOK:
15 minutes

YIELD:
4 to 6 servings

NOTES:
For a different dish, prepare as directed and refrigerate for a least 3 hours. Serve chilled. Noodles are al dente when cooked until tender but still crisp – not soft.

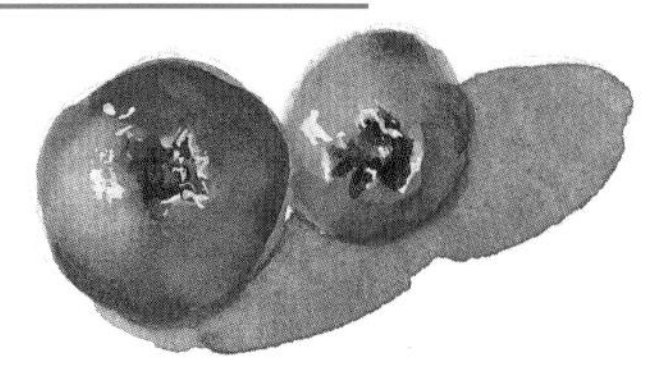

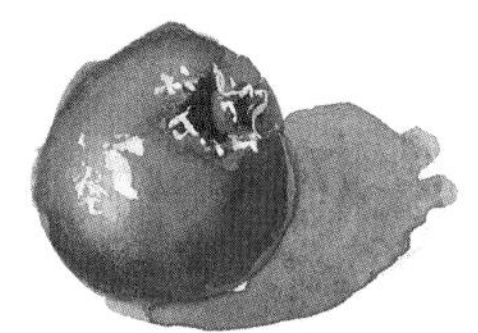

Eggs, Cheese & Pasta

A Pittock Picnic

Masses of marigolds, dahlias in bloom, full-blown chrysanthemums...what a lovely way to view the world: through a garden. When a gentle fall breeze blows through the tall evergreens, the spirit of Georgiana Burton Pittock and her love for flowers fills the Pittock Mansion grounds, which reign over Portland's northwest hills.

This French chateau, which commands a sweeping city view, is a monument to Henry and Georgiana Pittock. Their legacy is imprinted on the city, from the renowned June Rose Festival, which Georgiana inspired, to the nature trails winding through Macleay Park, which were one of Henry's favorite projects.

As part of its commitment to historic preservation, the Junior League of Portland turned the Pittock Mansion Gate Lodge, built as a caretaker's cottage, into a charming Tea Room in 1985. All proceeds from the Gate Lodge supported League projects.

Climb the Wildwood Trail to look out over Portland from the estate's romantic grounds. Then indulge in a picnic or brunch. Calico Quiche and Angel Hair Soufflé would have delighted Henry and Georgiana, too.

EGGS FLORENTINE

- *9 eggs, beaten*
- *1 pint small curd cottage cheese*
- *8 ounces Swiss cheese, grated*
- *8 ounces feta cheese, crumbled*
- *1/4 cup butter (1/2 cube), melted*
- *2 (10-ounce) packages frozen chopped spinach, thawed and squeezed dry*
- *1 teaspoon ground nutmeg*

Preheat oven to 350 degrees.

Grease a 9 x 13-inch ovenproof dish.

In a large mixing bowl, beat eggs slightly. Add cheeses and butter and mix well. Stir in spinach and nutmeg.

Pour into prepared pan. Bake for 60 minutes or until set.

THIS IS ONE WAY TO GET YOUR CHILDREN TO EAT THEIR SPINACH!

TEMPERATURE:
Preheat 350 degrees

BAKE:
60 minutes

YIELD:
8 servings

CREAMY SCRAMBLED EGGS WITH HERBS

- *6 eggs*
- *4 ounces cream cheese, cubed*
- *1/4 cup green onions, chopped*
- *1/4 cup fresh basil, chopped or 2 teaspoons dried basil*
- *2 tablespoons fresh parsley*
- *2 teaspoons fresh oregano, chopped, or 1/2 teaspoon dried oregano*
- *2 tablespoons milk*
- *Salt and pepper*
- *2 tablespoons butter*

In a small bowl, beat eggs. Add cream cheese, green onions, basil, parsley, oregano, milk, salt and pepper. Mix well.

In a sauté pan over medium heat, melt butter. Add eggs and stir until scrambled, about 6 minutes.

YIELD:
4 servings

NOTES:
Garnish with freshly-chopped tomatoes and crumbled feta cheese.

EGGS AU GRATIN

Temperature:
Preheat 400 degrees

Bake:
30 to 35 minutes

Yield:
4 to 6 servings

- 1 *teaspoon butter*
- 3/4 *pound salami, coarsely chopped*
- 8 *eggs, beaten*
- 6 *ounces mozzarella or Monterey Jack cheese, grated*
- 1 *Roma tomato, chopped and seeded*
- 3/4 *cup milk*
- 1 *teaspoon dried oregano*
- *Salt and pepper*

Preheat oven to 400 degrees.

Grease an 7 x 11-inch ovenproof dish.

In a sauté pan, melt butter and sauté salami until lightly browned. Drain off excess fat.

In a large mixing bowl, combine salami, eggs, cheese, tomato, milk, oregano, salt and pepper. Pour into prepared pan and bake for 30 to 35 minutes or until set.

CALICO QUICHE

Temperature:
Preheat 350 degrees

Bake:
35 to 40 minutes

Yield:
6 to 8 servings

- 1 *(9-inch) pie shell, homemade or frozen*
- 1/4 *cup red bell pepper, seeded, deveined and chopped*
- 1/2 *cup green bell pepper, seeded, deveined and chopped*
- 1 *cup Cheddar cheese, grated*
- 1 *cup Swiss cheese, grated*
- 1 *cup cooked chicken, cubed*
- 1/4 *cup butter (1/2 cube)*
- 1/2 *cup onion, coarsely chopped*
- 1 *tablespoon all-purpose flour*
- 1/2 *cup half and half*
- 1/2 *cup sour cream*
- 4 *eggs, beaten*
- 1/4 *teaspoon ground nutmeg*
- 1 *tablespoon parsley, chopped*

Preheat oven to 350 degrees.

In a pie shell, layer chopped peppers, cheeses and chicken.

In a sauté pan, melt butter and sauté onions until soft. Whisk in flour thoroughly. Stir in half and half and simmer until thickened, about 3 to 5 minutes. Let cool.

In a large bowl, combine sour cream, eggs, nutmeg and parsley. Stir into sautéed onion mixture.

Pour filling into pie crust. Bake 35 to 40 minutes or until set.

ZUCCHINI MUSHROOM FRITTATA

Temperature:
Preheat 350 degrees

Sauté:
5 minutes

Bake:
55 minutes

Yield:
6 to 8 servings

- 3 *tablespoons olive oil*
- 1 1/2 *cups zucchini (2 medium zucchini), chopped*
- 1 1/2 *cups mushrooms (8 large mushrooms), sliced*
- 3/4 *cup green bell pepper, seeded, deveined and chopped*
- 3/4 *cup onion, chopped*
- 1 *garlic clove, minced*
- 6 *eggs*
- 2 *(8-ounce) packages cream cheese, room temperature*
- 2 *cups cubed white bread, crusts trimmed, and divided*
- 1 1/2 *cups Cheddar cheese, grated*

Preheat oven to 350 degrees.

Grease a 10-inch springform pan.

In a large sauté pan, heat olive oil and sauté zucchini, mushrooms, pepper, onion and garlic for 5 minutes or until vegetables are tender. Cool.

In a large bowl, beat eggs. Add softened cream cheese, half of bread cubes, Cheddar cheese and vegetable mixture. Mix thoroughly.

Layer remaining bread cubes in prepared pan. Pour egg mixture over bread. Bake for 55 minutes or until set. Cool slightly before slicing and serving.

ITALIAN TORTE

This colorful side dish will enhance any buffet table.

Temperature:
Preheat 450 degrees/ lower to 375 degrees

Bake:
10 minutes/30 minutes

Yield:
6 servings

- 4 *eggs*
- 1 *(10-ounce) package frozen green beans, thawed*
- 1/4 *teaspoon garlic powder*
- 1 *tablespoon fresh parsley, chopped*
- 1/2 *cup freshly-grated Parmesan cheese*
- 1 *slice white bread, soaked in water*
- 1/4 *cup olive oil*

Preheat oven to 450 degrees.

Grease an 8 x 8-inch pan.

In a large mixing bowl, beat eggs, then add remaining ingredients. Pour into pan and bake at 450 degrees for 10 minutes. Reduce heat and bake at 375 degrees for 30 minutes.

Cut into squares and serve at room temperature.

CHEESE BLINTZ SOUFFLÉ

TEMPERATURE:
Preheat 350 DEGREES

BAKE:
50 to 60 minutes

YIELD:
6 to 8 servings

NOTES:
Can be prepared in a blender.

BLINTZ BATTER:

- 1/4 *cup butter (1/2 cube), room temperature*
- 1/3 *cup granulated sugar*
- 6 *eggs*
- 1 1/2 *cups sour cream*
- 1/2 *cup freshly-squeezed orange juice*
- 1 *cup all-purpose flour*
- 2 *teaspoons baking powder*

BLINTZ FILLING:

- 1 *(8-ounce) package cream cheese, cubed*
- 1 *pint small-curd cottage cheese*
- 2 *egg yolks*
- 2 *tablespoons granulated sugar*
- 1 *teaspoon vanilla*

Preheat oven to 350 degrees.

In a food processor, combine butter, sugar, eggs, sour cream, orange juice, flour and baking powder. Pulse 4 to 5 times until just combined.

Pour half of the batter into a buttered 9 x 13-inch baking pan. Set remaining batter aside.

FILLING:

In a food processor, combine cream cheese, cottage cheese, egg yolks, sugar and vanilla. Pulse until well mixed.

Drop filling by heaping spoonfuls over batter in baking dish. With a knife, spread filling evenly. (It will mix slightly with the batter.) Pour remaining batter over filling. (At this point, unbaked soufflé can be covered and refrigerated several hours or overnight. Bring to room temperature before baking.)

Bake uncovered for 50 to 60 minutes or until puffed and golden. Serve immediately with sour cream and syrup or jam.

CRÊPES BENGAL

This is a favorite from No Regrets, an earlier Junior League of Portland cookbook.

Temperature: Preheat 350 degrees

Bake: 25 minutes

Yield: 8 to 10 servings

CRÊPES:

- 8 eggs
- 1 cup all-purpose flour
- 1 teaspoon salt
- 2 tablespoons granulated sugar
- 1 1/4 cups whole milk
- 1/4 cup butter (1/2 cube), melted
- Additional butter for cooking

WHITE SAUCE:

- 1/2 cup plus 2 tablespoons butter, divided
- 1/2 cup all-purpose flour
- 2 cups milk, heated

FILLING:

- 2 tablespoons butter
- 3 shallots, minced
- 1 pound crab meat
- 2 teaspoons curry powder
- 1/2 teaspoon Worcestershire sauce
- 1/2 teaspoon salt
- 1/8 teaspoon cayenne pepper
- 1/2 cup white wine

GLAZE:

- 2 egg yolks, beaten
- 1/4 teaspoon salt
- 1/2 cup butter (1 cube), melted
- 2 tablespoons freshly-squeezed lemon juice
- 1 cup reserved white sauce
- 1/2 cup whipping cream, whipped
- Chutney

Preheat oven to 350 degrees.

CRÊPES:

In a food processor or blender, combine all crêpe ingredients. Blend only until flour is incorporated. Let stand a few minutes.

Heat 1/2 teaspoon butter to sizzling in a 6-inch crêpe pan or a 6-inch heavy skillet. Pour in 1/4 cup batter. Cook until gloss on top of crêpe disappears. (Cook only on 1 side.) Invert pan over waxed paper and remove crêpe. Set aside. Repeat with remaining batter.

WHITE SAUCE:

In a saucepan or microwave oven, melt butter and stir in flour. Add hot milk and cook until thickened. Reserve 1 cup. Set sauce aside.

FILLING:

In a small sauté pan, melt 2 tablespoons butter. Add shallots and lightly sauté. Add crab meat. Season with curry, Worcestershire, salt and cayenne. Add wine and all but 1 cup of white sauce.

GLAZE:

In a large mixing bowl, beat egg yolks, add salt. Beat in melted butter very gradually and add lemon juice. Fold in 1 cup reserved white sauce, then fold in whipped cream.

To assemble: Put about 2 tablespoons crab filling on unbrowned side of each crêpe and roll. Arrange rolled crêpe on 2 baking sheets and cover with glaze. (At this point, pans may be covered and refrigerated up to 24 hours. Bring to room temperature before baking.) Bake for 25 minutes. Garnish with a dollop of chutney.

BLUEBERRY PANCAKES

Here's an easy recipe when it's Dad's turn to cook. Mother's Day will never be the same.

2 cups all-purpose flour, sifted
3/4 teaspoon baking soda
1 teaspoon baking powder
3 tablespoons granulated sugar
1 teaspoon salt
1 package dry yeast, dissolved in 1/4 cup warm water
3 eggs, well-beaten
1/4 cup vegetable oil
1 1/2 cups buttermilk
2 cups blueberries, fresh or frozen, thawed

In a large bowl, combine flour, baking soda, baking powder, sugar, salt, yeast, eggs, oil and buttermilk. Whisk until smooth. Pour batter on hot, lightly greased griddle. Sprinkle each pancake with desired amount of berries. Turn when small bubbles begin to form throughout, and cook to golden brown on both sides. Serve hot with warmed syrup.

Yield:
8 to 10 servings

Notes:
A favorite from NO REGRETS, an earlier Junior League of Portland cookbook.

LIGHTEN-UP PANCAKES

This recipe has been a family tradition for generations!

2 eggs, separated
2 cups yogurt (See note.)
1 teaspoon salt
1 teaspoon baking soda
3/4 cup all-purpose flour

In a small mixing bowl, beat egg whites until soft peaks form. In another bowl, mix egg yolks and yogurt. Add salt, baking soda and flour; stir until just blended. Fold in egg whites.

Cook small pancakes (about 2 tablespoons batter each) on a preheated griddle or pan over medium heat until golden brown on each side.

Yield:
2 servings

Notes:
Use plain or flavored yogurt such as banana.

LEMON CLAM SPAGHETTI

YIELD:
6 servings

NOTES:
Lemon adds a tangy touch to this clam sauce.

- 1/2 *cup butter (1 cube), divided*
- 3 *tablespoons olive oil*
- 1/3 *cup onion, coarsely chopped*
- 2 *garlic cloves, minced*
- 2 *(7 1/2-ounce) cans chopped clams*
- 3 *tablespoons freshly-squeezed lemon juice*
- 1 *tablespoon fresh parsley, chopped*
- 2 *teaspoons grated lemon peel*
- 1/4 *teaspoon freshly-ground black pepper*
- 1 *bay leaf*
- 1 *tablespoon cornstarch dissolved in 1/4 cup cold water*
- 1 *pound spaghetti*
- 1 *cup freshly-grated Parmesan cheese*
- *Lemon wedges*

In a sauté pan over medium heat, melt 1 tablespoon butter. Add olive oil. Add onion and garlic and sauté until onion is tender. Drain clams and reserve juice.

Add clam juice, lemon peel, pepper, bay leaf, and cornstarch mixture to sauté pan. Raise heat and bring to a boil for 1 to 2 minutes.

Add drained clams and remaining butter. Stir until butter is melted and clams are heated through. Lower heat. Add lemon juice and parsley and stir.

Prepare pasta according to package directions. Pour clam sauce over noodles. Sprinkle with Parmesan cheese, toss well and serve with lemon wedges.

OREGONATA PASTA

The artichoke marinade adds a delicious touch.

Sauté: 5 minutes

Simmer: 20 minutes

- 1 *(6-ounce) jar marinated artichoke hearts, drained, coarsely chopped and liquid reserved*
- 1/2 *pound fresh mushrooms, sliced*
- 1 *tablespoon grated onion*
- 1 *garlic clove, minced*
- 1 *(15-ounce) can tomato sauce*
- 1 *cup dry white wine*
- 1 *(2 1/4-ounce) can sliced black olives, drained*
- 2 *teaspoons dried basil*
- 2 *teaspoons dried oregano*
- 1 *teaspoon salt*
- 1/2 *teaspoon fennel seed*
- 1/4 *teaspoon freshly-ground black pepper*
- 1 *pound spaghetti or other pasta*
- *Freshly-grated Parmesan cheese*

In a large sauté pan over medium-high heat, heat artichoke marinade until bubbly. Add mushrooms, onion and garlic to marinade and sauté over high heat for 5 minutes. Add artichokes and remaining ingredients (except pasta). Simmer uncovered for 20 minutes.

Meanwhile, cook pasta according to package directions. Pour sauce over pasta, sprinkle with Parmesan cheese and serve.

PASTA WITH FRESH HERB SAUCE

Take advantage of summer-fresh herbs.

Cook: 20 minutes

Yield: 6 servings

Notes: Suggested combinations of fresh herbs: chives, tarragon, cilantro, parsley, basil, rosemary, and watercress.

- 1 1/2 *cups half and half*
- 1/4 *cup butter (1/2 cube)*
- 1/2 *teaspoon salt*
- 1/8 *teaspoon freshly-ground pepper*
- 1/4 *cup Romano cheese, grated*
- 1 *cup mixed fresh herbs, finely chopped (See note.)*
- 1 *pound pasta, cooked*
- *Chopped tomato*
- *Freshly-grated Parmesan cheese*

In a saucepan over medium heat, combine half and half, butter, salt, and pepper. Simmer 15 minutes, or until sauce is slightly reduced and thickened.

Whisk in cheese and herbs and simmer for another 5 minutes. Taste and correct seasoning. Serve immediately over any type of cooked pasta. Sprinkle with chopped tomato and fresh Parmesan cheese.

LINGUINE WITH TOMATO-SEAFOOD SAUCE

SIMMER:
50 minutes

YIELD:
4 to 6 servings

NOTES:
Use any combination of shrimp, scallops, crab and lobster meat.

- *2 tablespoons olive oil*
- *1/2 cup onion, finely chopped*
- *1 (2-pound, 3-ounce) can Italian plum tomatoes*
- *1 teaspoon dried basil*
- *Salt and pepper*
- *1 cup whipping cream*
- *2 pinches cayenne pepper*
- *3/4 pound cooked shellfish (See note.)*
- *1 pound linguine*

In a large saucepan, heat oil, add onions, and sauté until tender.

Drain canned tomatoes and chop. Add chopped tomatoes to onion and season with basil, salt and pepper. Bring mixture to a boil. Cover and simmer for 30 minutes. Remove from heat and cool.

In a food processor or blender, purée cooled tomato mixture until smooth. Return purée to saucepan and add cream. Simmer tomato purée, stirring frequently, for 15 minutes until sauce is slightly reduced.

Stir in cayenne and cooked seafood. Adjust seasonings and simmer for 5 minutes.

While finishing final preparation of sauce, boil pasta according to package directions. Drain well. Transfer pasta to serving dish, and top with sauce. Toss well and serve.

GREEK PASTA

- 2 *tablespoons olive oil*
- 1 *garlic clove, minced*
- $3/4$ *cup cooked bay shrimp*
- 1 *pound feta cheese, rinsed and crumbled*
- 6 *green onions, finely chopped*
- 4 *fresh tomatoes, peeled, cored, seeded and finely chopped*
- *Salt and pepper (See note.)*
- 1 *pound pasta (See note.)*

In a large bowl, combine olive oil, garlic, shrimp, feta cheese, onions, tomatoes, salt and pepper. Toss to combine and let stand at room temperature for at least 1 hour.

Prepare pasta according to package directions and drain well.

Add hot pasta to sauce and toss. Serve immediately.

FETA CHEESE ADDS JUST THE RIGHT BITE TO THIS EASY DISH.

YIELD:
4 servings

NOTES:
Feta cheese is naturally salty so very little additional salt is needed. Try using orzo pasta and serve with barbecued lamb.

PROSCIUTTO AND ASPARAGUS PASTA

- $1/2$ *pound fresh asparagus spears or 1 (10-ounce) package frozen asparagus spears*
- 4 *ounces prosciutto ham, thinly sliced and cut into 1-inch strips (See note.)*
- $3/4$ *cup freshly-grated Parmesan cheese*
- $1/2$ *cup sour cream*
- $1/4$ *cup dry white wine*
- $1/4$ *cup butter ($1/2$ cube), melted*
- $1/2$ *pound linguine or fettuccine*

In a medium saucepan, steam or boil asparagus until crisp-tender. Drain and cut into bite-sized pieces.

In a medium bowl, combine asparagus and prosciutto. In a large bowl, combine cheese, sour cream, wine and butter. Mix well. Add asparagus-prosciutto mixture.

Cook pasta according to package directions. Drain well, but do not rinse. Transfer pasta to a warm serving platter and toss with sauce. Sprinkle with additional Parmesan, if desired. Serve immediately.

PERFECT FOR ENTERTAINING.

YIELD:
4 servings

NOTES:
Prosciutto is a cured ham that is available at specialty markets and delicatessens. Garnish with strips of sun-dried tomatoes.

SUN-DRIED TOMATO, ROASTED TOMATO AND GARLIC FETTUCCINE

ROASTING THE TOMATOES GIVES THIS PASTA DISH ITS DISTINCT FLAVOR.

TEMPERATURE:
Preheat 300 degrees/increase to 400 degrees

BAKE:
10 minutes/10 to 15 minutes

YIELD:
4 servings

NOTES:
Roma or plum tomatoes work best because of their low-moisture content. Reserve some basil leaves to julienne for garnish.

- 3 *tablespoons pine nuts*
- 2 *pounds Roma tomatoes, cored and cut into wedges*
- 3 *tablespoons extra virgin olive oil, divided*
- *Salt and pepper*
- 1 *cup fresh basil leaves, loosely packed, coarsely chopped, and divided (See note.)*
- 2 *tablespoons garlic, minced*
- 1/4 *cup oil-packed, sun-dried tomatoes, drained*
- 1/4 *cup white wine*
- 1/4 *cup chicken stock*
- 1/2 *teaspoon dried red pepper flakes*
- 1 *pound fresh pasta*
- *Freshly-grated Parmesan cheese*

Preheat oven to 300 degrees.

Spread pine nuts evenly over a cooking sheet. Toast pine nuts until lightly browned, approximately 10 minutes. Remove and set aside.

Increase oven temperature to 400 degrees.

Toss Roma tomatoes with 1 tablespoon olive oil, salt and pepper. Roast in a shallow pan until skins are slightly browned, approximately 10 to 15 minutes.

In a sauté pan, combine garlic with remaining 2 tablespoons olive oil, add roasted tomatoes, sun-dried tomatoes, toasted pine nuts, and fresh basil. Stir in wine and chicken stock and cook until slightly reduced. Season with red pepper flakes.

Place pasta in a serving bowl and pour sauce over top. Sprinkle with basil and Parmesan cheese. Serve immediately.

LINGUINE WITH WHITE CLAM SAUCE

- 1/2 *pound fresh linguine*
- 1 *cup whipping cream*
- 5 *tablespoons butter*
- 1/8 *teaspoon nutmeg*
- 4 *ounces cream cheese*
- 2 *tablespoons fresh basil, chopped*
- 2 *tablespoons fresh parsley, chopped*
- 2 *tablespoons fresh chives, chopped*
- 1 *garlic clove, minced*
- 3/4 *cup freshly-grated Parmesan cheese, divided*
- 2 *(5 1/2-ounce) cans whole baby clams*

Prepare linguine according to package directions. Drain well.

In a small saucepan, combine cream, butter and nutmeg. Simmer 10 minutes or until butter melts and mixture is well combined. Stir in cream cheese, chopped herbs and garlic. Add 1/4 cup Parmesan cheese and clams. Cook for an additional 5 minutes, stirring occasionally.

Pour sauce over linguine and toss. Garnish with remaining 1/2 cup Parmesan cheese and fresh parsley.

A "LIGHT" MEAL FOR COMPANY.

COOK:
15 MINUTES

YIELD:
4 servings

NOTES:
Serve with a salad and garlic rolls.

SCALLOP AND RED PEPPER LINGUINE

THE PEPPERS ADD A DELIGHTFUL COLOR AND FLAVOR.

YIELD:
4 to 6 servings

NOTES:
Either whole bay scallops or sea scallops sliced into thirds may be used.

- 1/2 *cup chicken broth*
- 2 *tablespoons freshly-squeezed lemon juice*
- 1 *pound scallops (See note.)*
- 3/4 *pound fresh linguine*
- 1 *tablespoon olive oil*
- 2 *garlic cloves, minced*
- 3 *red bell peppers, seeded, deveined and julienned*
- *Dash red pepper sauce*
- 1/2 *cup fresh parsley, finely chopped*

In a large sauté pan over high heat, combine chicken broth with lemon juice and bring to a boil. Add scallops and lower heat to maintain a low simmer. Poach scallops until opaque, about 3 minutes.

Drain scallops, reserving liquid. Set scallops aside. Measure liquid, and reduce, if necessary, to equal 1/2 cup of liquid. Set aside.

Prepare linguine according to package directions. Drain well and set aside.

In the same pan used for the scallops, heat olive oil and sauté garlic and red pepper strips until crisp-tender, about 2 to 3 minutes. Add drained linguine, scallops, reserved liquid, red pepper sauce and parsley. Toss lightly and serve.

ANGEL HAIR SOUFFLÉ

A pasta treat for Sunday brunch.

Temperature:
Preheat 375 degrees

Bake:
20 to 25 minutes

Yield:
4 servings

Notes:
Domestic or imported prosciutto is available at specialty markets and delicatessens. Boiled ham may be substituted.

- *4 ounces angel hair pasta*
- *8 egg whites*
- *6 egg yolks*
- *3/4 cup freshly-grated Parmesan cheese*
- *3/4 cup prosciutto ham, finely diced (See note.)*
- *1/2 teaspoon freshly-ground black pepper*
- *1/8 teaspoon red pepper sauce*

Preheat oven to 375 degrees. Grease a 2-quart soufflé dish.

Cook and drain pasta according to package directions.

In a large mixing bowl, beat 6 egg yolks with electric mixer until thick and lemon colored, approximately 5 minutes. (This may also be done in a food processor.) Stir in Parmesan cheese, ham, pepper, red pepper sauce and cooked pasta.

In another mixing bowl, beat 8 egg whites until soft peaks form. Fold about 1/2 cup of whites into yolk mixture to lighten it, then fold yolk mixture carefully into whites, using a rubber spatula and being careful not to over-mix.

Pour mixture into a prepared soufflé dish. Smooth the top, then draw a circle with your finger or a knife on top of soufflé about 2 inches from rim of dish. This causes the center to rise higher than sides and forms a cap. Bake at 375 degrees for 20 to 25 minutes.

BEEF, PORK & LAMB

RUSSET, RICH AND RARE

The seasons turn. Landscapes and colors change. A fall downpour scrubs the horizon clean. The air's fresh bite provides an irresistible urge to tramp across harvested fields. Drink in the rural palette of orange pumpkins, deep green and brown vines, ruby red apples and black-faced sheep.

Just a short drive south from Portland's urban center, the working farms of the Willamette Valley offer this opportunity. A city-dweller's pace is slowed by the unhurried gaze of animals, the underfoot rustle of cornstalks which used to whisper in the wind, and the world-famous vineyards dotting the hills.

Afterwards, a stop at a roadside stand provides ingredients for the feast to follow, one that might include BUTTERFLIED LEG OF LAMB WITH BLUE CHEESE, PEPPER PORK, or HAMBURGER PIE.

Growing tomatoes from seed calls for the same dedication as nurturing a project which will make a difference in someone's life. The League's work with the Resource Center for Child Abuse Prevention, Ronald McDonald House, and Boys and Girls Club is such a seed.

TERIYAKI FLANK STEAK

- 2 *tablespoons red wine vinegar*
- 3/4 *cup vegetable oil*
- 1/4 *cup soy sauce*
- 1/4 *cup honey*
- 1 *tablespoon fresh ginger, grated*
- 1 *large garlic clove, minced*
- 2 *tablespoons green onion, chopped*
- 2 *pounds flank steak*

MARINATE OVERNIGHT, ADD WILD RICE AND GREEN BEANS AND DINNER IS READY.

MARINATE:
8 hours or overnight

TEMPERATURE:
Preheat 500 degrees

BAKE:
14 minutes

YIELD:
4 to 6 servings

In a large bowl, whisk together vinegar, oil, soy sauce, honey, ginger and garlic. Add green onions and mix well.

In a large glass dish or non-reactive pan, place steak and cover with marinade. Place in the refrigerator and marinate for at least 8 hours, or overnight.

Preheat oven to 500 degrees.

Pour marinade into a saucepan, and warm over medium-high heat.

Place steak on the rack of a roasting pan and broil quickly, approximately 7 minutes per side.

To serve, slice steak very thinly on the diagonal. Arrange on a warm serving platter and drizzle with heated marinade. Serve extra marinade on the side.

SYMPHONY PICNIC ROAST WITH MUSTARD-CAPER SAUCE

This is terrific for those types of parties that rely on "heavy hors d'oeuvres." Or, the perfect picnic item for Portland's Washington Park Zoo concerts.

Grill:
32 minutes

Chill:
Several hours

Yield:
10 to 12 servings

- *1 4-pound beef tenderloin, trimmed*
- *3 tablespoons olive oil*
- *4 tablespoons dried marjoram, crumbled*

SAUCE:

- *3 tablespoons stone-ground mustard*
- *2 egg yolks*
- *1 small shallot, finely chopped*
- *Pinch of dried or fresh marjoram*
- *1 tablespoon freshly-squeezed lemon juice*
- *1 cup olive oil*
- *1/4 cup whipping cream*
- *1 1/2 tablespoons capers, drained*

Rub beef with olive oil.

Prepare barbecue. Sprinkle hot coals or gas grill with marjoram. Grill meat 8 minutes per side. Continue to sprinkle coals with marjoram during cooking. Beef will be rare.

Cool meat and slice pieces 3/4-inch thick.

SAUCE:

In a food processor, combine mustard, egg yolks, shallots, marjoram and lemon juice. Pulse to combine. With processor running, drizzle in olive oil until emulsified. Add whipping cream. Stop processor and stir in capers. Refrigerate sauce until ready to serve.

To serve, arrange beef slices on a platter in an overlapping pattern. Spoon a ribbon of sauce down the center and serve with remaining sauce.

POT ROAST SUPREME

- 1 *3-pound beef roast*
- 1/2 *cup all-purpose flour*
- 1/4 *cup vegetable oil*
- 6 *carrots, peeled and sliced*
- 6 *potatoes, peeled and quartered*
- 1 *(10 1/2-ounce) can onion soup, heated*

Preheat oven to 275 degrees.

Dredge meat in flour.

In a large stockpot, heat oil and brown meat. Add carrots and potatoes and pour heated soup into stockpot. Stir to combine ingredients, then transfer to an ovenproof casserole. Cover and bake at 275 degrees for 4 hours.

THIS IS TENDER, DELICIOUS AND A BUDGET HELPER.

TEMPERATURE:
Preheat 275 degrees

BAKE:
4 hours

YIELD:
6 servings

NOTES:
Serve with a tossed green salad topped with our CREAMY TARRAGON VINAIGRETTE, page 57, and HONEY WHOLE-WHEAT BREAD, page 64.

BURGUNDY BEEF

Fast and delicious; this is almost too good to be true.

Cook:
$2^1/2$ to 3 hours

Yield:
6 servings

Notes:
For an Irish version, add 2 sliced carrots, 4 small onions and 3 large, quartered potatoes 30 minutes before stew is finished.

- *1/2 cup olive oil*
- *3 pounds top round, cubed*
- *3 cups full-bodied red wine*
- *2 cups beef broth*
- *1 tablespoon tomato paste*
- *3 garlic cloves, minced*
- *1/2 teaspoon thyme*
- *1 bay leaf*
- *Salt*

In a large stockpot, heat oil. Add beef and brown evenly on all sides. Add wine, broth, tomato paste, garlic, thyme, bay leaf and salt. Bring to a boil. Cover and simmer for 2 1/2 to 3 hours, until beef is tender and liquid is thickened.

If broth needs additional thickening, mix 1 tablespoon water with 3 tablespoons flour and whisk until smooth. Add to stew.

PEPPERPOT BEEF

Just the ticket for a busy schedule!

Temperature:
Preheat 325 degrees

Bake:
2 hours

Yield:
8 servings

- 4 *tablespoons flour*
- 1 *teaspoon salt*
- 1/2 *teaspoon freshly-ground pepper*
- 1/2 *teaspoon ground ginger*
- 2 *pounds top round, cubed*
- 2 *tablespoons vegetable oil*
- 1 *(26-ounce) can peeled tomatoes*
- 1/4 *pound fresh mushrooms, sliced*
- 1 *bay leaf*
- *Dash of red pepper sauce*
- 1 1/4 *tablespoons Worcestershire sauce*
- 2 1/2 *tablespoons brown sugar*
- 2 1/2 *tablespoons red wine vinegar*
- 2 *garlic cloves, minced*
- 1 *(2-ounce) jar pimientos*
- 1 *(15-ounce) can kidney beans*

In a paper bag, combine flour, salt, pepper and ginger. Add meat, close bag and shake to coat each piece. Remove meat from bag.

In a large stockpot, heat oil. Add meat and brown quickly and evenly on all sides. Pour in tomatoes with liquid and stir to combine. Add mushrooms and bay leaf.

In a small bowl, combine red pepper sauce, Worcestershire, sugar, vinegar and garlic. Mix well, then add to stockpot. Stir thoroughly until all ingredients are well combined and transfer to a 2 1/2-quart casserole.

Cover and cook in a 325-degree oven for 1 1/2 hours.

Remove from oven, add pimiento and beans. Return to oven and continue cooking an additional 30 minutes.

CHEESY BEEF CASSEROLE

CHILL:
1 hour

BAKE:
1 hour

TEMPERATURE:
Preheat 375 degrees

YIELD:
6 to 8 servings

- *1 pound ground round*
- *2 (8-ounce) cans tomato sauce*
- *1 cup cottage cheese*
- *1 (8-ounce) package cream cheese*
- *1/4 cup sour cream*
- *1/3 cup green onions, chopped*
- *2 tablespoons butter, melted*
- *8 ounces egg noodles, cooked*

In a sauté pan over medium heat, brown meat. Drain grease. Stir in tomato sauce. Combine well and remove from heat.

In a 2-quart buttered casserole, place half of the noodles.

In a large bowl, combine cottage cheese, cream cheese, sour cream and onions. Spread over the noodles.

Cover with remaining noodles. Pour 2 tablespoons melted butter over noodles and top layer with tomato-meat sauce. Chill 1 hour before baking. Bake 1 hour at 375 degrees.

HAMBURGER PIE

A CLASSIC THAT WILL PLEASE EVERY FAMILY MEMBER.

TEMPERATURE:
Preheat 375 degrees

BAKE:
40 minutes

YIELD:
6 servings

- *1 pound extra lean ground beef*
- *1 (6-ounce) box seasoned croutons, divided*
- *1 (4-ounce) can tomato sauce*
- *2 teaspoons dried minced onion*
- *1/2 teaspoon salt*
- *2 eggs, beaten and divided*
- *1/2 cup mushrooms, sliced*
- *1 green bell pepper, seeded, deveined and chopped*
- *1 cup Cheddar cheese, grated*
- *1 tomato, sliced*

In a large bowl, combine beef, 1 cup seasoned croutons, tomato sauce, onion, salt and 1 egg. Mix well and press into sides and bottom of a 9-inch pie pan.

In a separate bowl, combine remaining croutons, egg, mushrooms, green pepper and cheese. Mix well and layer on top of beef crust. Arrange tomato slices over pie.

Bake at 375 degrees for 40 minutes.

LASAGNA WITH SPINACH AND MEAT SAUCE

File this one under "Sure hit." There won't be any leftovers.

Temperature:
Preheat 350 degrees

Bake:
60 minutes

Yield:
6 to 8 servings

- 2 *tablespoons olive oil, divided*
- 1 *medium onion, finely chopped*
- 1/2 *teaspoon crushed red pepper flakes*
- 3 *garlic cloves, minced*
- 1 *pound lean ground beef*
- 1/2 *pound mushrooms, sliced*
- 1 *(8-ounce) can tomato sauce*
- 1 *(28-ounce) can whole tomatoes, including liquid*
- 1 *(6-ounce) can tomato paste*
- 1 *teaspoon salt*
- 1 *teaspoon oregano*
- 1/2 *teaspoon basil*
- 1/2 *cup red wine*
- 1 *egg*
- 1 *(10-ounce) package frozen chopped spinach, thawed and well-drained*
- 1 *cup small curd cottage cheese or ricotta cheese*
- 1/2 *cup freshly-grated Parmesan cheese*
- 8 *ounces lasagna, cooked and drained*
- 1/2 *pound mozzarella cheese, thinly sliced*

Preheat oven to 350 degrees.

In a large sauté pan, heat oil. Sauté onion, red pepper flakes and garlic. Add ground beef and cook until brown.

Add mushrooms and sauté gently. Blend in tomato sauce, canned tomatoes with liquid, tomato paste, salt, oregano, basil and wine. Simmer about 15 minutes, breaking tomatoes into small pieces as mixture cooks.

In a medium bowl, mix egg with spinach, cottage cheese, Parmesan cheese and remaining 1 tablespoon oil.

To assemble, pour half of meat sauce into a 9 x 13-inch pan or lasagna pan and cover with a layer of lasagna noodles. Spread entire spinach mixture over lasagna noodles. Repeat, layering with remaining lasagna and meat sauce.

Cover and bake at 350 degrees for 45 minutes. Remove cover and arrange slices of cheese on top. Bake 15 minutes longer, until cheese is melted.

GREASY SPOON CHILI

NEXT TIME YOU HOST A SUPER BOWL PARTY, YOU'LL BE READY WITH THIS QUICK, SATISFYING CHILI.

COOK:
1 1/2 hours

YIELD:
10 to 12 servings

NOTES:
Serve with grated Cheddar cheese and chopped green onion as toppings.

- 2 *pounds ground beef*
- 1 *medium onion, coarsely chopped*
- 1 *cup celery (2 stalks), sliced*
- 1/2 *green bell pepper, seeded, deveined and chopped*
- 2 *garlic cloves, minced*
- 1 *(16-ounce) can whole tomatoes, chopped, with liquid*
- 1 *(16-ounce) can tomato sauce*
- 1 *(6-ounce) can tomato paste*
- 2 *teaspoons ground cumin*
- 1 *teaspoon granulated sugar*
- 3 *teaspoons chili powder*
- 2 *teaspoons crushed red pepper flakes*
- 2 *(15-ounce) cans kidney beans*

In a large sauté pan over medium heat, brown beef. Drain grease.

Add onion, celery, bell pepper and garlic. Sauté for 5 minutes.

Add tomatoes, tomato sauce, tomato paste, cumin, sugar, chili powder and red pepper flakes. Simmer for 1 hour. Add kidney beans, and simmer an additional 30 minutes.

GINGER-THYME PORK ROAST

Something special for winter entertaining.

Chill:
12 hours or overnight

Temperature:
Preheat 325 degrees

Bake:
1 hour 15 minutes

Yield:
4 to 6 servings

Notes:
1 1/2 teaspoon dried thyme can be substituted for fresh thyme. Delicious served with your favorite mashed potatoes.

- *1 3 to 4-pound pork roast, rolled and tied*
- *1 tablespoon fresh thyme, minced (See note.)*
- *2 1/2 teaspoons salt*
- *1 teaspoon pepper*
- *3 garlic cloves, divided*
- *1 bay leaf*
- *1/4 teaspoon ground ginger*
- *3 tablespoons oil*
- *1 large onion, thinly sliced*
- *1 large carrot, thinly sliced*
- *4 thyme sprigs or 1 teaspoon dried thyme*
- *1 bay leaf*

SAUCE:

- *3/4 teaspoon ground ginger*
- *1 cup dry white wine*
- *1 cup chicken broth*
- *4 gingersnaps, crumbled*
- *1/4 cup whipping cream*
- *1 tablespoon fresh thyme*
- *Oil and butter for browning*

Preheat oven to 325 degrees.

Untie roast and trim any fat.

In a food processor or blender, combine thyme, salt, pepper, 1 garlic clove, bay leaf and ginger. Pulse to combine. Rub roast with mixture. Wrap the roast with plastic wrap or place it in a plastic bag and refrigerate for 12 to 24 hours.

Re-roll and tie roast.

In a large heavy Dutch oven, heat oil and brown roast. Remove meat and discard oil.

In the same Dutch oven over medium heat, melt 2 tablespoons of butter. Add onion, carrot, thyme sprigs, 2 garlic cloves and bay leaf. Cover and cook for 5 minutes.

Add roast, lean-side down, and cook until sizzling. Place in oven, cover and roast for about 75 minutes, or until it tests done on a meat thermometer. (170 degrees is considered well-done.)

Remove roast to a heated platter and tent with foil to keep warm while making sauce.

SAUCE:

In the stockpot, combine ginger, wine, chicken stock, and crumbled gingersnaps. Simmer while stirring for 8 minutes. Add whipping cream and cook for 8 more minutes. Strain and add minced thyme.

Slice roast and arrange on platter. Pour some of the sauce over slices and pass the remainder. Garnish with fresh thyme sprigs.

PEPPER PORK

SAFFRON AND PEANUTS ADD UNUSUAL FLAVOR TO THIS EASY STEW.

SAUTÉ:
5 minutes

COOK:
1 hour

YIELD:
6 servings

NOTES:
Serve with a crusty bread and a Pinot Noir. This stew is best when made a day in advance, which allows flavors to blend.

1/4 cup olive oil
3 garlic cloves, minced
4 medium onions, coarsely chopped
2 pounds pork shoulder, cubed
3 tablespoons uncooked white rice
3 medium tomatoes, coarsely chopped
1/4 teaspoon crushed red pepper flakes
1/4 teaspoon ground cinnamon
1/8 teaspoon ground cloves
1 1/2 teaspoons salt
1/4 teaspoon saffron
1 (10 1/2-ounce) can condensed consommé, undiluted
3 medium potatoes, quartered
1/4 cup whipping cream
1 tablespoon molasses
1/4 cup peanuts, finely chopped

In a large Dutch oven, heat olive oil. Add garlic and onions and sauté 5 minutes.

Add pork and brown well on all sides. Add rice. Stir in tomatoes, red pepper flakes, cinnamon, cloves, salt, saffron and consommé.

Simmer, covered, for 30 minutes.

Add potatoes and simmer 15 minutes.

Stir in whipping cream, molasses and peanuts and simmer until meat and potatoes are tender, about 15 minutes.

SPIT-ROASTED CINNAMON PORK

An East Coast dad likes this so much, he sent it to his daughter on the West Coast.

- *1* *$3\frac{1}{2}$ to 4-pound center cut pork loin, boned*
- *2* *tablespoons ground cinnamon*
- *2* *teaspoons salt*
- *1* *teaspoon white pepper*
- *2* *teaspoons granulated sugar*
- *1* *onion, finely chopped*
- *4* *garlic cloves, minced*
- *1 to 3* *tablespoons soy sauce*

Score pork with a sharp knife. Incisions should be 1/8 to 1/4-inch deep.

In a small bowl, combine cinnamon, salt, pepper, sugar, onion and garlic. Mix well. Whisk in 1 tablespoon soy sauce. If mixture is not spreadable, add another 1 to 2 tablespoons soy sauce to thin.

Rub mixture into loin as completely as possible, rubbing deeply into the scored lines. Refrigerate pork overnight. Bring to room temperature before grilling.

Secure pork on a spit. Arrange coals for indirect heat cooking method. Set drip pan under spit and insert spit when fire is ready.

Roast for 1½ to 2 hours or until pork is slightly pink inside. Baste with juices from drip pan; do not overcook. Allow to rest for 5 to 10 minutes before cutting into thin slices.

Chill:
Overnight

Roast:
1½ to 2 hours

Yield:
6 servings

Notes:
To grill indirectly, allow coals to become white-hot. Push coals to sides of barbecue and place drip pan in middle of coals. Coals should surround drip pan; no coals should be underneath pan. Cover barbecue and cook as directed.

APRICOT AND PINE NUT-STUFFED PORK TENDERLOIN

TEMPERATURE:
Preheat 500 degrees

BROIL:
23 to 25 minutes

YIELD:
6 servings

NOTES:
Add 1/4 cup pine nuts to saucepan and sauté with celery and onion mixture for a little added crunch.

1 1-pound pork tenderloin
2/3 cup chicken stock
1/3 cup chopped dried apricots
1/4 cup pine nuts (optional)
2 tablespoons onion, chopped
2 tablespoons celery, chopped
1 tablespoon margarine or butter
1/8 teaspoon ground cinnamon
Dash of pepper
2 cups whole wheat bread cubes

SAUCE:
1 1/2 teaspoons cornstarch
Dash of ground nutmeg
1 cup apricot nectar

Split tenderloin lengthwise, cutting to, but not through, opposite side. Lightly pound tenderloin with meat mallet to a 10 x 6-inch rectangle.

FILLING:

Pour chicken stock over apricots. Let stand 5 minutes. In a small saucepan, cook onion and celery in margarine until tender but not brown. Remove from heat. Add cinnamon and pepper. In a large mixing bowl combine bread cubes, onion mixture and apricot mixture; toss lightly to moisten.

Spread filling evenly over tenderloin. Starting from short side, roll up jellyroll style. Secure meat with wooden toothpicks or tie with string at 1-inch intervals beginning 1/2 inch from end. Cut meat roll into six 1-inch slices.

Place meat slices on rack of unheated broiler pan, cut-side down. Broil 4 inches from heat for 12 minutes. Turn; broil 11 to 13 minutes more or until done. Remove toothpicks or string and transfer meat to a serving platter.

SAUCE:

Combine cornstarch and nutmeg. Stir in apricot nectar. Cook and stir until mixture is bubbly. Cook and stir 2 minutes more. Serve with meat slices.

SUMMER PORK CHOPS

- 1/2 *cup vegetable oil*
- 1 *cup soy sauce or teriyaki sauce*
- 3 *tablespoons brown sugar*
- 3 *garlic cloves, minced*
- 1 *tablespoon fresh ginger, grated*
- 2 *tablespoons cooking sherry*
- 4 *pork chops, boneless and 1-inch thick*

In a large bowl, whisk together oil, soy sauce, sugar, garlic, ginger and sherry. Transfer marinade to a shallow dish.

Add pork chops and marinate overnight, turning at least once.

Prepare barbecue. Grill chops over hot coals, using indirect grilling method. Cook for 20 minutes per side. (Direct heat will take less time.) Baste meat with marinade while grilling.

MARINATE:
Overnight

YIELD:
4 servings

NOTES:
Chops may also be broiled. Continue to baste with marinade while broiling. For indirect grilling method, see Notes, page 150.

PORK CHOPS WITH CHUTNEY

- 1/2 *cup ketchup*
- 1/3 *cup freshly-squeezed lemon juice*
- 3 *tablespoons brown sugar*
- 2 *tablespoons Worcestershire sauce*
- 1/2 *cup water*
- 1 *cup chutney (See note.)*
- 4 *pork chops, at least 1 1/2 inches thick*

Preheat oven to 350°.

SAUCE:

In a bowl, combine ketchup, lemon juice, sugar, Worcestershire, water and chutney. Whisk thoroughly.

Pour sauce into a roasting pan and heat for 10 minutes in preheated oven.

Remove pan from oven. Add chops and turn to coat evenly. Return to oven and bake for 1 1/2 hours, basting occasionally.

TEMPERATURE:
Preheat 350 degrees

BAKE:
1 1/2 hours

YIELD:
4 servings

NOTES:
Use pear, apple, or tomato chutney, or try our PEACH CHUTNEY, page 23.

LEMON HAZELNUT PORK CHOPS

COOK:
10 to 15 minutes

YIELD:
4 servings

NOTES:
Pecans or walnuts can be substituted for hazelnuts.

4	*boneless pork loin chops, 1/2-inch thick and trimmed*
1/2	*teaspoon garlic salt*
1/4	*teaspoon lemon pepper seasoning*
1	*tablespoon butter*
2	*tablespoons finely-chopped hazelnuts*
4	*tablespoons freshly-squeezed lemon juice*
1	*teaspoon freshly-grated lemon peel*
	Fresh lemon slices for garnish

In a large sauté pan over medium heat, melt butter. Season chops on both sides with garlic salt and lemon pepper. Place chops in sauté pan and brown until pork is tender; 5 to 7 minutes per side. Remove chops to serving plate. Sprinkle with hazelnuts and set aside.

Stir lemon juice into drippings in sauté pan and heat for 1 minute, stirring constantly. Spoon over cooked chops and sprinkle with lemon peel. To serve, garnish each chop with a fresh lemon slice.

CLASSIC PORK CHOP CASSEROLE

- 4 *pork chops*
- 1 *cup uncooked brown rice*
- 1/2 *cup green bell pepper, seeded, deveined and chopped*
- 2 *tablespoons butter*
- 1 *(14-ounce) can tomatoes*
- 2 *teaspoons salt*
- 1/2 *(14-ounce) can water*
- *Freshly-ground black pepper*
- 1 *onion, chopped*

Preheat oven to 350 degrees.

In a large sauté pan, melt butter and brown pork chops. Season with salt and pepper. Remove chops and set aside. Reserve 6 tablespoons fat drippings from pork.

Wash and drain rice. In sauté pan, heat fat drippings and add rice. Brown rice, stirring often to avoid scorching.

Add green pepper, tomatoes, salt, water and onion. Sprinkle with pepper.

Remove rice mixture from sauté pan and place in a casserole. Layer chops on top. Cover and bake in oven at 350 degrees for 1 hour.

THIS CASSEROLE IS QUICK TO ASSEMBLE AND HAVE READY WHEN DINNER HOUR ARRIVES.

TEMPERATURE:
Preheat 350 degrees

BAKE:
1 hour

YIELD:
4 servings

ISLAND RIBS

Savor the flavor of the South Pacific with these delicious ribs!

Marinate:
3 hours; 2 at room temperature, 1 in refrigerator

Temperature:
Preheat 350 degrees

Bake:
1 hour

Yield:
2 to 3 servings

Notes:
Use this marinade for chicken, too.

- *1/2 cup soy sauce*
- *1/2 cup ketchup*
- *3 tablespoons brown sugar*
- *3 tablespoons fresh ginger, grated*
- *4 to 5 pork ribs*
- *1/4 cup sugar*
- *1 teaspoon salt*

In a bowl, whisk together soy sauce, ketchup, sugar and ginger. Let stand overnight.

Preheat oven to 350 degrees.

Rub ribs on both sides with sugar and salt; let stand 2 hours. Brush with marinade. Marinate in refrigerator for at least 1 hour.

Bake for 1 hour at 350 degrees, turning after 30 minutes.

HAM AND ENDIVE AU GRATIN

TEMPERATURE:
Preheat 450 degrees

COOK:
30 minutes

BAKE:
15 minutes

YIELD:
3 to 4 servings

- *1/2 cup butter (1 cube), divided*
- *1/3 cup freshly-squeezed lemon juice*
- *6 to 8 Belgian endives, roots trimmed*
- *Salt*
- *1/4 cup all-purpose flour*
- *1/4 teaspoon cayenne pepper*
- *Dash nutmeg*
- *2 cups milk*
- *3/4 cup Swiss cheese, grated and divided*
- *6 to 8 thin slices cooked ham*
- *Paprika*

In a large sauté pan, combine 1/4 cup butter, lemon juice and 2 tablespoons water. Place endive in sauté pan and sprinkle with salt. Simmer, covered, 30 minutes. Check occasionally and add a little water if needed.

Preheat oven to 450 degrees.

In a saucepan, melt remaining butter. Remove from heat. Stir in flour, cayenne, nutmeg and milk. Return to heat and bring to a boil, stirring constantly. Reduce heat and add 1/2 cup Swiss cheese. Simmer over low heat until thickened and cheese has melted.

Drain cooked endives. Wrap each with a ham slice, leaving ends uncovered. Arrange endives in a baking dish. Cover with sauce and top with remaining Swiss cheese and paprika.

Bake at 450 degrees for 15 minutes.

BAKED HAM-ASPARAGUS ROLLS

THIS IS EXCELLENT FOR LUNCH OR A SUNDAY EVENING SUPPER.

TEMPERATURE:
Preheat 350 degrees

BAKE:
25 to 30 minutes

YIELD:
4 servings

NOTES:
Try this with CLASSIC FRUIT SALAD, page 40 and SOUR CREAM CRESCENT ROLLS, page 62.

3	*tablespoons butter*
3	*tablespoons all-purpose flour*
3/4	*teaspoon salt*
2	*cups milk*
1	*cup Swiss cheese, grated*
1 1/3	*cups cooked rice*
8	*slices cooked ham*
24 to 32	*slender fresh or frozen asparagus spears, cooked and drained*
1/4	*cup freshly-grated Parmesan cheese*

In a saucepan, melt butter. Whisk in flour and salt. Stir in milk and cook, stirring constantly, until thickened.

Add cheese, stirring until just melted.

Blend 1 cup of the sauce into rice.

Spoon an equal amount of rice mixture onto each ham slice. Top with 3 or 4 asparagus spears placed diagonally, and roll ham around filling.

Secure with toothpicks.

Arrange rolls in a shallow 2-quart baking dish. Pour remaining sauce over top and sprinkle with Parmesan cheese. Bake at 350 degrees for 25 to 30 minutes.

BUTTERFLIED LEG OF LAMB WITH BLUE CHEESE

- 1 *garlic clove, minced*
- 1 *teaspoon ground ginger*
- 4 *tablespoons brown sugar*
- 1/2 *cup red or dry white wine*
- 1/2 *cup soy sauce*
- 1/2 *cup olive oil*
- 1 *5-pound leg of lamb, butterflied (See note.)*

SAUCE:

- 2 *ounces blue cheese, crumbled*
- 4 *tablespoons butter (1/2 cube)*
- 4 *green onions, chopped*
- 1 *tablespoons freshly-squeezed lemon juice*

In a small bowl, combine garlic, ginger and sugar. Mix well. Whisk in wine, soy sauce and olive oil to make marinade.

Cover lamb with marinade and refrigerate for 2 days, turning every 4 to 6 hours.

While coals are burning to embers, prepare blue cheese mixture.

In a small bowl, combine blue cheese, butter, green onions and lemon juice.

Place lamb on grill, cover and barbecue approximately 1 hour or until internal temperature reaches 150 degrees (medium) or 180 (well done).

Place barbecued lamb on a baking sheet. Spoon blue cheese mixture over lamb and place under the broiler for 4 to 5 minutes or until cheese melts & bubbles.

To serve, thinly slice lamb.

BRING ON SPRING WITH THIS UNIQUE DISH.

MARINATE:
2 DAYS

GRILL:
Approximately 1 hour

BROIL:
4 TO 5 MINUTES

YIELD:
6 to 8 servings

NOTES:
Ask the butcher to butterfly the lamb.

GRILLED LEG OF LAMB

GRILL:
Approximately 1 hour

YIELD:
6 to 8 servings

NOTES:
Have your butcher bone the lamb. If you do not have a mortar and pestle, use 2 pieces of waxed paper and a rolling pin to grind herbs. For indirect grilling method, see Notes, page 150, SPIT ROASTED CINNAMON PORK.

- *1/3 cup dried oregano*
- *3 teaspoons garlic powder*
- *2 teaspoons dill*
- *1 teaspoon ground thyme*
- *1 teaspoon salt*
- *1 teaspoon pepper*
- *1/2 cup olive oil, divided*
- *1 3 to 4-pound leg of lamb, butterflied (See note.)*

With mortar and pestle, grind oregano, garlic, dill, thyme, salt and pepper together, to a fine, but not powdery, texture.

Rub half the oil on 1 side of the lamb, then sprinkle with half the spice mixture. Pound the herbs into surface of the lamb with a meat mallet.

Turn lamb to the other side and repeat process with remaining oil and herbs.

Starting with the short end, tightly roll leg of lamb. Tie securely in several places with twine.

Place meat thermometer in middle of lamb and grill over medium coals in covered barbecue using indirect heating method. Cook for approximately 1 hour or until meat thermometer registers 150 degrees. Turn meat after first 30 minutes of cooking.

RACK OF LAMB

1/4	*cup seasoned bread crumbs*
4	*tablespoons Dijon mustard*
1	*garlic clove, minced*
2	*tablespoons soy sauce*
1/2	*cup olive oil*
1	*3-pound rack of lamb*

Preheat oven to 375 degrees.

Cut all fat from lamb.

In a small bowl, combine bread crumbs, mustard and garlic. Whisk in soy sauce. Slowly whisk in olive oil until bread crumb mixture is soft and sticks together quite well.

Spread mixture on top and sides of lamb. Place lamb on the rack of a roasting pan in center of oven.

Bake lamb in a 375-degree oven for 45 minutes.

If crust begins to burn while cooking, cover loosely with foil.

RICE PILAF WOULD BE A HARMONIOUS ADDITION TO THE MENU.

TEMPERATURE:
Preheat 375 degrees

COOK:
45 minutes

YIELD:
2 to 4 servings

LAMB CHOPS WITH FETA CHEESE

This dish explains Greeks' love of lamb!

Marinate:
Overnight

Broil:
10 to 14 minutes

Yield:
4 servings

Notes:
Substitute 8 small rib chops for shoulder chops.

2 cups olive oil, divided
2 cups dry white wine, divided
Dash of fresh rosemary
4 whole allspice
2 bay leaves
2 garlic cloves, minced
4 ounces feta cheese, cubed
4 to 6 shoulder-blade chops

In a large bowl, whisk together 1 cup oil, 1 cup wine, rosemary, allspice and bay leaf. Cover lamb with marinade and refrigerate overnight.

In a separate bowl, combine remaining oil and wine with garlic. Mix well and pour over feta cheese. Marinate cheese overnight.

Broil chops 5 to 7 minutes per side. Just before second side is done, place a small mound of cheese on each chop and return to broiler. Cook until cheese melts.

LAMB CHOP STEW

12 to 14 lamb chops
2 tablespoons vegetable oil
1 (10 1/2-ounce) can French onion soup
1 (10 1/2-ounce) can cream of tomato soup
1 (14 1/2-ounce) can chicken broth
2 carrots, sliced
3 medium potatoes, quartered
1 cup (2 stalks) celery, sliced

Preheat oven to 375 degrees.

In a large sauté pan, heat oil and brown lamb chops on both sides. Slice meat from bone and cut into bite-sized pieces.

In a large Dutch oven with lid, combine meat, onion soup, tomato soup, chicken broth and vegetables. Place in a 375-degree oven and bake for 1 to 2 hours or until meat is very tender.

This is quick and delicious. On extra busy nights, substitute 1 (16-ounce) bag frozen mixed vegetables.

Temperature:
Preheat 375 degrees

Bake:
1 to 2 hours

Yield:
4 to 6 servings

Notes:
To thicken stew, add beurre manie. To make beurre manie, combine 2 tablespoons butter and 2 tablespoons flour. Rub mixture together between fingers to form small balls. Drop into simmering stew and blend until stew thickens. Repeat process, if needed.

Poultry & Game

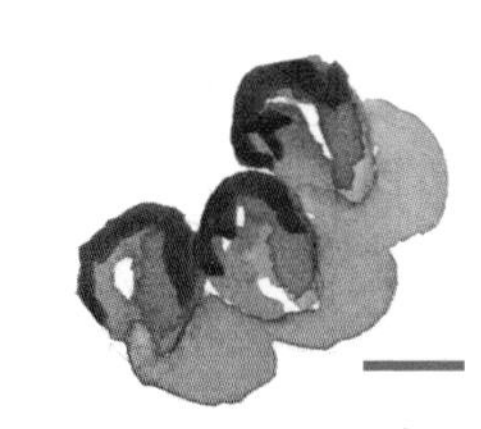

FOWL IN FOUL WEATHER

Fog steals over the Willamette River. Trees stripped bare by November squalls afford a dramatic view of the arching St. John's bridge. Hidden in the hills above the river are homes in what residents call "old Portland" style. Hunters head north to Sauvie Island.

When Portlanders draw indoors to combat damp days and chilly nights, a warming meal restores the glow to a winter evening. With the gleam of tall, creamy candles reflected in their holders, the deep red of CRANBERRY CHICKEN or the crispy gold of LEMON-ROASTED GAME HENS brings heart to the hearth.

For more than 80 years, the Junior League of Portland has cast its own glow on the Portland community. With projects like ArtSource, YWCA Transitional School for the Homeless, Alzheimer's Community Outreach and Women Helping Women, volunteers improve the quality of life for all Portlanders.

THAI CHICKEN CURRY

- 2 *tablespoons corn oil*
- 2 *teaspoons mild curry paste (See note.)*
- 2 *chicken breast halves, boneless and skinless, cut into 1/4-inch strips*
- 2 *tablespoons granulated sugar*
- 2 *tablespoons soy sauce*
- 1/4 *teaspoon salt*
- 1 *garlic clove, minced*
- 2 *tablespoons butter*
- 2 *tablespoons all-purpose flour*
- 1/4 *teaspoon salt*
- *Dash of white pepper*
- 1 *cup milk*
- 2 *cups broccoli florets*
- 1/4 *cup salted peanuts*

BROCCOLI ENHANCES THIS CLASSIC CURRY DISH.

YIELD:
2 servings

NOTES:
Curry paste is available in specialty markets.

In a wok or sauté pan over low heat, combine oil and curry paste. Cook for 1 minute, stirring well. Increase heat to medium-high and add chicken, sugar, soy sauce, salt and garlic. Stir-fry until chicken is done.

In a medium saucepan over low heat, melt butter. Blend in flour, salt and pepper, then add milk in a steady stream. Cook and stir over medium-high heat until thick and bubbly, about 5 minutes.

Add chicken, broccoli and peanuts to sauce and cook until heated through. Serve on a bed of steamed rice.

CHICKEN OLÉ

YOUR FAMILY WILL REQUEST THIS AGAIN AND AGAIN.

MARINATE:
30 minutes

YIELD:
6 servings

NOTES:
This goes very well with Spanish rice.

- *1 cup chunky salsa, medium hot*
- *1/4 cup Dijon mustard*
- *3 tablespoons freshly-squeezed lime juice*
- *6 chicken breast halves, boneless and skinless*
- *3 tablespoons butter*
- *1/2 cup plain yogurt or sour cream*
- *1 lime, cut into 6 thin slices*

In a large bowl, combine salsa, mustard and lime juice. Add chicken, turning to coat. Marinate in refrigerator for at least 30 minutes.

In a large sauté pan, melt butter over medium heat until foamy. Remove chicken from marinade and place in frying pan. Cook, turning frequently, until well-browned on all sides.

Add marinade to sauté pan and cook for 5 minutes more or until fork can be inserted into chicken with ease and marinade is slightly reduced and beginning to glaze.

Remove chicken to heated serving platter. Raise heat to high and boil marinade 1 minute to reduce liquid. Pour over chicken. Garnish with 1 tablespoon of yogurt or sour cream and a lime slice on each piece of chicken.

CHICKEN MARSALA

4	*chicken breast halves, boneless and skinless*
1/4	*cup all-purpose flour*
	Salt and pepper
3	*tablespoons butter*
2	*tablespoons olive oil*
1/2	*cup dry Marsala wine*
1/2	*cup chicken broth*
1/4	*cup freshly-grated Parmesan cheese*
1/4	*cup freshly-squeezed lemon juice*

SAUTÉ:
6 MINUTES

YIELD:
4 servings

NOTES:
Serve with angel hair pasta or POTATOES FRANCAISE, page 115.

Place chicken between sheets of waxed paper and flatten with a mallet.

In a shallow dish, combine flour, salt and pepper. Dredge chicken pieces until well-coated, shaking off excess flour.

In a sauté pan over medium-high heat, melt butter and olive oil. Add chicken and brown well, turning often to prevent sticking, for approximately 2 to 3 minutes.

Add Marsala wine and chicken broth. Cover, reduce heat to low and simmer for 3 minutes. Sprinkle with Parmesan cheese and cover until cheese has melted.

Remove chicken and place on warmed plate. Pour lemon juice into pan and whisk pan juices and browned bits together. Pour sauce over chicken. Serve immediately.

CHICKEN WELLINGTON

Vicki Yates recommended '93.

TEMPERATURE:
Preheat 400 degrees

BAKE:
25 minutes

YIELD:
4 servings

NOTES:
Chicken breasts can be prepared ahead, wrapped in wax paper and refrigerated. The sauce can be made ahead and reheated.

4 chicken breast halves, boneless and skinless
1 (16 1/2-ounce) can chicken broth
1/2 cup white wine
1 sheet frozen puff pastry dough (1/2 of 17 1/4-ounce package), thawed until pliable (about 1/2 hour)
1 1/2 cups Cheddar cheese, grated

SAUCE:

3 tablespoons butter
3 tablespoons all-purpose flour
Poaching liquid from chicken breasts
3 tablespoons lemon juice
Pinch of nutmeg
Salt and pepper

Preheat oven to 400 degrees.

In a deep sauté pan over high heat, combine chicken broth and white wine. Bring to a boil. Add chicken and gently simmer for 10 minutes. Remove chicken and reserve broth.

Cut puff pastry into four rectangles. Roll out each rectangle until large enough to fold over chicken breast. Split each breast lengthwise and stuff with 4 tablespoons of cheese.

Place each chicken breast on a rectangle of pastry. Fold pastry over chicken, pinching seams for a tight seal. Bake seam-side down in a 400-degree oven for 25 minutes.

SAUCE:

In a saucepan over medium heat, melt butter and stir in flour. Gradually add reserved broth, lemon juice and seasonings. Cook and stir until thick and bubbly. Pour sauce over chicken and serve.

Large servings! Try cutting in half.

MU SHU YOU CAN DO

THE TITLE SAYS IT ALL!

YIELD:
4 servings

NOTES:
Garnish with vertically sliced leeks.
Pancakes should be made ahead so they are ready for filling.

- 5 *chicken breast halves, boneless and skinless*
- 1 *tablespoon dry sherry*
- 2 *teaspoons dark soy sauce*
- 1 *tablespoon plus 2 teaspoons cornstarch, divided*
- 1 *tablespoon water*
- 3 *tablespoons plus 2 teaspoons peanut oil, divided*
- 1 *cup bean sprouts*
- 1/3 *cup sliced mushrooms*
- 2 *cups shredded green or Chinese cabbage*
- 3 *green onions, shredded*
- 4 *eggs*
- 2 *garlic cloves, finely minced*
- 2 *teaspoons fresh ginger, finely minced*
- 3/4 *cup hoisin sauce*

SAUCE:

- 3 *tablespoons chicken stock*
- 2 *tablespoons dry sherry*
- 1 *tablespoon dark soy sauce*
- 1 *tablespoon sesame oil*
- 1/2 *teaspoon granulated sugar*
- 1/4 *teaspoon freshly-ground black pepper*

PANCAKES:

- 1 3/4 *cup all-purpose flour*
- 3/4 *cup boiling water*
- 2 *teaspoons sesame or cooking oil*

Cut chicken lengthwise into very thin slices. Place slices together and cut crosswise into 1-inch lengths.

In a large bowl, mix chicken with sherry, soy sauce, 2 teaspoons cornstarch and 2 teaspoons peanut oil. Refrigerate until ready to cook.

In another large bowl, combine bean sprouts, mushrooms, cabbage and green onions. In a small bowl beat eggs well. Set aside.

SAUCE:

In a small bowl, combine chicken stock, sherry, soy sauce, sesame oil, sugar and pepper. Mix well and set aside.

In another small bowl, dissolve 1 tablespoon cornstarch in 1 tablespoon of water and set aside.

In a heavy saucepan or wok over high heat, add 1 tablespoon of peanut oil. Add eggs and stir-fry quickly, until they become firm, about 1 minute. Place cooked eggs in a bowl.

about 2 minutes. Transfer chicken to bowl with eggs. Add final tablespoon of oil to wok along with garlic and ginger. Sauté a few seconds, then add vegetables and stir-fry until crisp-tender, about 2 to 3 minutes.

Return eggs and chicken to wok and pour in sauce mixture. When sauce comes to a low boil, stir in a little of the cornstarch/water mixture until sauce glazes the food. Transfer to a heated platter.

Serve with hot pancakes and hoisin sauce. To serve, spread a little hoisin sauce on each pancake. Place 1/2 cup filling on top of sauce, then roll pancake into a cylinder, folding bottom end up to keep filling from escaping. Filled pancakes are eaten with fingers.

PANCAKES:

In a medium bowl, combine flour and boiling water and mix with a spoon. Cool slightly. When cool enough to handle, knead hot dough together until smooth, about 3 minutes.

Cover bowl with a damp towel and set aside to cool. When dough is cool, form into a 12-inch long cylinder. Cut into rounds 1-inch thick.

Brush each side of round with oil and flatten with palm of your hand. Roll with rolling pin into flat pancakes.

In an ungreased sauté pan, fry each pancake over medium-low heat for 1 minute on the first side and 30 seconds on the second side.

In a colander over boiling water, steam stacked pancakes for 10 minutes.

POLLO GENOVESE

- *2 pounds chicken breasts, boneless and skinless*
- *4 tablespoons butter (1/2 cube)*
- *4 tablespoons olive oil*
- *All-purpose flour seasoned with salt and pepper for dredging*
- *4 garlic cloves, minced*
- *1 (6-ounce) can pitted olives, drained*
- *1 cup fresh mushrooms, sliced*
- *1 (26-ounce) can stewed tomatoes, with liquid*
- *1/4 cup parsley, chopped*
- *2 tablespoons capers, drained*
- *1 tablespoon dried basil*
- *1 cup white wine*

Add pasta and dinner is ready!

Temperature:
Preheat 350 degrees

Sauté:
15 minutes

Bake:
20 to 30 minutes

Yield:
6 servings

Preheat oven to 350 degrees.

Place chicken breasts between sheets of waxed paper and pound with a mallet until very thin. Cut chicken into bite-sized pieces.

In a large sauté pan, heat butter and olive oil. Dredge chicken in flour and sauté in small batches until golden brown. Place chicken in greased ovenproof casserole dish.

If necessary, add 1 additional tablespoon olive oil to pan and sauté olives, mushrooms and garlic for 4 to 5 minutes. Add tomatoes, parsley, capers, basil and wine and bring to boil. Continue boiling for about 5 minutes to slightly reduce liquid.

Pour sauce over chicken. Bake in a 350-degree oven for 20 to 30 minutes.

CHICKEN AND ARTICHOKE CACCIATORE

Temperature:
Preheat 350 degrees

Bake:
1 hour and 10 minutes

Yield:
4 servings

Notes:
Spinach linguine and crusty sourdough bread add just the right touch.

- *4 chicken breast halves, boneless and skinless*
- *All-purpose flour seasoned with salt and pepper for dredging*
- *2 tablespoons olive oil*
- *1 (6-ounce) jar marinated artichoke hearts; do not drain*
- *1 (15-ounce) can stewed tomatoes; do not drain*
- *2 garlic cloves, minced*
- *1/2 teaspoon dried oregano*
- *1/2 teaspoon dried basil*
- *1/2 teaspoon pepper*
- *1/2 pound fresh mushrooms, sliced*
- *1/4 cup sherry*

Preheat oven to 350 degrees.

Dredge chicken in seasoned flour.

In a large Dutch oven, heat olive oil. Add chicken and brown over medium-high heat. Add artichoke hearts, stewed tomatoes, garlic, herbs, pepper and mushrooms. Remove from heat. Cover and bake in a 350-degree oven for 1 hour. Add sherry and bake an additional 10 minutes.

Serve over pasta or rice.

HONEY-MUSTARD CHICKEN

Be prepared for many requests for this recipe!

Yield:
8 servings

Notes:
Garnish this dish with lemon and orange slices and scattered pomegranate seeds.

- *1 cup honey*
- *1 1/3 cups Dijon mustard*
- *2 cups seasoned bread crumbs*
- *8 chicken breast halves, boneless and skinless*
- *1/2 to 1 cup butter (1 to 2 cubes), divided*

In a medium bowl, combine honey and mustard. Mix well. Put bread crumbs in a flat dish or pie pan. Dredge chicken breasts in honey-mustard mixture, then in bread crumbs.

In a sauté pan over medium heat, melt 1/2 cup (1 cube) butter. Add chicken, turning as it cooks. Add more butter as necessary. Sauté until chicken is done, approximately 10 to 15 minutes.

CHICKEN-DIJON RIGATONI

Yield:
6 servings

Notes:
Tarragon can be substituted for parsley.

- 1/4 *cup butter (1/2 cube)*
- 6 *chicken breast halves, boneless, skinless and cubed*
- 2 *cups half and half*
- 1 *tablespoon olive oil*
- *Salt and pepper*
- 1 *pound medium rigatoni*
- 1/3 *cup Dijon mustard*
- 3 *tablespoons fresh parsley, chopped*

In a large sauté pan over medium-high heat, melt butter until bubbly. Add chicken and sauté until tender, about 3 to 5 minutes. Remove chicken from pan and set aside.

Add half and half to pan and stir to blend with butter. Add salt and pepper. Bring to a boil. Reduce heat and simmer until mixture is reduced and slightly thickened, about 5 minutes.

Meanwhile, bring 4 quarts water to a boil with olive oil and salt. Add pasta and cook according to package directions. Transfer pasta to a warmed serving dish.

Whisk mustard into cream mixture. Return chicken to pan, reduce heat to low and cook until heated through. Do not boil. Spoon chicken mixture over pasta. Add parsley and toss thoroughly. Serve immediately.

CRANBERRY CHICKEN

TAKE ADVANTAGE OF WONDERFUL NORTHWEST CRANBERRIES FOR THIS SPECIAL DISH.

TEMPERATURE:
Preheat 400 degrees

BAKE:
45 minutes

YIELD:
6 servings

- *1 tablespoon butter*
- *1 small onion, coarsely chopped*
- *3 pounds chicken thighs, skinned*
- *2/3 cup ketchup*
- *1/3 cup brown sugar, firmly packed*
- *1 tablespoon cider vinegar*
- *1 teaspoon dry mustard*
- *1 1/2 cup fresh or frozen cranberries, rinsed*

Preheat oven to 400 degrees.

In a 10 x 15-inch baking pan, combine butter and onion. Roast uncovered until onion is pale gold, stirring occasionally. Push onion to one side of pan. Place chicken thighs side by side in pan (not on top of onion). Bake uncovered for 25 minutes.

In a bowl, combine ketchup, brown sugar, vinegar, mustard and cranberries. Scoop browned onions out of pan and stir into mixture. Space chicken evenly in pan and spoon cranberry mixture over chicken.

Bake about 20 minutes more, until cranberry mixture is slightly caramelized and chicken is no longer pink at the bone in the thickest part. (Cut with a small sharp knife to test.)

DIJON CHICKEN AND ARTICHOKES

SAUTÉ:
4 TO 5 MINUTES

COOK:
10 minutes

YIELD:
4 servings

- *4 chicken breasts, boneless, skinless and pounded flat*
- *2 tablespoons butter*
- *1/2 cup onions, thinly sliced*
- *1 cup fresh mushrooms, sliced*
- *2 garlic cloves, minced*
- *1 (6-ounce) jar marinated artichoke hearts, drained*
- *2 tablespoons Dijon mustard*
- *1 cup dry white wine*
- *1/2 cup whipping cream*
- *2 tablespoons fresh parsley, chopped*

In a sauté pan, brown chicken breasts in butter. Remove from pan and keep warm.

Add onion, mushrooms and garlic and sauté lightly. Add artichoke hearts and mustard. Add wine; allow to simmer until reduced by half. Stir in cream.

Return chicken to sauté pan, cook 5 to 10 more minutes or until no longer pink in middle. Check for doneness. Remove chicken to serving dish. Pour sauce over and sprinkle with parsley.

Serve with rice or pasta.

CHICKEN BREASTS STUFFED WITH PESTO BUTTER

- 6 *chicken breast halves, boneless and skinless*
- 1/2 *cup fresh basil leaves, washed and dried*
- 1/4 *cup freshly-grated Parmesan cheese*
- 1 *garlic clove, minced*
- 1/2 *cup butter (1 cube), room temperature*
- 1/3 *cup all-purpose flour seasoned with salt and pepper*
- 1 *egg, well beaten*
- 3/4 *cup fine dry bread crumbs (made from French or Italian bread)*
- 2 *tablespoons butter*
- 2 *tablespoons olive oil*

Place chicken between sheets of waxed paper and pound with a mallet until very thin, being careful not to tear meat.

In a food processor or blender, combine basil, cheese and garlic. Mix until a thick paste is formed. Add butter and blend. Shape into a 3-inch square. Chill until firm. Slice chilled square into 6 sticks, 1/2-inch wide and 3-inches long.

Lay out the flattened chicken breasts. Place a stick of pesto butter to one side of each piece of meat (preferably to the larger side). Fold the remaining side over butter, then fold down the two ends. Press meat together on all sides to securely enclose butter.

Using 3 separate pie plates, place seasoned flour in one, beaten egg in another and bread crumbs in the third.

Dredge each chicken breast in flour and shake off excess. Dip into egg, then roll in bread crumbs. Firmly pat bread crumbs onto chicken.

Refrigerate chicken rolls for at least 1 hour to allow crumbs to adhere. At this point chicken rolls may be frozen, but thaw completely before cooking.

In a large sauté pan, heat butter and olive oil. Sauté chicken on medium to medium-high heat for about 15 minutes, turning chicken until golden brown on all sides and meat is white all the way through.

EXCELLENT WHEN SERVED WITH SPINACH FETTUCCINE AND FRESH TOMATOES.

CHILL:
1 hour

SAUTÉ:
15 minutes

YIELD:
6 servings

NOTES:
May be kept warm in a 200-degree oven for up to 30 minutes before serving.

CILANTRO CHICKEN

A WELCOME ADDITION TO ANY RECIPE LIBRARY, THIS RENDITION HAS NO SALT OR OIL.

TEMPERATURE:
Preheat 350 degrees

SAUTÉ:
4 TO 5 MINUTES

BAKE:
30 minutes

YIELD:
4 servings

- 1 *pound chicken breasts, boneless and skinless*
- 1/2 *cup dry white wine*
- 1 *bunch cilantro, stems removed, washed and dried*
- 4 *garlic cloves*
- 4 *tablespoons freshly-squeezed lime juice*
- 1 *tomato, skinned, seeded and diced*

Preheat oven to 350 degrees.

In a large non-stick sauté pan over medium-high heat, brown chicken on both sides. Transfer chicken to a casserole dish with a cover or a Dutch oven.

Pour white wine into sauté pan and scrape pan to remove any browned bits. Bring wine to a boil. Pour over chicken.

In a food processor or blender, combine cilantro and garlic. Mix well. Sprinkle over chicken and add lime juice and tomato. Bake, covered, for 30 minutes, until chicken is cooked through.

ITALIAN STUFFED CHICKEN BREASTS

MAKES A TERRIFIC PRESENTATION!

TEMPERATURE:
Preheat 350 degrees

BAKE:
40 minutes

YIELD:
6 servings

NOTES:
Although prosciutto is becoming much more common, it is sometimes hard to find. Check specialty markets and grocery stores equipped with expanded delicatessens.

- 6 *chicken breast halves, boneless and skinless*
- *Salt and pepper*
- *Thyme*
- *Marjoram*
- 12 *pieces oil-packed, sun-dried tomatoes, drained*
- 6 *ounces mozzarella cheese, cut into 1-ounce sticks*
- 6 *thin slices proscuitto ham (See note.)*
- 3 to 4 *tablespoons butter*

Preheat oven to 350 degrees.

Place chicken between sheets of waxed paper and pound with a mallet until very thin.

Sprinkle chicken with salt, pepper, thyme and marjoram.

Wrap each mozzarella stick with 1 slice prosciutto. Place sun-dried tomatoes and wrapped mozzarella in center of each chicken breast. Roll chicken breasts around filling. Place close together in a baking dish and baste with butter. Bake at 350 degrees for 40 minutes, basting every 15 minutes.

TANGY CHICKEN AND PEA PODS

A crowd-pleaser for all ages!

Marinate: 4 hours or overnight

Temperature: Preheat 350 degrees

Bake: 40 minutes

Yield: 10 servings

Notes: Leftovers are terrific hot or cold!

- *10 chicken breast halves, boneless and skinless*
- *2 cups freshly-squeezed lemon juice*
- *1 cup all-purpose flour*
- *1 teaspoon salt*
- *2 teaspoons paprika*
- *1 teaspoon freshly-ground black pepper*
- *1 cup vegetable oil*
- *2 tablespoons lemon zest*
- *1/4 cup brown sugar, firmly packed*
- *1/4 cup chicken broth*
- *1 teaspoon lemon extract*
- *2 lemons, thinly sliced*
- *1 pound Chinese snow pea pods*
- *1 (15-ounce) can water-packed baby ears of corn, drained*
- *4 garlic cloves, minced*
- *2 tablespoons vegetable oil*
- *1 tablespoon butter*

Preheat oven to 350 degrees.

In a large bowl, combine chicken and lemon juice. Marinate overnight, if possible, or for a minimum of 4 hours.

Remove chicken from marinade and pat dry. In a shallow dish, combine flour, salt, paprika, and pepper. Dredge chicken pieces and coat each one well. Shake off excess flour.

In a large sauté pan over medium-high heat, add oil. When oil is hot, add chicken (being careful not to overcrowd pan) and fry until chicken is browned and crispy.

In a small bowl, combine chicken broth and lemon extract. Place chicken pieces in a 9 x 13-inch glass baking dish and cover with broth mixture. Garnish with lemon slices and bake in a 350-degree oven for 40 minutes.

Clean and stem pea pods, removing any strings. In a large sauté pan or wok, heat oil. Add pea pods, corn, and garlic. Stir-fry until pea pods are crisp-tender. Combine with baked chicken and serve over rice.

SESAME CHICKEN

GREAT FOR A LAST-MINUTE DINNER PARTY!

MARINATE:
1 to 2 hours

TEMPERATURE:
Preheat 500 degrees

BAKE:
5 to 10 minutes

YIELD:
4 servings

1/4 cup soy sauce
1 tablespoon honey
1 tablespoon dry white wine
1 teaspoon ginger
2 garlic cloves, minced
3 pounds chicken breasts, boneless and skinless
2 eggs, beaten
1/2 cup all-purpose flour
1/2 cup sesame seeds
2 tablespoons butter
2 tablespoons olive oil

In a large bowl, whisk together soy sauce, honey, wine, ginger and garlic. Add chicken to bowl and cover with marinade. Refrigerate for 1 to 2 hours.

Heat a large cast-iron skillet in a 500-degree oven.

Remove chicken from marinade.

In a medium bowl, beat eggs. Combine flour and sesame seeds in a paper bag. Dip chicken in eggs, then shake chicken in bag until well-coated with sesame seeds.

When pan is hot, add butter and oil. Place chicken in a single layer in the pan and turn to coat with melted butter and oil. Bake 5 to 10 minutes or until chicken is no longer pink when cut.

ELEGANT CHICKEN POT PIE

Temperature:
Preheat 350 degrees

Cook:
30 minutes

Bake:
30 minutes

Yield:
6 to 8 servings

- 1 *sheet frozen puff pastry, thawed*
- 1 *egg yolk, beaten with 1 tablespoon water*
- 8 *chicken breast halves, boneless and skinless*
- 2 *(14 1/2-ounce) cans chicken broth*
- 1 *cup dry white wine*
- 1 *large onion, coarsely chopped*
- 3 *medium carrots, thickly sliced*
- 3 *stalks celery, sliced*
- 3 *bay leaves*
- 2 *tablespoons parsley, chopped*
- 1 *cup peas, fresh or frozen*
- 1/2 *pound fresh mushrooms, thickly sliced*
- 1/2 *pound cooked ham, cut in 1-inch cubes*
- 1/4 *cup butter (1/2 cube)*
- 1/4 *cup all-purpose flour*
- 2 *egg yolks*
- 1 *cup whipping cream*
- 1/4 *teaspoon mace*
- 1/4 *teaspoon freshly-ground pepper*
- 1 *teaspoon fines herbs or herbs de provence*
- *Salt*

Preheat oven to 350 degrees.

Roll out thawed puff pastry, cut to fit dimensions of 9 x 13-inch baking dish. Place on baking sheet. Use scraps to decorate (flowers, leaves, etc.) Brush pastry with egg yolk/water mixture and bake for 20 to 25 minutes, until puffed and lightly browned. Reserve for the top of the pie.

In a large sauté pan, combine chicken, broth and wine. Bring to a boil. Add onion, carrots, celery, bay leaves and parsley. Cover and simmer for 30 minutes or until vegetables are tender. With slotted spoon, remove vegetables and chicken. Strain broth and reserve.

Skin chicken and cut into 1-inch chunks. Arrange the chicken, cooked vegetables, peas, sautéed mushrooms, and ham in 9 x 13-inch dish.

In medium sauté pan, melt butter, stir in flour and cook for a few minutes. Stir in 2 cups reserved broth and cook until thickened.

Beat egg yolks and stir into sauce. Add cream and stir to thicken but do not boil. Add seasonings and salt to taste.

Pour sauce over chicken, ham, and vegetables in pan. Cover with foil and bake at 350 degrees for 25 minutes. Remove foil, top with puff pastry crust, and bake 5 minutes more.

SPICY CHICKEN CHILI

After a day on the slopes, this quick, easy dinner will satisfy even your hungriest skier.

Sauté:
5 to 7 minutes

Cook:
20 minutes

Yield:
4 to 6 servings

Notes:
Garnish individual servings with grated cheese, chopped green onions, chopped avocado and sour cream or sprigs of cilantro.

- 6 *chicken breast halves, boneless and skinless, cubed*
- 1 *cup onion, coarsely chopped*
- 1 *green bell pepper, seeded, deveined and chopped*
- 2 *garlic cloves, minced*
- 2 *tablespoons olive oil*
- 2 *(15 1/2-ounce) cans Mexican-style stewed tomatoes*
- 2 *(15 1/2-ounce) cans pinto beans, drained*
- 1/2 *cup picante sauce (hot, medium or mild)*
- 1 *teaspoon ground cumin*
- 1 *teaspoon chili powder*
- 1/2 *teaspoon salt*

In a large sauté pan over medium-high heat, warm oil. Add chicken, onion, pepper and garlic. Sauté 5 to 7 minutes or until chicken is no longer pink.

Add remaining ingredients and simmer 20 minutes. Serve over steamed rice.

FAR EAST CHICKEN

When barbecue season arrives, try this!

Marinate:
6 hours or overnight

Temperature:
Preheat 350 degrees

Bake:
1 hour

Yield:
4 servings

Notes:
Two Cornish game hens, halved, can be substituted. Grill skewers of pineapple and water chestnuts to serve alongside.

- 1/2 *cup soy sauce*
- 1/2 *cup sherry*
- 1/2 *cup pineapple juice*
- 1 *teaspoon curry powder*
- 1 *teaspoon Dijon mustard*
- 1 *whole fryer chicken, cut into serving pieces (See note.)*

In a large bowl, combine soy sauce, sherry, pineapple juice, curry and mustard and mix well. Add chicken and coat well. Cover and marinate in refrigerator overnight, or for a minimum of 6 hours.

Place chicken on a rack over a pan and bake in a 350-degree oven for 1 hour, or grill on the barbeque.

GREEN CHICKEN ENCHILADAS

Temperature:
Preheat 350 degrees

Bake:
20 minutes

Yield:
6 to 8 servings

- 1 *(18-ounce) package flour tortillas*
- 1 *cup Cheddar cheese, grated*
- 2 *cups Monterey Jack cheese, grated*
- 2 *cups cooked, cubed chicken*
- 1/2 *medium onion, chopped*
- 1/2 *cup sliced black olives*
- 1 1/2 *cups sour cream*
- 2 *tablespoons parsley, chopped*
- 3/4 *teaspoon freshly-ground pepper*

SAUCE:

- 2 *tablespoons butter*
- 2 *tablespoons all-purpose flour*
- 1/2 *cup milk*
- 1 1/2 *cups chicken broth*
- 1 *(10-ounce) package frozen spinach, cooked, drained and coarsely chopped*
- 2/3 *cup sour cream*
- 4 *tablespoons green chilies, chopped*
- 1/2 *medium onion, chopped*
- 1 *clove garlic, minced*
- 3/4 *teaspoon cumin*

GARNISH:

Additional shredded cheese
Lime slices
Tomato slices

Preheat oven to 350 degrees.

In a large bowl, mix together cheeses, chicken, onion, olives, sour cream, parsley and pepper and set aside.

In a sauté pan, heat butter over low heat. Add flour and cook for a few minutes, stirring constantly. Stir in milk and 1/2 cup chicken broth. Bring to a boil; while stirring, boil for 1 minute.

Add remaining chicken broth, cook and stir until hot and thickened, add spinach, sour cream, green chilies, onion, garlic and cumin.

Dip each tortilla into sauce, coating both sides. Spoon about 1/4 cup filling onto each tortilla and roll up. Place seam-side down in an ungreased 9 x 13-inch baking dish. Pour remaining sauce over enchiladas and bake uncovered in a 350-degree oven about 20 minutes until bubbly.

Garnish with shredded cheese, lime and tomato slices.

ROMANO CHICKEN

TEMPERATURE:
Preheat 350 degrees

BAKE:
1 hour

YIELD:
4 servings

NOTES:
Freshly-grated Parmesan cheese can be substituted for Romano cheese.

- *3 cups fresh white bread crumbs*
- *1 cup freshly-grated Romano cheese*
- *1 teaspoon salt*
- *1/3 cup fresh parsley, chopped and washed*
- *1/2 cup butter (1 cube)*
- *1 garlic clove, minced*
- *2 teaspoons Dijon mustard*
- *1 teaspoon Worcestershire sauce*
- *1 whole fryer chicken, cut into pieces*

Preheat oven to 350 degrees.

In a food processor, combine bread crumbs, cheese and salt. Add washed parsley and process for just a few seconds or the whole mixture turns too green!

In a saucepan over medium heat, melt butter. Add garlic, mustard, and Worcestershire and let cool slightly. Dip chicken pieces in butter mixture and roll in crumb/cheese mixture. Be sure each piece is coated well. Pat coating on with your hands.

Place chicken on shallow baking tray. Pour any remaining butter mixture over chicken. Bake in a 350-degree oven for 1 hour, until golden and tender.

GRILLED HERBED CHICKEN

MARINATE:
8 hours or overnight

GRILL:
45 minutes to 1 hour

YIELD:
6 servings

- *2 tablespoons fresh oregano leaves*
- *2 tablespoons fresh thyme leaves*
- *2 tablespoons fresh rosemary leaves*
- *2 to 3 garlic cloves, minced*
- *1/2 teaspoon salt*
- *1/4 teaspoon freshly-ground pepper*
- *1/2 cup freshly-squeezed lemon juice*
- *1/4 cup olive oil*
- *3 to 4 pounds chicken breasts, chicken pieces or halved Cornish game hens*

In a food processor or blender, combine oregano, thyme, rosemary and garlic. Mix well. Add salt, pepper and lemon juice. Let stand for a few minutes. With processor running, drizzle in oil.

In a bowl with a lid, or in a plastic bag, combine chicken and marinade. Refrigerate all day or overnight.

Drain chicken. Grill on barbecue or indoor broiler for 45 minutes to 1 hour, turning to prevent burning. Baste frequently with marinade.

BARBECUED CHICKEN ORIENTAL

Marinate:
4 hours

Temperature:
Preheat 375 degrees

Bake:
45 minutes

Yield:
4 servings

- 1 *garlic clove, minced*
- 1 *small onion, quartered*
- 1/4 *cup water*
- 2 *tablespoons olive oil*
- 6 *tablespoons soy sauce*
- 2 *tablespoons freshly-squeezed lemon juice*
- 2 *tablespoons honey*
- 1/2 *teaspoon pepper*
- 1 *whole fryer chicken, cut into serving pieces*

In a food processor or blender, place garlic and onion. Pulse until finely chopped. With processor running, add water and drizzle in olive oil until well combined.

Pour mixture into a small saucepan and simmer for 10 minutes, stirring occasionally. Remove from heat and stir in soy sauce, lemon juice, honey and pepper.

Place chicken in a large bowl or plastic bag and add marinade. Refrigerate for at least 4 hours.

Bake in a 375-degree oven for 45 minutes to 1 hour, or grill on the barbecue, basting occasionally with marinade. If barbecuing, turn frequently to prevent marinade from burning.

CURRIED TURKEY AND ARTICHOKE BAKE

A GREAT BUFFET DISH.

CHILL:
1 HOUR

TEMPERATURE:
Preheat 350 degrees

BAKE:
1 hour if cold/45 minutes if not chilled first

YIELD:
4 servings

NOTES:
Fresh spinach (1 bunch) can be substituted for frozen. Serve with basmati rice. Substitute turkey for shrimp or crab meat, or try it without any meat.

1 (10-ounce) package frozen chopped spinach (See note.)
2 cups white or brown rice, cooked
4 tablespoons butter, room temperature, divided
1 (6-ounce) jar marinated artichoke hearts, drained
1 1/2 cups diced cooked turkey or chicken
1 cup Monterey Jack cheese, grated
1 garlic clove, finely minced
1/4 pound fresh mushrooms, sliced
2 tablespoons all-purpose flour
1/2 teaspoon curry powder
1 teaspoon Dijon mustard
1 cup milk
Salt and pepper

Preheat oven to 350 degrees.

Cook frozen spinach and squeeze out excess liquid, or blanch fresh spinach by dropping into pot of boiling water for 1 to 2 minutes, drain, pat dry and chop.

In a large bowl, combine spinach with rice and 2 tablespoons of butter. Press rice mixture evenly over bottom and sides of a well-greased, 10-inch pie pan or 9 x 13-inch glass baking dish. Cover and chill 1 hour.

Cut artichoke hearts into bite-sized pieces. Arrange evenly over rice, top with turkey, then cheese.

In a medium sauté pan, melt remaining 2 tablespoons of butter. Add garlic and mushrooms, sauté until golden. Stir in flour, curry powder and mustard. Cook until bubbly. Gradually add milk and cook until thickened. Season with salt and pepper and pour over spinach/rice/artichoke mixture. Can be made ahead, cooled, covered and refrigerated at this point.

Place casserole in a 350-degree oven and bake 45 minutes, or if chilled, bake 1 hour.

LEMON-ROASTED CORNISH GAME HENS

A simple but impressive dish.

Temperature:
Preheat 375 degrees

Bake:
50 minutes

Yield:
4 servings

- 3 *tablespoons butter, room temperature*
- 1 *teaspoon salt*
- 1/4 *teaspoon freshly-ground pepper*
- 1 *teaspoon finely-grated lemon zest*
- 2 *teaspoons fresh mint, chopped (or 1/2 teaspoon dried mint)*
- 4 *Cornish game hens*
- *2 tablespoons olive oil*
- 1 *small onion, coarsely chopped*
- 1 *garlic clove, minced*
- 2 *tablespoons lemon peel, julienned*
- 1 *cup chicken broth*
- 2 *teaspoons cornstarch*
- 1/4 *cup freshly-squeezed lemon juice*
- 2 *tablespoons parsley, washed and chopped*

Preheat oven to 375 degrees.

In a small mixing bowl, combine butter, salt, pepper, lemon zest and mint. Rub mixture over game hens.

Place hens in a large roasting pan. Bake at 375 degrees for about 50 minutes, until golden brown and juices run clear when skin is pierced with a fork.

In a medium sauté pan, heat oil and sauté onion for 5 minutes. Stir in julienned lemon peel and garlic. Cook and stir for 1 minute. Stir in chicken broth and bring to a boil.

Mix cornstarch with 1 tablespoon water and stir into hot mixture. Boil 1 minute until thickened. Stir in lemon juice and remove from heat.

Place hens on serving platter. Spoon a little sauce over each hen and sprinkle with chopped parsley. Pass remainder of sauce separately.

EASY CHICKEN ELEGANCE

NOT ONLY IS THIS EASY, IT CAN BE MADE IN ADVANCE AND REHEATED. IT LOOKS LIKE YOU SLAVED FOR HOURS!

TEMPERATURE:
Preheat 425 degrees

BAKE:
25 minutes

YIELD:
4 servings

NOTES:
Substitute parsley, chives, or green onions for watercress.

1 *sheet frozen puff pastry (1/2 of 17 1/4-ounce package)*
4 *chicken breast halves, boneless and skinless*
1 *(8-ounce) package cream cheese, room temperature*
2 *garlic cloves, minced*
2 *tablespoons watercress leaves, chopped (See note.)*
Salt and pepper
1 *egg, beaten*

Remove puff pastry from freezer, unwrap and let thaw 20 to 30 minutes.

Preheat oven to 425 degrees.

In a large bowl, combine cream cheese, watercress, garlic, salt and pepper to taste. Mix well.

Roll out puff pastry 1/8- to 1/4-inch thick on lightly-floured surface. Cut rectangles large enough to cover and seal around each chicken breast.

Spread rectangles with cream cheese mixture. Place chicken breast on top and seal tightly by first brushing seam of pastry with beaten egg, then pressing edges together across top.

Place seam-side down on an ungreased baking sheet. Brush completely with beaten egg. Bake at 425 degrees for 25 minutes.

CHICKEN GILLESPIE

Even your finicky eaters will love this.

Yield:
4 servings

- 4 *chicken breast halves, boneless and skinless*
- 1/2 *cup all-purpose flour*
- 1/2 *teaspoon salt*
- 1/2 *teaspoon freshly-ground pepper*
- 2 *eggs*
- 1/3 *cup Parmesan cheese, grated*
- 1/4 *cup butter (1/2 cube)*
- 1/2 *cup white wine*
- 4 *slices mozzarella cheese*

In a shallow dish, combine flour, salt, and pepper. In a separate shallow dish, beat eggs. In a third shallow dish, place Parmesan cheese.

Dip chicken into seasoned flour, then into egg, and finally into Parmesan cheese. (Can repeat this process if a thicker crust is desired.)

In a large sauté pan over medium heat, melt butter. Add chicken and sauté until golden brown. Add wine and cook until chicken is no longer pink in the middle, about 10 minutes. Place mozzarella slices on top, cover and cook until cheese is melted, about 3 minutes. Sprinkle with parsley and serve.

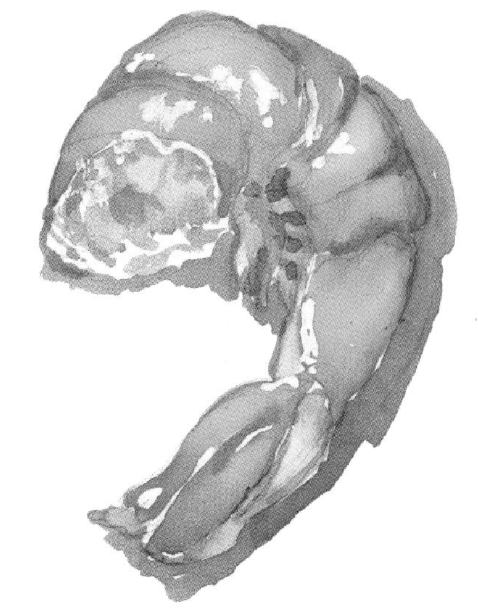

Seafood & sauces

SALMON, SCALLOPS AND SEA

Ah, summer...a dazzling season for dinner alfresco. In Oregon, where river and sea meet at the mouth of the Columbia, warm-weather menus demand fresh seafood in all of its glorious guises. PEPPERED SHRIMP, GRILLED CITRUS SALMON, even BROILED SHERRIED HALIBUT give the dinner (or picnic) table a summery snap. Add in the abundance of Oregon's berries and fruits, and a meal is made.

Portland's waterfront provides undiscovered possibilities and a backdrop for festive gatherings of family and friends. With new fountains and memorial gardens beckoning, the sun's heat shimmering off the river's waters, and the scent of TURKISH SWORDFISH grilling over hot coals, Portland is the best of all worlds. Bring on the bread and beverages.

The Junior League of Portland, the first League on the West Coast and fourth in the nation, shares a rich heritage with the pioneers who carved the Oregon Trail to the Northwest. In 1910, Mrs. Henry L. Corbett founded the League because she saw its need in a rapidly growing population.

PEPPERED SHRIMP

Sauté:
6 minutes

Yield:
4 servings

- 1/4 *pound unsalted butter (1 cube), divided*
- 1/4 *cup green onion, finely diced*
- 1/4 *cup red onion, chopped*
- 1/2 *teaspoon garlic, minced*
- 2 *tablespoons red pepper, seeded, deveined and chopped*
- 2 *tablespoons green pepper, seeded, deveined and chopped*
- 1/2 *teaspoon cayenne pepper*
- 1/4 *teaspoon freshly-ground black pepper*
- 1/2 *teaspoon dried basil*
- 3/4 *pound medium to large shrimp, peeled and deveined*
- 1/3 *pound sliced fresh mushrooms (7 to 10 mushrooms)*
- 6 *tablespoons chicken broth, divided*
- 2 *tablespoons chopped parsley*

In a large sauté pan over medium heat, melt half of the butter. Add onions, garlic, peppers and seasonings and sauté until ingredients soften, about 4 to 5 minutes.

Stir in shrimp and cook 1 minute or until shrimp turn pink on both sides.

Add mushrooms and 1/4 cup of broth to shrimp and stir. Add remaining butter, parsley and remaining broth. Cook until sauce thickens slightly.

Serve immediately over pasta or rice.

SHRIMP CURRY LEONE

THIS MAKES AN EXCELLENT DISH FOR A "HANDS ON" DINNER PARTY.

SAUTÉ:
10 minutes

YIELD:
8 servings

NOTES:
Have guests place rice on their plates, then top with shrimp curry sauce and various condiments.

- *3/4 cup all-purpose flour*
- *4 to 5 teaspoons curry powder*
- *1 teaspoon salt*
- *1 teaspoon ground ginger*
- *2 teaspoons granulated sugar*
- *1 cup onion (1 large onion), minced*
- *1 cup green apple, chopped*
- *3/4 cup butter (1 1/2 cubes) plus 3 tablespoons, divided*
- *1 quart chicken broth*
- *2 cups milk*
- *3 pounds medium to large raw shrimp, peeled and deveined*
- *2 tablespoons freshly-squeezed lemon juice*
- *1/2 cup ripe olives, chopped*
- *4 hard-boiled eggs (yolk only), chopped*
- *1/2 pound bacon, cooked and crumbled*
- *1/2 cup coconut, lightly toasted*
- *1/2 cup green onions, chopped*
- *1 (9-ounce) jar mango chutney, chopped*

In a small bowl, mix flour, curry, salt, ginger and sugar. Set aside.

In a sauté pan over medium heat, melt 3/4 cup butter. Cook onions and apples until apples are tender. Blend in flour and curry mixture. Slowly stir in the chicken broth and milk. Stir occasionally until sauce has thickened, approximately 2 to 3 minutes.

In a separate sauté pan over high heat, melt 3 tablespoons of butter. Cook shrimp, stirring frequently for 4 to 5 minutes, or until shrimp just begins to turn pink. Drain. Add shrimp and lemon juice to curry sauce and heat through.

Pour into a heated chafing dish and serve accompanied with rice and individual bowls of olives, egg yolk, bacon, coconut, green onions and chutney as garnishes.

SASSY SEAFOOD SAUTÉ

SAUTÉ:
8 minutes

YIELD:
4 to 6 servings

- 2 *green onions, chopped*
- 2 *tablespoons ketchup*
- 1 *tablespoon cocktail sauce*
- 1 *tablespoon sherry*
- 1 *tablespoon soy sauce*
- 1 *tablespoon granulated sugar*
- 1/4 *teaspoon salt*
- 1/4 *teaspoon dry mustard*
- 4 *tablespoons olive oil*
- 5 *garlic cloves, finely minced*
- 1/2 *teaspoon crushed red pepper flakes*
- 1 *pound medium shrimp, peeled and deveined*
- 1 *pound scallops*
- 1/4 *cup fresh parsley, minced*

In a small bowl, combine onions, ketchup, cocktail sauce, sherry, soy sauce, sugar, and mustard. Set aside.

In a large skillet, warm olive oil over medium heat. Add garlic and crushed red pepper and sauté until fragrant and golden.

Add shrimp and scallops and cook 2 to 3 minutes or until shrimp turns pink.

Add sauce mixture and cook 1 minute or until heated through.

Serve immediately over rice or pasta.

PRAWNS IN VERMOUTH

This last-minute entrée is for those who enjoy cooking with guests.

Cook:
5 minutes

Yield:
6 to 8 servings

- 2 *tablespoons olive oil*
- 2 *pounds large shrimp, peeled and deveined*
- 3 *tablespoons butter*
- 2 *garlic cloves, finely minced*
- 1/2 *teaspoon salt*
- 1/4 *teaspoon freshly-ground black pepper*
- 6 *tablespoons freshly-squeezed lemon juice*
- 3 *ounces (6 tablespoons) dry vermouth*

In a sauté pan, warm olive oil over medium heat. Add shrimp and cook until shrimp are just pink. Remove shrimp and turn onto a warm serving plate.

Lower heat and add butter, garlic, salt and pepper and stir until blended. Turn heat to high and add lemon juice and vermouth.

Cook about 1 minute, stirring constantly. Pour sauce over shrimp and serve immediately.

SCAMPI

This recipe is easily doubled to serve eight or more. It is very rich and sweet.

Temperature:
Preheat 400 degrees

Cook:
8 to 10 minutes

Yield:
4 servings

Notes:
Do not make any substitutions for Cointreau. A smaller shrimp may be used.

- 1 *pound jumbo shrimp, peeled and deveined (See note.)*
- 1/2 *cup whipping cream*
- 2 *tablespoons melted butter*
- 1/4 *cup Cointreau (See note.)*
- 2 *teaspoons garlic, minced*
- 1/4 *cup parsley, chopped (reserve some parsley for garnish)*
- 1 *teaspoon paprika*
- *Kosher salt*
- *White pepper*

Preheat oven to 400 degrees.

In an ovenproof serving dish, arrange shrimp. In a bowl, combine cream, butter, Cointreau, garlic, parsley, paprika, salt and pepper and pour over shrimp.

Bake uncovered at 400 degrees for 8 minutes or until cooked through. Sprinkle with extra parsley. Serve over a bed of rice.

GRILLED CITRUS SALMON

- 1 1/2 *tablespoons freshly-squeezed lemon juice*
- 2 *tablespoons olive oil*
- 1 *tablespoon butter*
- 1 *tablespoon Dijon mustard*
- 4 *garlic cloves, minced*
- 2 *dashes cayenne pepper*
- 2 *dashes salt*
- 1 *teaspoon dried basil*
- 1 *teaspoon dried dill*
- 2 *teaspoons capers*
- 3 *pounds fresh salmon fillets*

In a small sauté pan over medium heat, combine lemon juice, olive oil, butter, mustard, garlic, pepper, salt, basil, dill, and capers. While stirring, bring to a boil. Reduce heat and simmer for 5 minutes.

Place salmon fillets skin-side down on a piece of heavy-duty foil with edges folded up, to make a pan. Pour sauce evenly over fish.

Place fish on grill and cover with a lid.

Barbecue over medium-hot coals for 10 to 12 minutes, depending on thickness of fillets. Fish will be flaky and light pink in color when cooked.

THIS IS DELICIOUS!

GRILL:
10 to 12 minutes

YIELD:
6 servings

NOTES:
As an alternative, wrap fish in foil and bake in a 350-degree oven for 15 to 20 minutes.

SZECHUAN SALMON

BROIL :
15 to 18 minutes

YIELD:
8 servings

NOTES:
Try this recipe on your barbecue when warm weather arrives.

8 salmon fillets (1/4 to 1/3-pound each)
2 cups bread crumbs
1/3 cup butter (5 1/3 tablespoons), melted
4 teaspoons red, pink and/or black peppercorns
1 1/2 large garlic cloves, minced

BEURRE BLANC SAUCE:

1/4 cup dry white wine with splash of dry vermouth
2 teaspoons freshly-squeezed lemon juice
2 teaspoons freshly-squeezed lime juice
1/2 cup whipping cream
1 cup butter (2 cubes), room temperature
White pepper

Broil salmon fillets until half-done (approximately 10 minutes). Mix bread crumbs, butter, peppercorns and garlic together until crumbs become moist. Top each fillet with bread crumb mixture.

Return fillets to broiler until done, approximately 5 to 8 minutes depending on thickness. Bread crumb mixture should be evenly browned.

Serve fish on a pool of beurre blanc sauce. (Prepare sauce while fish is in final broil.)

BEURRE BLANC SAUCE:

In a saucepan over high heat, combine wine, vermouth, lemon and lime juices. Cook over high heat until mixture almost evaporates, about 1 minute.

Lower heat, add cream and cook until slightly thickened, about 2 minutes. Remove from heat.

Just before serving, whisk butter and a dash of white pepper into cream mixture and continue whisking until butter is completely melted.

NORTHWEST SALMON CAKES WITH MUSTARD SAUCE

TEMPERATURE:
Preheat 250 degrees

COOK:
15 to 20 minutes

YIELD:
4 to 6 servings
3/4 cup sauce

NOTES:
Sauce can be made up to 4 days in advance and refrigerated.

- *7 slices white bread, broken into pieces*
- *1 teaspoon dried minced onion, softened in 1/2 teaspoon water*
- *1 teaspoon dried thyme*
- *1/2 teaspoon salt*
- *1/4 teaspoon cayenne pepper*
- *3 large shallots*
- *2/3 cup freshly-grated Parmesan cheese*
- *1 egg*
- *1 tablespoon mayonnaise*
- *1 teaspoon Dijon mustard*
- *1 teaspoon freshly-squeezed lemon juice*
- *1 1/2 cups salmon (10 ounces), cooked and coarsely flaked*
- *Vegetable oil (for frying)*

MUSTARD SAUCE:

- *1/4 cup fresh parsley, loosely packed*
- *1 small garlic clove*
- *1 small shallot*
- *1/2 small jalapeño pepper, seeded*
- *1 egg yolk*
- *8 tablespoons olive oil*
- *1 teaspoon Dijon mustard*
- *2 tablespoons prepared mild horseradish*
- *1/8 teaspoon granulated sugar*
- *1/8 teaspoon Worcestershire sauce*
- *Dash of salt*

In a food processor, combine bread, onion, thyme, salt and cayenne. Process to fine crumbs, about 1 to 2 minutes, and transfer to shallow pie plate.

With processor running, drop shallots through feed tube and mince. Add cheese and process until minced.

Add 1 1/2 cups bread crumb mixture, egg, mayonnaise, mustard and lemon juice and blend, pulsing approximately 3 to 4 times.

Add salmon and blend just until combined, pulsing briefly; do not overprocess. (Can be prepared 1 day ahead. Cover salmon mixture and chill. Cover remaining bread crumb mixture separately and keep at room temperature.)

Position rack in center of oven and preheat to 250 degrees. Line baking sheet with several layers of paper towels.

Shape salmon mixture into twelve 1-inch thick patties, using about 2 1/2 tablespoons for each. Dredge in remaining bread crumb mixture to coat thoroughly.

Heat 1/4-inch oil in a large, heavy skillet over medium heat. Add several patties and cook until crisp and golden, about 1 minute per side.

Gently transfer to prepared sheet; keep warm in oven.

Cook remainder, adding more oil if necessary. Serve immediately, accompanied by Mustard Sauce.

MUSTARD SAUCE:

In a food processor, add parsley and with machine running, drop garlic, shallot and jalapeño pepper through feed tube and mince.

Add egg yolk, 2 tablespoons oil and mustard. Process until slightly thickened, about 20 seconds.

With machine running, slowly drizzle remaining oil through feed tube in a thin steady stream.

Add horseradish, sugar, Worcestershire and salt and blend 10 seconds. Adjust seasonings. This makes 3/4 cup of sauce.

SALMON FLORENTINE

THIS RICH DISH MAKES A PERFECT WINTER MEAL.

- 4 *sheets frozen puff pastry*
- 2 *(10-ounce) packages frozen chopped spinach*
- 6 *ounces crab meat*
- 8 *ounces freshly-grated Parmesan cheese*
- 4 *eggs, beaten*
- 1/2 to 3/4 *cup whipping cream*
- 1/2 *cup sherry*
- *Salt and pepper*
- 2 *cups fresh mushrooms (10 large mushrooms), chopped*
- 3 to 4 *tablespoons butter*
- 5 *pounds salmon fillets*
- 1 *egg white, slightly beaten*

LEMON HOLLANDAISE SAUCE:

- 3 *egg yolks*
- 1 1/2 *tablespoons freshly-squeezed lemon juice*
- 4 *tablespoons cold unsalted butter, divided*
- 12 *tablespoons unsalted butter, melted*
- *Salt and freshly-ground white pepper*

Allow frozen pastry to stand at room temperature for 20 minutes.

Cook spinach according to package directions, undercooking slightly to allow for baking later. Drain thoroughly.

In a large bowl, mix together spinach, crab meat, grated Parmesan cheese, eggs, cream, sherry, salt and pepper.

In a sauté pan, melt butter and cook mushrooms until just tender and liquid evaporates. Lift out of butter with a slotted spoon and add to spinach mixture.

Use remaining butter to brush one side of each pastry sheet.

Place 1 sheet of puff pastry, buttered-side up, on a greased roasting pan. Brush with egg whites. Lay 2 salmon fillets down the center of the pastry.

Spread half of spinach mixture on salmon and cover with another sheet of pastry, buttered-side down. Shape and cut into the form of a fish, crimping the edges together to create the appearance of fish scales on top. Brush top of pastry with egg white.

Repeat with the remaining pastry, salmon fillets and spinach filling. Bake on a rack in a preheated 350-degree oven for 20 to 30 minutes, until top is browned. Serve with Lemon Hollandaise Sauce.

TEMPERATURE:
Preheat 350 degrees

BAKE:
20 to 30 minutes

COOK:
3 to 4 minutes

YIELD:
16 servings
1 cup sauce

NOTES:
Make an eye and fins out of pastry scraps, attaching with slightly beaten egg white.
You can flavor the hollandaise, with white wine, herbs, vermouth, or shallots. Boil over high heat to reduce liquid to 1/4 cup, and add seasonings, substituting them for the lemon juice.

LEMON HOLLANDAISE SAUCE:

In a saucepan, vigorously whisk egg yolks for 1 minute, or until they are thick and pale yellow, then whisk in lemon juice.

Add 2 tablespoons of cold butter. Set pan over low heat. Watch carefully and continue whisking. (The bottom of the pan will be visible between strokes when sauce is done.) Remove from heat and add remaining butter, beating in one tablespoon at a time to stop cooking.

Drizzle in warm melted butter and continue beating to make a thick sauce. Add seasoning and more lemon juice as necessary. Serve immediately.

BAKED HALIBUT FILLETS

PUT THIS IN YOUR FILES UNDER "DINNER, QUICK".

TEMPERATURE:
Preheat 350 degrees

BAKE:
20 minutes

YIELD:
2 to 3 servings

NOTES:
Yogurt can be substituted for the sour cream.

- *1 pound halibut fillets*
- *1/4 cup chives, chopped*
- *1/2 cup sour cream*
- *Salt and freshly-ground black pepper*
- *1/4 cup freshly-grated Parmesan cheese*

Place halibut in a buttered ovenproof serving dish.

In a mixing bowl, combine chives, sour cream, pepper, salt and cheese and pour mixture over top of halibut.

Bake in a 350-degree oven for 20 minutes.

Garnish with lemon wedges and fresh parsley.

BROILED SHERRIED HALIBUT

- 2 *halibut steaks*
- 1 *cup medium-dry sherry*
- 1/2 *cup bread crumbs*
- 1/2 *cup mayonnaise or yogurt*
- 1/2 *cup sour cream*
- *Dash paprika*

MARINATE:
2 hours

COOK:
15 minutes

YIELD:
2 servings

NOTES:
Fish is done when it just becomes firm to the touch and flakes with a fork.

In a glass or non-reactive dish, marinate halibut in sherry for two hours. Turn steaks after first hour and continue to marinate.

Remove halibut from marinade and pat dry. Dredge halibut steaks in bread crumbs to lightly coat.

Place fish on broiling pan.

Combine mayonnaise and sour cream. Spread a generous amount on top of each steak. Sprinkle with additional bread crumbs and a dash of paprika.

Broil at 500 degrees for approximately 15 minutes, longer if steaks are very thick. Check for doneness.

TURKISH SWORDFISH (KYLYEH SHEESH)

MARINATE:
5 to 6 hours

GRILL:
10 to 12 minutes

YIELD:
2 servings

NOTES:
This also works with whole swordfish steaks.

1 pound swordfish, cubed (See note.)
1 tablespoon lemon juice
1 tablespoon olive oil
1 tablespoon onion, finely minced
1/4 tablespoon paprika or crushed red pepper flakes
10 to 15 bay leaves

LEMON SAUCE:

3 tablespoons freshly-squeezed lemon juice
1 1/2 tablespoons olive oil
1/3 cup fresh parsley, grated
Pinch of salt

Marinate swordfish in lemon juice, oil, onion and red pepper for 5 to 6 hours.

LEMON SAUCE:

In the meantime, in a small bowl, mix lemon juice, olive oil, parsley and salt. Set aside.

Thread fish cubes onto skewers, placing one-half bay leaf between each cube and at each end. Grill fish over coals, turning frequently for about 10 to 12 minutes.

Remove from skewers, discard bay leaves and serve with lemon sauce.

DUNGENESS CRAB FONDUE

A GREAT TREAT!

COOK:
20 minutes

YIELD:
6 servings

NOTES:
Serve with a green salad and crisp apple slices.

- *2 tablespoons butter*
- *1 tablespoon shallots, finely chopped*
- *1 garlic clove, minced*
- *2 tablespoons all-purpose flour*
- *1 cup milk*
- *4 ounces cream cheese, cubed*
- *3 ounces Muenster cheese, grated*
- *2 ounces extra sharp Cheddar cheese, grated*
- *1 teaspoon freshly-squeezed lemon juice*
- *Red pepper sauce*
- *1/4 cup white vermouth*
- *3/4 pound Dungeness crab meat*

In a sauté pan over medium heat, melt butter. Sauté shallots and garlic for a few minutes until soft. Whisk in flour. Cook over low heat until mixture is bubbly. Remove from heat.

Blend in milk. Return to burner and bring to a boil, stirring constantly, for 1 minute. Remove from heat.

Gradually add cheeses. Over low heat, stir until cheese melts to a smooth consistency. Add lemon juice, red pepper sauce, and vermouth. Add crab meat and stir occasionally until sauce is heated through.

Pour into a fondue pot or a chafing dish. If using a chafing dish, place over a pan of hot water. Serve warm with chunks of sourdough French bread or dark rye bread.

SANTA FE RED CHILI AND CRAB ENCHILADAS

These enchiladas capture the spicy flavors of the Southwest.

Temperature:
Preheat 425 degrees

Bake:
25 minutes

Yield:
8 servings

Notes:
Substitute dried Anaheim chilies for poblanos. Garnish with cilantro and avocado for another variation.

SAUCE:

- *4 garlic cloves*
- *1 (3-ounce) package dried red poblano chilies*
- *1 to 2 cups hot water*
- *Salt*
- *1 tablespoon all-purpose flour*
- *1 teaspoon ground cumin*
- *1 tablespoon olive oil*
- *1/4 cup whipping cream*
- *1 (12-ounce) package corn, flour, or whole wheat tortillas*
- *1 cup Dungeness crab meat*
- *1/2 medium onion, diced*
- *2 cups Monterey Jack cheese, grated*

SAUCE:

In a medium bowl, soak chilies in hot water for 30 minutes. Drain.

In a food processor, mince garlic. Add chilies and purée. Add flour, cumin, olive oil and dash of salt. Process a few seconds. Drizzle in 1/4 cup whipping cream. Pour mixture into a saucepan and simmer over low heat.

Meanwhile, assemble each enchilada. Spread each tortilla with 1 tablespoon chili sauce, 1 tablespoon crab, onion and cheese. Roll tightly and place side by side in a greased 9 x 13-inch glass casserole dish seam-side down.

Spoon remaining chili sauce over tops of enchiladas and cover with grated cheese.

Cover with foil and bake at 425 degrees for 25 minutes. To serve, garnish top with shredded iceberg lettuce, chopped tomatoes and a dollop of sour cream.

SWORDFISH SERENADE

- 1 *tablespoon lemon peel, grated*
- 1/3 *cup freshly-squeezed lemon juice*
- 1/4 *cup dry white wine*
- 3 *tablespoons safflower oil*
- 2 *tablespoons light soy sauce*
- 1/4 *teaspoon freshly-ground black pepper*
- 1/4 *cup green onions, minced*
- 1 *tablespoon fresh ginger, finely minced*
- 2 *garlic cloves, finely minced*
- 2 *pounds firm fish, such as swordfish, tuna or shark*

MARINATE:
1 hour

TEMPERATURE:
Preheat 550 degrees

BROIL:
8 to 12 minutes

YIELD:
4 to 6 servings

NOTES:
Swordfish, tuna and shark are done when the fish just becomes firm to the touch and flakes with a fork.

In a large bowl, combine lemon peel and lemon juice. Whisk in wine, oil and soy sauce. Add black pepper, green onions, ginger and garlic and mix well. Set aside.

Place fish in a glass or non-reactive dish and cover with marinade. Let marinate for 1 hour.

Remove fish from marinade. Pour marinade into a small saucepan over high heat and bring to a vigorous boil. Remove from heat.

Prepare a charcoal fire and grill fish over medium heat, brushing marinade over fish as it cooks.

If using an oven, preheat to 550 degrees, and broil fish on highest rack for about 8 to 12 minutes, turning fish once and basting with marinade.

Place fish on heated plates and drizzle with remaining marinade. Serve immediately.

ORANGE-SOY MARINADE

This tangy marinade works equally well for fish or meat.

Yield:
2 cups

- 3/4 *cup orange juice*
- 1/2 *cup teriyaki sauce*
- 3/4 *cup soy sauce*
- 2 *tablespoons olive oil*
- 1/2 *teaspoon garlic powder*
- 2 *tablespoons fresh parsley, chopped*
- 1 *tablespoon fresh basil, chopped*

In a medium bowl, combine orange juice, teriyaki sauce, soy sauce, garlic powder, parsley and basil. Cover and refrigerate.

DIJON-DILL SAUCE

This delicious sauce is great for a quick weeknight meal, served on any fish.

Yield:
4 tablespoons

Notes:
You can make this sauce ahead and refrigerate it. If fresh dill is available, substitute it for dried dill.

- 2 *tablespoons good-quality mayonnaise*
- 2 *tablespoons Dijon mustard*
- 2 *teaspoons dried dill*

In a small bowl, mix mayonnaise, mustard and dill. Spread on top of fish and barbecue, bake or broil fish until flaky.

CREOLE SAUCE

COOK:
2 hours

YIELD:
20 servings

NOTES:
If using fresh tomatoes, plunge tomatoes into boiling water, drain, remove skins and chop. Sauce can be stored in refrigerator for up to two weeks or frozen in pint or quart containers.

- *1/2 cup butter (1 cube), melted*
- *3 tablespoons olive oil*
- *1 large onion, chopped*
- *1 cup celery (2 stalks), chopped*
- *2 large green bell peppers, seeded, deveined and sliced*
- *6 garlic cloves, minced*
- *2 cups water*
- *3 tablespoons tomato paste*
- *3 tablespoons fresh parsley, chopped*
- *2 tablespoons Worcestershire sauce*
- *1 tablespoon salt*
- *1 tablespoon dried basil, crushed*
- *1 teaspoon dried thyme*
- *1 bay leaf, crumbled*
- *3 (26-ounce) cans whole tomatoes or 20 small fresh tomatoes (See note.)*
- *1/2 teaspoon white or black pepper*
- *Cayenne pepper*

In a heavy sauté pan, melt butter and oil over medium heat.

Add onion, celery, green bell peppers and garlic and sauté until vegetables are tender.

Add water, tomato paste, parsley, Worcestershire, salt, basil, thyme, bay leaf, tomatoes and pepper.

Reduce heat and simmer for 1 1/2 to 2 hours, stirring occasionally.

Serve over shrimp, crab, or other seafood with rice.

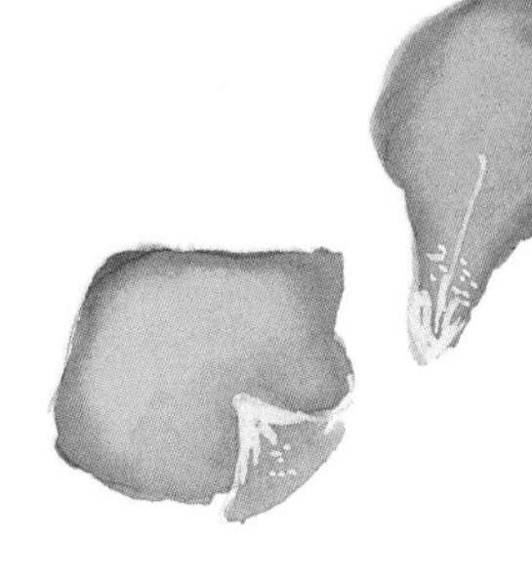

Cakes & Pastries

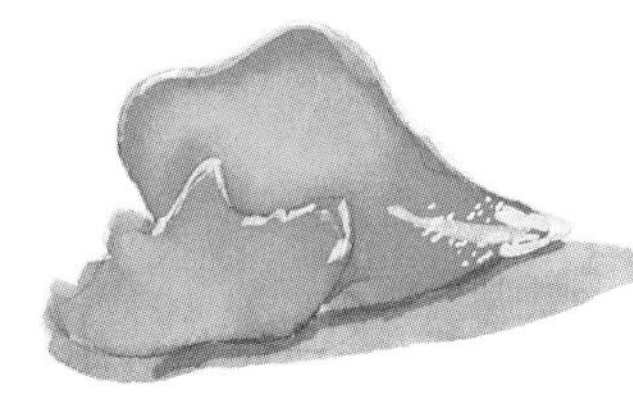

Gazebos, Gateaux and Guests

Fleecy clouds dance across a blue August sky. Gentle winds caress the flowers. Who could ask for a more perfect wedding day in a Portland park?

More than 200 parks grace the city with their welcoming presence, among them Peninsula Park, a North Portland neighborhood treasure. Designed in 1912, this park is Portland's second oldest playground. A community center and gazebo add to the natural setting.

Wedding guests begin to gather. Last-minute touches are made to the enticing dessert table. Careful hands place a pink rose bud next to a Lemon Chiffon Cake. Almond Cake with Raspberry Sauce is a colorful counterpoint. Shifting the Chocolate Lace Cookie plate to the side allows the dazzling floral arrangement to dominate the table setting.

The string quartet pauses. The bride appears.

The Junior League's presence in North Portland has included volunteer service with the North Portland Community Health Clinic, Columbia Villa, and Emanuel Hospital Pre-surgery Puppets.

CHOCOLATE LACE COOKIES

- 1/2 *cup butter (1 cube), room temperature*
- 1 *cup granulated sugar*
- 1/4 *cup dark corn syrup*
- 1 *teaspoon vanilla extract*
- 3/4 *cup all-purpose flour*
- 1/2 *teaspoon salt*
- 1/2 *teaspoon baking powder*
- 1/4 *cup milk*
- 1 *cup old-fashioned rolled oats*
- 1 *cup almonds, blanched and finely chopped*
- 1 *(12-ounce) package semi-sweet chocolate*

In a medium bowl, cream butter and sugar until light and fluffy. Beat in corn syrup and vanilla.

Sift flour with salt and baking powder. Add flour to creamed mixture, alternating with milk, beating until smooth. Stir in rolled oats and almonds.

Drop by rounded teaspoonfuls onto a lightly-greased cookie sheet. (Space 3 inches apart to allow for spreading.)

Bake at 325 degrees, 12 to 14 minutes or until edges are well browned and cookies are bubbling.

Let cool slightly. Remove from pan to racks to cool completely.

In a microwave oven or in a double boiler over hot water, melt chocolate.

Spread the melted chocolate on the bottoms of the cookies, or dip half of each cookie into melted chocolate. Place cookie on waxed paper.

THIS IS NOT YOUR AVERAGE COOKIE.

TEMPERATURE:
Preheat 325 degrees

BAKE:
12 to 14 minutes

YIELD:
4 dozen

NOTES:
Store the cookies in a tightly-sealed container with waxed paper between each layer.

CHOCOLATE-HAZELNUT CLUSTERS

INDULGE! SERVE THESE COOKIES WITH A BOWL OF VANILLA ICE CREAM AND HOT FUDGE SAUCE.

CHILL:
1 hour

TEMPERATURE:
Preheat 350 degrees

BAKE:
8 to 10 minutes

YIELD:
2 1/2 dozen

- *1/2 cup unsalted butter (1 cube), room temperature*
- *1/2 cup dark brown sugar, firmly packed*
- *1/2 cup granulated sugar*
- *1 teaspoon vanilla extract*
- *1 egg*
- *1/2 teaspoon baking powder*
- *1 teaspoon water*
- *3/4 cup all-purpose flour*
- *1 1/2 cups old-fashioned rolled oats*
- *1/2 cup hazelnuts, coarsely chopped*
- *12 ounces dark chocolate chips or coarsely-chopped bittersweet chocolate bars*

In a large mixing bowl, cream butter, brown sugar, sugar and vanilla. Beat in egg, baking powder and water until well blended. Stir in flour, oats, hazelnuts and chocolate. Refrigerate until dough is firm, about 1 hour.

Preheat oven to 350 degrees.

Grease 2 cookie sheets. Drop by teaspoonfuls onto greased cookie sheets. Bake at 350 degrees, 8 to 10 minutes until cookie springs back. Do not overbake. Cool on cookie sheets for 2 minutes and then remove onto a wire rack.

CHOCOLATE MOCHA DOTS

- 1 *cup butter (2 cubes), room temperature (See note.)*
- 1/2 *cup granulated sugar*
- 1/2 *cup brown sugar, firmly packed*
- 1 *tablespoon instant coffee*
- 1 *teaspoon hot water*
- 2 *ounces unsweetened chocolate, melted and cooled*
- 1 *egg*
- 2 *cups all-purpose flour*
- 1 *teaspoon cinnamon*

GLAZE:

- 2 *cups semi-sweet or milk chocolate chips*
- 6 *tablespoons butter*
- 3/4 *cup almonds, blanched, toasted and chopped*

CHILL:
Several hours

TEMPERATURE:
Preheat 350 degrees

BAKE:
8 to 10 minutes

YIELD:
40 cookies

NOTES:
Do not substitute margarine for butter.

Preheat oven to 350 degrees.

In a medium bowl, cream butter, sugar and brown sugar. In a small bowl, dissolve coffee in hot water. Add coffee, melted chocolate and egg to butter mixture and beat well. Add flour and cinnamon and beat until well-mixed.

Cover and chill at least one hour or until firm. Divide dough in half and shape into two 7-inch logs, approximately 1 1/2 inches in diameter. Chill several hours or overnight. At this point, logs may be wrapped and frozen up to 2 weeks.

When ready to bake, slice logs into 1/4-inch slices and place on ungreased cookie sheet. Bake at 350 degrees, 8 to 10 minutes. Cookies should be soft.

Let cool on pan for 1 minute, then transfer to rack. While cookies cool, melt chocolate and butter in small saucepan. Stir until well-blended. Keep chocolate over low heat.

When cookies have completely cooled, dip half of cookie into the melted chocolate. If necessary, tip pan when dipping cookie to allow entire half of cookie to be coated. Place on waxed paper. Sprinkle chopped almonds on warm chocolate.

NUTMEG COOKIES

TEMPERATURE:
Preheat 350 degrees

BAKE:
12 to 15 minutes

YIELD:
3 dozen

NOTES:
Cut with seasonal cookie cutters, these will make a special addition to your next holiday party.

3 cups flour
1 teaspoon nutmeg
1 cup butter, softened
3/4 cup sugar
1 egg
2 teaspoons vanilla extract
2 teaspoons rum extract

FROSTING:

3 tablespoons butter (2 cubes), room temperature
1/2 teaspoon vanilla extract
1 teaspoon rum extract
2 1/2 cups powdered sugar
2 to 3 tablespoons milk
Nutmeg

Preheat oven to 350 degrees. Sift together flour and nutmeg. Set aside. Cream butter and sugar. Beat in egg, vanilla and rum extract. Add dry ingredients and mix. Chill slightly, if needed, for easier handling.

On a slightly floured surface, roll dough to 1/4-inch thickness and cut with a cookie cutter into 1/4-inch thickness. Bake 12 to 15 minutes. Let cool.

FROSTING:

Cream butter with vanilla and rum extract. Gradually beat in powdered sugar, alternating with milk until creamy and desired consistency. Frost cookies. Sprinkle with nutmeg while frosting is soft.

CHEWY CHOCOLATE NUT COOKIES

- *1 1/2 cups butter (3 cubes), room temperature*
- *2 cups granulated sugar*
- *2 eggs*
- *2 teaspoons vanilla extract*
- *2 cups all-purpose flour*
- *3/4 cup cocoa powder*
- *1 teaspoon baking soda*
- *1/2 teaspoon salt*
- *1 (12-ounce) package chocolate chips or M&M's® candies*
- *1 cup hazelnuts or pecans, chopped*

A GLASS OF COLD MILK IS ALL YOU NEED.

TEMPERATURE:
Preheat 350 degrees

BAKE:
8 to 9 minutes

YIELD:
3 to 4 dozen

Preheat oven to 350 degrees.

In a medium bowl, cream together butter and sugar until light and fluffy. Add eggs and vanilla extract. Beat well.

Combine flour, cocoa, baking soda and salt and gradually blend into creamed mixture.

Stir in chocolate chips and nuts.

Drop by teaspoonfuls onto ungreased cookie sheet.

Bake at 350 degrees, 8 to 9 minutes. Do not overbake; cookies will be soft. (They will puff while baking and flatten while cooling.)

Cool slightly and remove from baking sheet.

EBONY AND IVORY COOKIES

WATCH THESE DISAPPEAR LIKE MAGIC.

TEMPERATURE:
Preheat 350 degrees

BAKE:
8 to 10 minutes

YIELD:
3 dozen

- *1/2 pound unsalted butter (2 cubes), room temperature*
- *1 3/4 cups granulated sugar*
- *2 large eggs, room temperature*
- *1 1/2 teaspoons vanilla extract*
- *1 ounce bittersweet (not unsweetened) or semi-sweet chocolate, melted and cooled*
- *1/4 cup sour cream*
- *3/4 pound white chocolate, coarsely chopped*
- *2 1/2 cups all-purpose flour*
- *1 cup unsweetened cocoa*
- *1/2 teaspoon baking soda*
- *1/2 teaspoon baking powder*
- *1/2 teaspoon salt*
- *1 cup hazelnuts, pecans or walnuts, coarsely chopped*

Preheat oven to 350 degrees.

In a large bowl, cream together butter and sugar until light and fluffy. Beat in eggs, one at a time. Blend in vanilla, bittersweet chocolate and sour cream. Fold in chopped white chocolate.

In a large bowl, sift together flour, cocoa, baking soda, baking powder and salt.

Mix into butter mixture. Stir in nuts.

Drop by rounded tablespoonfuls of dough onto prepared sheets, spacing 2 inches apart.

Bake 8 to 10 minutes until firm, but still soft to touch in center. Transfer to wire racks to cool completely.

SUGAR PECAN CRISPS

- *3/4 cup butter (1 1/2 cubes), room temperature*
- *2/3 cup granulated sugar*
- *1 egg*
- *1 teaspoon vanilla extract*
- *1/4 teaspoon salt*
- *1 3/4 cups all-purpose flour*
- *1/2 cup pecans, finely chopped*

In a medium bowl, cream butter with sugar until light and fluffy.

Add egg, vanilla extract and salt. Beat well. With mixer at low speed, gradually add flour.

Cover bowl and chill dough 30 minutes or until firm enough to handle.

Shape chilled dough into a 12-inch log, then roll in pecans to coat outside of log. Wrap in plastic wrap or waxed paper and chill several hours or overnight.

Cut dough into 1/4-inch slices and place on ungreased cookie sheet. Bake at 350 degrees, 10 to 12 minutes or until lightly browned.

Remove from cookie sheet and cool on wire rack.

LAST-MINUTE COOKIES STRAIGHT FROM YOUR PANTRY.

CHILL:
Several hours or overnight

TEMPERATURE:
Preheat 350 degrees

BAKE:
10 to 12 minutes

YIELD:
3 to 4 dozen

KAHLUA BARS

Looks like a simple chocolate brownie until you take your first bite!

Temperature:
Preheat 350 degrees

Bake:
25 to 30 minutes

Yield:
24 to 32 bars

- *4 ounces unsweetened chocolate*
- *2/3 cup butter, room temperature*
- *2 cups granulated sugar*
- *4 eggs*
- *1 teaspoon vanilla extract*
- *1/2 cup Kahlua*
- *1 1/4 cups all-purpose flour*
- *1 teaspoon baking powder*
- *1 teaspoon salt*

FROSTING:

- *2 tablespoons Kahlua*
- *1 teaspoon instant coffee*
- *1/2 cup butter (1 cube), room temperature*
- *2 cups powdered sugar*
- *1/2 teaspoon vanilla extract*
- *2 to 3 teaspoons milk*

TOPPING:

- *1 ounce semi-sweet chocolate*
- *1 tablespoon butter*

Preheat oven to 350 degrees. Grease a 9 x 13-inch baking pan.

In a medium saucepan over low heat, melt the chocolate and butter together. Remove pan from heat and mix in sugar, eggs, vanilla and Kahlua. Stir in flour, baking powder and salt.

Spread in prepared pan. Bake at 350 degrees, 25 to 30 minutes or until batter starts to pull away from sides of pan. Cool.

FROSTING:

In a small bowl, mix Kahlua with instant coffee, stirring until coffee is dissolved. In a medium bowl, cream butter, powdered sugar and vanilla together. Add coffee mixture and beat until well blended. Add milk to desired consistency. Spread frosting over cooled brownies.

TOPPING:

In a small saucepan, melt chocolate and butter together. Cool slightly, then drizzle topping over frosting. Cool until chocolate is set. Cut into bars.

ROCKY ROAD FUDGE BARS

TEMPERATURE:
Preheat 350 degrees

BAKE:
32 minutes

YIELD:
36 bars

COOKIES:

- *1/2 cup butter (1 cube)*
- *1 ounce unsweetened chocolate*
- *1 cup granulated sugar*
- *1 cup all-purpose flour*
- *1 teaspoon baking powder*
- *1 teaspoon vanilla extract*
- *2 eggs*
- *1 cup walnuts, chopped*

FILLING:

- *6 ounces cream cheese, room temperature*
- *1/2 cup granulated sugar*
- *2 tablespoons all-purpose flour*
- *1/4 cup butter, room temperature*
- *1 egg*
- *1/2 teaspoon vanilla extract*
- *1/4 cup walnuts, chopped*
- *1 cup semi-sweet chocolate pieces*
- *2 cups miniature marshmallows*

FROSTING:

- *1/4 cup butter (1/2 cube)*
- *1 ounce unsweetened chocolate*
- *2 ounces cream cheese*
- *1/4 cup milk*
- *1 pound powdered sugar*
- *1 teaspoon vanilla extract*

Preheat oven to 350 degrees. Grease and flour a 9 x 13-inch pan.

In a large saucepan over low heat, melt 1/2 cup of butter and unsweetened chocolate. Remove from heat.

Add sugar, flour, baking powder and vanilla. Mix well. Beat in eggs. Stir in chopped walnuts. Spread in prepared pan.

FILLING:

In a small bowl, combine cream cheese with sugar, flour, butter, egg and vanilla. Blend until smooth and fluffy. Stir in 1/4 cup chopped walnuts. Spread over chocolate mixture. Sprinkle with semi-sweet chocolate.

Bake 25 to 30 minutes until toothpick inserted comes out clean. Sprinkle with marshmallows and bake 2 minutes longer.

FROSTING:

In a large saucepan over low heat, melt butter, chocolate and cream cheese. Stir in milk. Whisk in powdered sugar and vanilla until smooth. Immediately pour over marshmallows and swirl together with a knife. Store bars in refrigerator.

PARTY PECAN BARS

TEMPERATURE:
Preheat 350 degrees

BAKE:
45 minutes

YIELD:
36 bars

CRUST:

- *2/3 cup powdered sugar*
- *2 cups all-purpose flour*
- *1 cup butter, room temperature*

TOPPING:

- *2/3 cup butter, melted*
- *1/2 cup honey*
- *3 tablespoons whipping cream*
- *1/2 cup dark brown sugar, firmly-packed*
- *3 1/2 cups pecans, coarsely chopped*

Preheat oven to 350 degrees. Grease a 9 x 13-inch baking pan.

CRUST:

In a medium bowl, sift sugar and flour together. With a pastry blender, cut in butter. Press into prepared baking pan. Bake at 350 degrees for 20 minutes. While bars are baking, prepare topping.

TOPPING:

In a medium bowl, combine melted butter, honey, whipping cream and brown sugar. Stir in pecans, being sure to coat thoroughly.

Remove baked bars from oven and spread pecan mixture over crust. Return to oven and bake at 350 degrees for 25 minutes. Allow to cool completely before cutting into bars.

CHOCOLATE CHEESECAKE BROWNIES

TEMPERATURE:
Preheat 350 degrees

BAKE:
40 minutes

YIELD:
32 bars

CHILL:
Several hours

BROWNIE LAYER:

- *1 tablespoon butter*
- *2 ounces unsweetened chocolate*
- *1/2 cup butter (1 cube)*
- *1 cup granulated sugar*
- *1/2 teaspoon vanilla extract*
- *2 eggs*
- *1/3 cup all-purpose flour*
- *1 cup chopped nuts (pecans, walnuts or hazelnuts)*

CHEESECAKE LAYER:

- *1 (8-ounce) package cream cheese, room temperature*
- *1/2 cup granulated sugar*
- *2 tablespoons unsweetened cocoa powder*
- *1/2 teaspoon vanilla extract*
- *2 eggs*
- *1 tablespoon all-purpose flour*

Preheat oven to 350 degrees. Adjust oven rack one-third up from bottom of oven.

Line a 9 x 9-inch pan with a 12-inch square of aluminum foil. Place 1 tablespoon butter in pan and melt it in the oven, then brush it on bottom and sides of pan. Set pan aside.

BROWNIE LAYER:

In a heavy saucepan over medium heat, melt chocolate and butter, stirring occasionally. Whisk in sugar and vanilla. Remove pan from heat and beat in eggs one at a time.

Add flour and stir well, then add chopped nuts. Turn batter into pan and smooth top. Set aside.

CHOCOLATE CHEESECAKE LAYER:

In a small bowl, beat cream cheese until soft. Add sugar, cocoa and vanilla and beat. Then add flour and eggs one at a time, beating well after each addition.

Pour cheesecake mixture over brownie layer. Smooth top.

Marbleize the mixtures slightly by inserting a knife almost to the bottom of one corner of pan and cutting through batter in a wide zigzag pattern. Smooth top.

Bake at 350 degrees, about 40 minutes, or until a toothpick inserted in the center comes out clean. Cool. Refrigerate for several hours or freeze for about an hour until firm.

TO REMOVE AND CUT BROWNIES:

Cover top of pan with a sheet of waxed paper, then a cookie sheet. Invert onto cookie sheet and peel off foil.

Invert again right-side up. The cheesecake layer will now be on top. Cut into 32 bars or triangles, cleaning blade after each cut. Store in a single layer in refrigerator or freezer. Serve chilled.

PUMPKIN SQUARES

Moist, yummy frosting. Take along a basketful of these sweet treats for your next outdoor adventure!

Temperature: Preheat 350 degrees

Bake: 25 to 30 minutes

Yield: 2 dozen squares

- *4 eggs*
- *1 2/3 cups granulated sugar*
- *1 cup oil*
- *1 (16-ounce) can pumpkin*
- *2 cups all-purpose flour*
- *2 teaspoons baking powder*
- *2 teaspoons cinnamon*
- *1 teaspoon salt*
- *1 teaspoon baking soda*
- *1/8 teaspoon nutmeg*

FROSTING:

- *2 (3-ounce) packages cream cheese*
- *1 cup butter (2 cubes)*
- *2 teaspoons vanilla extract*
- *3 3/4 cups powdered sugar*

In a large mixing bowl, beat together eggs, sugar, oil and pumpkin until light and fluffy.

In another bowl, sift together flour, baking powder, cinnamon, salt, baking soda and nutmeg. Add to pumpkin mixture and mix thoroughly.

Spread batter in ungreased 15 x 10-inch jelly roll pan. Bake at 350 degrees, 25 to 30 minutes. Cool.

FROSTING:

Cream together cream cheese and butter. Stir in vanilla. Add powdered sugar and stir until mixture is smooth. Frost and cut into squares.

BLUE RIBBON CARROT CAKE

EXTREMELY MOIST, RICH CAKE.

CHILL:
Several hours

TEMPERATURE:
Preheat 350 degrees

BAKE:
45 to 55 minutes

YIELD:
20 to 24 servings

NOTES:
The cake may be baked, glazed, frozen and frosted later or frosted and refrigerated for several days.

CAKE:

- 2 *cups all-purpose flour*
- 2 *teaspoons baking soda*
- 2 *teaspoons cinnamon*
- 1/2 *teaspoon salt*
- 3 *eggs*
- 3/4 *cup vegetable oil*
- 3/4 *cup buttermilk*
- 2 *cups granulated sugar*
- 2 *teaspoons vanilla extract*
- 1 *(8-ounce) can pineapple, crushed and drained*
- 2 *cups carrots, grated*
- 3 1/2 *ounces shredded coconut*
- 1 *cup seedless raisins*
- 1 *cup walnuts, coarsely chopped*

GLAZE:

- 1 *cup granulated sugar*
- 1/2 *teaspoon baking soda*
- 1/2 *cup buttermilk*
- 1/4 *cup butter (1/2 cube)*
- 1 *tablespoon light corn syrup*
- 1 *teaspoon vanilla extract*

FROSTING:

- 1/4 *cup butter (1/2 cube), room temperature*
- 1 *(8-ounce) package cream cheese, room temperature*
- 1 *teaspoon vanilla extract*
- 2 *cups powdered sugar*
- 1 *teaspoon freshly-squeezed orange juice*
- 1 *teaspoon orange peel, grated*

Preheat oven to 350 degrees.

Generously grease a 9 x 13-inch baking pan or two 9-inch cake pans.

CAKE:

Sift flour, baking soda, cinnamon and salt together; set aside.

In a large bowl, beat eggs. Add oil, buttermilk, sugar and vanilla and mix well. Add flour mixture, pineapple, carrots, coconut, raisins and walnuts and stir well.

Pour into prepared pan. Bake 45 to 55 minutes or until a toothpick inserted in the center comes out clean.

BUTTERMILK GLAZE:

In a small saucepan over high heat, combine sugar, baking soda, buttermilk, butter and corn syrup. Bring to a boil. Cook 5 minutes, stirring occasionally.

Remove from heat and stir in vanilla. Set glaze aside until cake is baked.

Remove cake from oven and slowly pour glaze over the hot cake. Cool cake in pan until glaze is totally absorbed, about 15 minutes.

FROSTING:

In a large bowl, cream butter and cream cheese until fluffy. Add vanilla, powdered sugar, orange juice and orange peel. Mix until smooth. Frost cake and refrigerate until frosting is set. Serve cake chilled.

WALNUT-LEMON TART

CRUST:

- 1 *cup all-purpose flour*
- 6 *tablespoons butter, chilled and cut into 6 equal pieces*
- 2 *tablespoons granulated sugar*
- 1 *egg yolk*
- 1 *tablespoon cold water*
- 1/8 *teaspoon salt*

FILLING:

- 3/4 *cup light corn syrup*
- 6 *tablespoons butter*
- 1/2 *cup brown sugar, firmly-packed*
- 2 *tablespoons all-purpose flour*
- 3 *eggs*
- 1/4 *cup freshly-squeezed lemon juice*
- 2 1/2 *teaspoons lemon rind, grated*
- 1 1/2 *cups walnuts, coarsely chopped*
- *Zest of lemon*
- *Whipped cream for garnish*

TEMPERATURE:
Preheat 375 degrees

BAKE:
7 to 9 minutes/
40 minutes

CHILL:
Several hours

YIELD:
8 to 10 servings

NOTES:
If you do not have a lemon zester, use a sharp knife to remove thin, narrow strips of yellow portion of lemon rind.

CRUST:

In a food processor with metal blade in place, combine flour, butter, sugar, yolk, water and salt. Process for 5 seconds, turning machine on and off rapidly. Continue processing until a ball of dough forms on the blade. Chill dough for several hours until firm.

Roll out and fit into a 9-inch tart pan. Line tart pastry with foil and fill with dried beans or metal pastry weights.

Preheat oven to 375 degrees.

Partially bake in a 375-degree oven for 5 to 6 minutes. Remove the weights and foil and continue baking for 2 or 3 minutes more, until shell is starting to color and just beginning to shrink from sides of pan.

Remove from oven and set aside.

FILLING:

In a large bowl, combine corn syrup, butter, sugar and flour. Add eggs, lemon juice and lemon rind. Mix until smooth. Stir in nuts and pour mixture into crust.

Bake at 375 degrees for 40 minutes, then remove from oven. The filling will not be completely set. Cool on a rack for 20 minutes.

Just before serving, use a lemon zester to cut strips of lemon rind. Sprinkle on tart. Decorate with whipped cream.

LEMON CHIFFON CAKE

THIS LIGHT, TART DESSERT IS THE PERFECT ENDING TO A SUMMER MEAL.

YIELD:
10 to 12 servings

CHILL:
Several hours

NOTES:
Spread top of cake with a thin layer of GRANDMOTHER'S LEMON CURD, page 257. About an hour before serving, spread top with 3/4 cup whipped cream or pipe whipped cream rosettes against inside edge of ladyfingers. Garnish with candied violets or candied lemon rind.

- *8 egg yolks, beaten*
- *2 cups granulated sugar, divided*
- *1 cup freshly-squeezed lemon juice*
- *1/2 teaspoon salt*
- *1 1/2 tablespoons unflavored gelatin*
- *1/2 cup cold water*
- *3 teaspoons lemon peel, finely grated*
- *8 egg whites*
- *1 1/4 cups whipping cream, whipped*
- *3/4 cup whipping cream, whipped*
- *12 ladyfinger cakes, split*
- *Candied violets, candied lemon rind (See note.)*

In the top of a double boiler, combine egg yolks, 1 cup of sugar, lemon juice and salt. Cook over boiling water until slightly thickened, approximately 10 to 15 minutes.

In a small bowl, combine gelatin and water and stir. Add to yolk mixture and stir until dissolved. Stir in lemon peel. Cool mixture until partially set.

In another large bowl, beat egg whites. Add 1 cup sugar and continue beating until very stiff. Fold yolk mixture into egg whites and combine thoroughly until no streaks appear. Gently fold in 1 1/4 cups whipped cream.

Grease a 9-inch springform pan. Line pan with ladyfingers vertically and fill with mixture. (The mousse holds the ladyfingers in place.) Chill several hours before serving.

ALMOND CAKE WITH RASPBERRY SAUCE

A simple and elegant dessert, especially for almond lovers!

Temperature:
Preheat 350 degrees

Bake:
45 to 50 minutes

Yield:
8 to 12 servings

3	*eggs, lightly beaten*
1	*(8-ounce) can almond paste*
3/4	*cup granulated sugar*
1/2	*cup unsalted butter, room temperature*
1/4	*cup all-purpose flour*
	Powdered sugar

SAUCE:

4	*cups fresh raspberries*
1	*cup powdered sugar*
3 to 4	*tablespoons freshly-squeezed lemon juice*

Preheat oven to 350 degrees.

Grease and flour one 8-inch round cake pan.

In a large mixing bowl, beat 1 egg, almond paste and sugar. Beat in remaining eggs. Add butter and beat until creamed. Stir in flour until blended. Pour into prepared pan.

Bake at 350 degrees for 45 to 50 minutes or until a knife inserted into the center comes out clean.

When cooled, invert onto a platter and sift powdered sugar over the top.

SAUCE:

In a food processor or blender, purée fresh raspberries, sugar and lemon juice. Press gently through a sieve with the back of a wooden spoon to remove seeds. Slice cake and serve on a pool of raspberry sauce.

FESTIVE CRANBERRY TORTE

For the final course of your holiday feast, serve this delicious torte.

Freeze:
Overnight

Yield:
8 to 10 servings

Notes:
Decorate with holly leaves and cranberries.

CRUST:

- 1 *cup vanilla wafer cookies, crushed*
- 1/3 *cup walnuts, chopped*
- 3 *tablespoons granulated sugar*
- 1/4 *cup butter (1/2 cube), melted*

FILLING:

- 1 1/2 *cups fresh cranberries, finely chopped*
- 1 *cup granulated sugar*
- 2 *egg whites, unbeaten, room temperature*
- 1 *tablespoon freshly-squeezed orange juice*
- 1 *teaspoon vanilla extract*
- 1 *cup whipping cream*
- *Additional whipped cream, for garnish*
- *Additional cranberries, for garnish*

CRUST:

In a medium mixing bowl, combine crust ingredients and blend well. Press into bottom of a 9-inch springform pan and chill.

FILLING:

In a large bowl of an electric mixer, combine cranberries and sugar. Let stand 5 minutes. Add egg whites, orange juice and vanilla. Beat on slow speed until frothy, then at high speed 8 to 10 minutes until stiff peaks form.

In a separate bowl, beat whipping cream until soft peaks form. Fold whipped cream into cranberry mixture.

Pour into prepared crust and seal with plastic wrap. Freeze until firm, preferably overnight.

Serve with whipped cream and cranberries.

DOUBLE CHOCOLATE FUDGE

Extremely easy with luscious results!

Chill:
Several hours

Yield:
5 pounds fudge

- 4 *cups granulated sugar*
- 1 *(12-ounce) can evaporated milk*
- 8 *ounces semi-sweet chocolate*
- 8 *ounces unsweetened chocolate*
- 7 *ounces marshmallow cream*
- 3/4 *cup butter (1 1/2 cubes), room temperature*
- 2 *teaspoons vanilla extract*
- 2 *cups nuts, chopped (optional)*

In a heavy saucepan over medium heat, combine sugar and milk. Bring to a boil for 6 minutes, stirring occasionally.

Remove from heat and add chocolates, marshmallow cream, butter, vanilla and nuts.

Stir until all ingredients are well mixed.

Pour into a greased 9 x 13-inch pan and refrigerate until firm. Cut into squares.

TOFFEE SURPRISE

A quick and easy treat for kids who deserve a surprise!

Temperature:
Preheat 400 degrees

Bake:
6 minutes

Yield:
2 to 3 dozen pieces

Notes:
Substitute sliced almonds for walnuts.

- 35 *single saltine crackers*
- *Vegetable oil spray*
- 1 *cup butter*
- 1 *cup sugar*
- 1 *16-ounce package chocolate chips*
- 1 *cup ground walnuts*

Preheat oven to 400 degrees.

Line a jellyroll pan or cookie sheet with aluminum foil placed shine-side down. Spray with vegetable oil. Place crackers on pan in a single layer, sides touching.

Combine butter and sugar in a small saucepan. Bring to a rolling boil, stirring frequently, and boil for 2 to 3 minutes, until mixture is thick and fluffy. Pour over crackers.

Bake at 400 degrees for 6 minutes. Remove from oven and cool 1 minute.

Sprinkle chocolate chips on top and let melt a few minutes, then spread. Sprinkle top with nuts. Chill. To serve, break into irregular pieces.

SNACK ATTACK CHOCOLATE CAKE

TEMPERATURE:
Preheat 400 degrees

BAKE:
25 minutes

YIELD:
16 to 20 servings

NOTES:
Substitute whipped cream for frosting for a lighter dessert. For a layer cake, use two 9-inch round cake pans.

2 cups all-purpose flour
2 cups granulated sugar
1 cup butter (2 cubes)
4 tablespoons cocoa
1 cup water
1/2 cup buttermilk
2 eggs, slightly beaten
1 teaspoon baking soda
1 teaspoon vanilla extract

FROSTING:

1/2 cup butter (1 cube)
4 tablespoons cocoa
5 tablespoons buttermilk
4 cups (1 box) powdered sugar, sifted
1 teaspoon vanilla extract
1 cup walnuts, chopped

Preheat oven to 400 degrees. Grease a 9 x 13-inch pan.

Sift together flour and sugar. Set aside.

In a saucepan over high heat, bring butter, cocoa and water to boil, then pour over sugar and flour mixture. Mix well.

Add buttermilk, eggs, baking soda and vanilla to flour mixture and mix well.

Pour into prepared pan.

Bake 25 minutes at 400 degrees or until toothpick inserted in center of cake comes out clean.

FROSTING:

In a saucepan over high heat, bring butter, cocoa and buttermilk to boil. Remove from heat. Add sugar, vanilla, and walnuts and beat with a wire whisk until well blended. While frosting is still warm, spread on cooled cake.

CLASSIC CHOCOLATE FUDGE CAKE

TEMPERATURE:
Preheat 350 degrees

BAKE:
30 to 35 minutes

YIELD:
8 servings

- 3 *squares baking chocolate, unsweetened*
- 1/2 *cup butter (1 cube), room temperature*
- 2 1/4 *cups brown sugar, firmly packed*
- 3 *eggs*
- 2 *teaspoons vanilla extract*
- 2 1/4 *cups cake flour, sifted*
- 2 *teaspoons baking soda*
- 1/2 *teaspoon salt*
- 1 *cup sour cream*
- 1 *cup boiling water*

CHOCOLATE FUDGE FROSTING:

- 4 *squares unsweetened baking chocolate*
- 1/2 *cup butter (1 cube)*
- 1 *pound powdered sugar*
- 1/2 *cup milk*
- 2 *teaspoons vanilla*

Preheat oven to 350 degrees.

In a metal bowl over hot (but not boiling) water, slowly melt chocolate, stirring gently. Cool.

Grease two 9-inch round layer cake pans and line with waxed paper.

In a large mixing bowl, cream butter; add sugar and eggs. Beat at high speed for five minutes until light and fluffy. Be sure to scrape bottom and sides of pan to mix thoroughly. Beat in vanilla and cooled chocolate.

Sift together flour, baking soda and salt. Mix into creamed mixture alternating with sour cream, beginning and ending with dry ingredients. When thoroughly blended, stir in boiling water. Batter will be thin.

Pour immediately into prepared pans. Bake for 30 to 35 minutes or until cake tests done. Cool in pans 15 minutes. Finish cooling on wire racks.

FROSTING:

In a small saucepan over low heat, combine chocolate and butter. Slowly melt, stirring gently. In a medium bowl, combine sugar, milk, and vanilla and beat until smooth. Add chocolate/butter mixture. Set pan in bowl of ice. Beat until thick. Spread one layer, top with second cake layer and spread frosting evenly over entire cake.

CHOCOLATE MERINGUE TORTE

TEMPERATURE:
Preheat 275 degrees

BAKE:
45 minutes

FREEZE:
6 hours

YIELD:
8 to 10 servings

NOTES:
In the spring, garnish with fresh strawberries or raspberries.

4	*large egg whites*
3/4	*teaspoon cream of tartar*
1	*cup granulated sugar*
1	*cup pecans, chopped*
2	*cups whipping cream*
1	*cup chocolate syrup*
1 1/2	*teaspoons vanilla extract*
	Chocolate shavings
	Pecan halves
	Strawberries

Preheat oven to 275 degrees.

In a large mixing bowl, beat egg whites until foamy. Add cream of tartar and beat until soft peaks form. Gradually add sugar, a little at a time, and continue beating until very stiff peaks form. Fold in pecans.

Cover 2 baking sheets with brown paper. Draw an 8 to 10-inch circle on each paper. Divide and spread meringue over each circle, shaping into flat shells.

Bake for 45 minutes. Turn off oven. Do not remove meringues for another 45 minutes. DO NOT OPEN DOOR. Remove and cool. (Meringues may even be left in oven overnight.)

TO ASSEMBLE:

In a medium mixing bowl, beat cream until very stiff. Fold in chocolate syrup and vanilla.

Spread meringue layer with half of chocolate cream. Add second meringue and cover top with remaining cream. Decorate with chocolate shavings and pecan halves. Freeze at least 6 hours. Remove from freezer 10 minutes before serving.

CHOCOLATE VELVET

A cake for a very special occasion.

Chill:
8 hours or overnight

Yield:
12 servings

Notes:
Garnish with chocolate leaves and a single fresh flower, such as a camellia or a rose, or garnish with small flowers, such as pansies and violets. A ribbon may be tied around the ladyfinger sides, using red or gold for Christmas or pastel colors for spring.

- *24 ladyfinger cakes, split*
- *1 pound semi-sweet chocolate*
- *3 eggs, separated*
- *1 tablespoon kirsch*
- *1 tablespoon rum*
- *1 tablespoon creme de cacao*
- *1 1/2 teaspoons instant coffee powder (optional)*
- *3 tablespoons butter, melted*
- *3 tablespoons powdered sugar*
- *1 cup whipping cream*

Split the ladyfingers in half and line the bottom and sides of a 9-inch springform pan with them, reserving enough to cover the top.

In the top of a double boiler over simmering water, melt 12 ounces of semi-sweet chocolate. Remove from heat and add 3 egg yolks and kirsch, rum, creme de cacao and coffee powder. Beat until smooth. Stir in melted butter.

In a small bowl, beat 3 egg whites until foamy. Add powdered sugar and beat until stiff peaks form. Carefully fold into chocolate mixture.

In a separate bowl, whip cream until soft peaks form and carefully fold into chocolate mixture. Pour into prepared pan, smooth top, and cover with reserved ladyfingers. Cover and chill 8 hours or overnight.

Several hours before serving, remove cake from refrigerator. In the top of a double boiler over simmering water, melt remaining 4 ounces chocolate and stir in 6 to 7 tablespoons hot water. Pour over top of cake and chill until firm. Before serving, run a knife around edge of pan and release springform pan sides.

Remove cake to a serving platter.

FROZEN CHOCOLATE MOUSSE TORTE

VERY REFRESHING AND SATISFYING.

TEMPERATURE:
Preheat 375 degrees

BAKE:
15 minutes

CHILL OR FREEZE:
Overnight

YIELD:
10 servings

1 (8-ounce) can almond paste
1 tablespoon cocoa
5 eggs, divided
6 ounces semi-sweet chocolate, melted
2 teaspoons instant coffee powder, dissolved in 1 teaspoon hot water
1 tablespoon brandy
2 tablespoons granulated sugar
1/2 cup whipping cream
Semi-sweet chocolate curls or whipped cream for garnish

Preheat oven to 375 degrees.

Grease and flour a 9-inch springform pan.

In a food processor with a metal blade, crumble almond paste. Add cocoa and 2 of the eggs and blend until smooth. Pour into prepared pan and bake at 375 degrees for 15 minutes.

Cool on a wire rack.

In a small metal bowl placed over very hot, but not boiling water, melt chocolate, stirring gently.

Separate 2 of the remaining eggs. In a large bowl, beat the 2 egg yolks with remaining whole egg. Beat in dissolved coffee, brandy and melted chocolate.

In a separate mixing bowl, beat 2 egg whites until foamy. Gradually add sugar until moist, stiff peaks form.

Fold egg whites into chocolate mixture.

In another bowl, whip cream. Fold into chocolate mixture. Spread evenly over cooled cake.

Freeze overnight.

Thaw 10 minutes before serving. Garnish with chocolate curls and/or whipped cream.

WHITE CHOCOLATE MOUSSE PIE

YIELD:
8 servings

CRUST:

- 2 *cups chocolate wafers, crushed*
- 1 *tablespoon granulated sugar*
- 1/2 *cup butter (1 cube), melted*

FILLING:

- 12 *ounces white chocolate baking bars*
- 1/4 *cup milk*
- 1 *teaspoon vanilla extract*
- 3 *egg whites*
- 1/4 *teaspoon salt*
- 2 *cups whipping cream*
- *Granulated sugar for whipping cream (optional)*

In a medium bowl, combine wafers, sugar and butter. Mix thoroughly. Press into bottom of 10-inch springform pan. Chill while making filling.

In a metal mixing bowl over hot (not boiling) water, combine white chocolate and milk. Stir until chocolate is melted and smooth. Whisk in vanilla. Transfer to a large bowl and set aside 15 minutes.

In a medium bowl, beat egg whites and salt. Beat until stiff peaks form. Gently fold egg whites into chocolate mixture.

In a medium bowl, whip cream with dash of sugar until stiff peaks form. Gently fold half the cream into the chocolate mixture. Spread mixture into crust shell. Decorate top of pie with remaining cream.

CHOCOLATE CHIP-LOVERS' PIE

TEMPERATURE:
Preheat 350 degrees

BAKE:
35 to 40 minutes

YIELD:
8 servings

- *1 cup butter (2 cubes), room temperature*
- *1 cup granulated sugar*
- *1 teaspoon vanilla extract*
- *2 eggs*
- *1/2 cup all-purpose flour*
- *6 ounces chocolate chips*
- *3/4 cup pecans, chopped*
- *1/2 cup flaked coconut*
- *1 unbaked, 9-inch pie shell*
- *Whipped cream or ice cream for garnish*

Preheat oven to 350 degrees.

In a medium mixing bowl, cream butter and sugar. Add vanilla. Add eggs and beat well. Stir in flour.

Gradually stir in chocolate chips, pecans and coconut. Pour mixture into pastry shell.

Bake at 350 degrees for 35 to 40 minutes. Top will be a deep golden color while center may still be soft.

KIDS' ICE CREAM

KIDS ARE THE SECRET INGREDIENT.

YIELD:
6 servings and lots of fun!

- 1 *3-pound empty coffee can with plastic lid*
- 1 *1-pound empty coffee can with plastic lid*
- 1 *cup whipping cream*
- 1 *cup whole milk*
- 3/4 *cup granulated sugar*
- 1 1/2 *teaspoons vanilla extract*
- *Ice cubes*
- 3/4 *cup rock salt*

In a medium bowl, combine cream, milk, sugar, vanilla and mix well. Put mixture into a small 1-pound coffee can and close with the plastic lid.

Place ice cubes and rock salt in large 3-pound coffee can. Put small can holding the cream mixture inside the large can with rock salt and ice. Close the lid.

Have two kids sit on the floor opposite each other and roll the can back and forth for 20 minutes.

If more than two kids want to join in, have them sit in a circle and roll the can around in a circle from one child to the next.

Ice cream should be ready to eat after 20 minutes of rolling.

CHILLY CAPPUCCINO

SO EASY, SO DELICIOUS!

CHILL:
Several hours

YIELD:
4 to 6 servings

- 1 *pint coffee ice cream, room temperature*
- 1 *pint chocolate fudge ice cream, room temperature*
- 1/3 *cup brandy*
- 1/4 *cup milk*

In a blender or food processor fitted with a metal blade, combine all ingredients and mix until well blended. Pour into parfait or wine glasses. Freeze until firm. Serve with a dollop of whipped cream.

MOCHA-CHOCOLATE CHIP CHEESECAKE

TEMPERATURE:
Preheat 200 degrees

BAKE:
2 hours

CHILL:
12 hours or overnight

YIELD:
8 generous slices

NOTES:
Cake will appear soft after baking is completed.

CRUST:

- *1 1/2 cups chocolate wafer crumbs*
- *4 tablespoons butter, melted*
- *1/3 cup granulated sugar*

FILLING:

- *3 (8-ounce) packages cream cheese, room temperature*
- *1 cup granulated sugar*
- *4 eggs, room temperature*
- *1/3 cup whipping cream*
- *1 tablespoon instant coffee*
- *1 teaspoon vanilla extract*
- *1 cup miniature chocolate chips*

Preheat oven to 200 degrees. Position rack in center of oven.

CRUST:

Butter sides and bottom of a 9-inch springform pan. In a medium bowl, combine chocolate wafer crumbs, butter and sugar. Pat evenly onto bottom and sides of prepared pan. Chill crust while making filling.

FILLING:

In a large mixing bowl, beat cream cheese until fluffy. Beat in sugar gradually. Add eggs one at a time, beating well after each addition.

Add whipping cream, coffee and vanilla and beat until coffee is dissolved and mixture is well blended, about 3 minutes.

Turn mixture into prepared crust. Top with chocolate chips and swirl through with spatula.

Set pan on baking sheet. Bake 2 hours or until toothpick inserted in center of cake comes out clean. Cool completely, then refrigerate 12 hours or overnight.

Garnish with whipped cream and chocolate-covered espresso beans.

WALNUT-PUMPKIN CHEESECAKE

This rich dessert makes a terrific alternative to pumpkin pie.

Temperature: Preheat 325 degrees

Bake: 1 1/2 hours

Yield: 8 large slices or 16 small slices

Chill: Several hours

CRUST:

- 1 cup graham cracker crumbs
- 2 tablespoons granulated sugar
- 4 tablespoons butter (1/2 cube), melted

FILLING:

- 2 (8-ounce) packages cream cheese, room temperature
- 1/2 cup granulated sugar
- 1/2 cup brown sugar, firmly packed
- 4 eggs
- 1/3 cup whipping cream
- 1 cup plus 3 tablespoons canned pumpkin
- 1/2 teaspoon cinnamon
- Pinch of nutmeg
- Pinch of cloves

TOPPING:

- 1/3 cup brown sugar, firmly packed
- 1/2 cup walnuts, chopped
- 1 tablespoon butter, room temperature
- Whipped cream

Position one rack in center of oven, with a second rack placed on lowest oven rack setting. Preheat oven to 325 degrees. Grease bottom of 9-inch springform pan. Set aside.

CRUST:

In a small bowl, combine graham cracker crumbs, sugar and butter until well-blended. Press into bottom of springform pan and refrigerate.

FILLING:

In a large mixing bowl on high speed, cream together cream cheese, sugar and brown sugar. Add eggs one at a time, mixing thoroughly after each addition. Add whipping cream and beat for 3 minutes.

Add pumpkin, cinnamon and clove. Beat for 1 minute. Pour into prepared springform pan.

Place a jelly roll pan on the bottom rack of oven and fill with 1/2-inch of water. Bake cheesecake on the center rack for 1 1/2 hours or until knife inserted comes out clean.

TOPPING:

In small bowl, combine brown sugar, walnuts and butter until crumbly.

When cheesecake is done, turn oven off, sprinkle topping on and return to oven. Remove cheesecake after 1/2 hour. Refrigerate until well chilled. Garnish with whipped cream.

COMPANY CHEESECAKE

TEMPERATURE:
Preheat 500 degrees/250 degrees

BAKE:
15 minutes/1 hour and 30 minutes

YIELD:
12 generous slices

NOTES:
This is delicious when topped with BLUEBERRY SAUCE, page 257.

CRUST:

- *1 cup graham cracker crumbs*
- *2 1/4 cups granulated sugar, divided*
- *1/4 cup butter (1/2 cube), melted*

FILLING:

- *5 (8-ounce) packages cream cheese*
- *1/4 cup all-purpose flour*
- *1/4 teaspoon salt*
- *6 eggs*
- *1 teaspoon freshly-squeezed lemon juice*
- *1/2 cup whipping cream*

Preheat oven to 500 degrees. Grease sides and bottom of 9-inch springform pan.

CRUST:

In a medium bowl, combine crumbs with 1/4 cup sugar and butter. Press crumb mixture into bottom of pan. Chill crust while making filling.

FILLING:

In a large mixing bowl, beat cream cheese until fluffy.

Mix 2 cups sugar with flour and salt. Slowly add to cheese mixture. Add eggs one at a time, mixing thoroughly after each addition.

Beat in lemon juice and whipping cream until smooth.

Bake 15 minutes at 500 degrees.

Reduce heat to 250 degrees and continue baking for 1 hour and 30 minutes.

Cool before removing from pan.

PEANUT BUTTER PANACHE

Old partners, chocolate and peanut butter, meet up for this distinctive, chilled dessert.

Chill:
2 hours

Yield:
8 servings

CRUST:

- 3/4 *cup peanuts, finely chopped*
- 1 *cup graham cracker crumbs*
- 1/4 *cup granulated sugar*
- 1/3 *cup butter, melted*

CHOCOLATE FILLING:

- 1/2 *cup butter (1 cube), room temperature*
- 3/4 *cup powdered sugar*
- 1 *egg, room temperature*
- 1/2 *cup semi-sweet chocolate, melted*
- 1 *teaspoon vanilla extract*

PEANUT BUTTER FILLING:

- 1 *(8-ounce) package cream cheese, room temperature*
- 1/2 *cup creamy peanut butter*
- 2 *tablespoons sugar*
- 1/4 *cup butter (1/2 cube), room temperature*
- 1/2 *cup whipping cream*
- 1 *tablespoon vanilla extract*

CHOCOLATE GLAZE:

- 2 *cups (12 ounces) semi-sweet chocolate, coarsely chopped*
- 1 *cup whipping cream*
- 1/2 *cup peanuts, coarsely chopped*

CRUST:

Grease sides and bottom of a 9-inch springform pan. In a medium bowl, combine peanuts, crumbs, sugar and butter and mix well. Press crumb mixture into bottom of prepared pan. Chill while making filling.

CHOCOLATE FILLING:

In a medium mixing bowl, cream butter and powdered sugar together until fluffy. Add egg and beat until well blended. Add semi-sweet chocolate and vanilla and mix well. Spread chocolate mixture over crust. Chill while preparing peanut butter filling.

PEANUT BUTTER FILLING:

In a medium mixing bowl, beat together cream cheese, peanut butter, sugar and butter until fluffy. In a separate bowl, beat whipping cream and vanilla until stiff peaks form. Fold into peanut butter mixture. Chill while preparing chocolate glaze.

CHOCOLATE GLAZE:

Place chocolate in a medium bowl.

In a small saucepan over medium-high heat, pour cream. Heat until almost boiling. Pour over chocolate and let stand 2 to 3 minutes. Mix chocolate and cream together and pour over peanut butter filling. Sprinkle chopped peanuts on top. Chill for 2 hours.

CHERRY-BERRY COMPOTE

A perfect picnic-basket take-along for a summer concert.

Chill:
Several hours

Yield:
6 to 8 servings

- 1/2 *cup granulated sugar*
- 1/4 *cup water*
- 2 *tablespoons raspberry liqueur*
- 2 *tablespoons kirsch*
- 2 *cups each red raspberries, strawberries, and dark sweet cherries, pitted*
- *Mint leaves*

In a saucepan over high heat, combine sugar and water and bring to a boil. Remove from heat and add liqueurs. Chill.

Place fruit in a medium bowl. Pour chilled syrup over the fruit and refrigerate 1 to 2 hours before serving.

Serve in chilled dessert bowls or goblets with a sprig of fresh mint.

RASPBERRIES WITH ALMOND CREAM

Refreshing on a summer night.

Chill: 6 hours

Yield: 4 servings

Notes: Substitute blueberries or blackberries for raspberries.

- *1 (3-ounce) package cream cheese, room temperature*
- *1/2 cup powdered sugar*
- *2 tablespoons almond-flavored liqueur*
- *1 cup whipping cream*
- *2 cups fresh raspberries*
- *Almonds, toasted for garnish*

In a large mixing bowl on high speed, beat cream cheese, sugar and liqueur until smooth. While beating, slowly pour in cream. Mixture should be stiff consistency at all times. Do not add too much whipping cream at one time; keep beating until completely incorporated.

Cover and refrigerate up to 6 hours. Line the bottom of each of 4 dessert bowls with 1/2 cup of raspberries. Mound almond cream over each. Top with remaining berries and garnish with whole almonds.

EDWARDIAN CREAM

An English recipe, delicious and truly decadent.

Chill: 2 to 3 hours

Yield: 6 servings

- *1 cup unsalted butter (2 cubes), room temperature*
- *1 (8-ounce) package cream cheese, room temperature*
- *1 1/2 tablespoons granulated sugar*
- *2 1/2 teaspoons freshly-squeezed lemon juice*
- *2 teaspoons vanilla*
- *10 ounces fresh fruit purée such as strawberry, peach or blended fruits*

In a large bowl, whip all ingredients, except fruit purée, until light and fluffy. Divide the mixture into 6 dessert cups or glasses. Chill 2 to 3 hours.

Pass fruit purée through a sieve to remove seeds.

Before serving, spoon purée over the chilled cream.

STRAWBERRY PIZZA

TEMPERATURE:
Preheat 325 degrees

BAKE:
15 minutes

YIELD:
10 servings

NOTES:
For fruit variations, arrange sliced kiwi with strawberries and drizzle on melted chocolate, or white chocolate. Or, top with peach jam and sliced peach rounds. Recipe may be made ahead and refrigerated.

CRUST:

1	*cup all-purpose flour*
1/4	*cup powdered sugar*
1/2	*cup butter (1 cube)*

FILLING:

1	*(8-ounce) package cream cheese, room temperature*
1/2	*teaspoon vanilla extract*
1/2	*cup granulated sugar*
1/4	*teaspoon freshly-squeezed lemon juice*

TOPPING:

1	*cup fresh strawberries, mashed*
4	*tablespoons granulated sugar*
1	*tablespoon cornstarch*
8 to 10	*strawberries, sliced*

CRUST:

In a medium bowl, combine flour, sugar and butter. Form into a ball with hands and press into a 14-inch ungreased pizza pan.

Bake at 325 degrees for 15 minutes. Cool.

FILLING:

In a medium bowl, combine cream cheese, vanilla, sugar and lemon juice. Spread on cooled crust.

TOPPING:

In a saucepan over medium heat, combine strawberries, sugar and cornstarch. Simmer until thick and glossy. Cool. Spread on top of cheese filling.

Cut fresh strawberries crosswise to make rounds that resemble pepperoni; place on pizza and serve.

RASPBERRY-RHUBARB PIE

- 2 *9-inch pie crusts (See note.)*
- 1 1/3 *cups granulated sugar*
- 3 *tablespoons cornstarch*
- 1/2 *teaspoon grated orange peel*
- 2 *cups fresh rhubarb, cut into 1/2-inch pieces*
- 2 *cups fresh or frozen raspberries (if using frozen berries, do not thaw)*
- 2 *tablespoons butter*
- 1 *tablespoon granulated sugar*

Preheat oven to 425 degrees.

In a small bowl, combine sugar, cornstarch and orange peel. Set aside.

In a separate bowl, combine rhubarb and raspberries. Place half the fruit in an unbaked, pastry-lined pie pan and sprinkle with half the sugar mixture.

Repeat with remaining fruit and sugar and dot with butter.

Cover with top crust, seal and flute edges. Cut slits in top crust and sprinkle with sugar. Cover edge with strips of aluminum foil to prevent over-browning.

Bake pie at 425 degrees, for 30 minutes. Remove aluminum foil and bake about 15 minutes longer or until crust is brown and juice bubbles through slits in crust.

A TRADITIONAL PIE, WITH THE ADDED FLAVOR OF GRATED ORANGE PEEL.

TEMPERATURE:
Preheat 425 degrees

BAKE:
45 minutes

YIELD:
8 servings

NOTES:
Use our BASIC PIE CRUST, this page.

BASIC PIE CRUST

- 2 *cups all-purpose flour*
- 3/4 *cup shortening*
- 4 *tablespoons water*

In a medium mixing bowl, cut shortening into flour. Add 4 tablespoons water. Work into dough.

Quickly form into a ball, but do not work with dough too long. Divide dough into 2 equal balls.

Roll out each ball of dough between 2 pieces of plastic wrap to fit a 9-inch pie plate.

FLAKY AND DELICIOUS – YOU CAN'T MISS WITH THIS ONE.

YIELD:
2 9-inch pie crusts

NOTES:
Use for any of your pastry needs and bake as your recipe directs.

GALA STRAWBERRY PIE

STRAWBERRY SEASON TAKES ON A WONDERFUL NEW MEANING WITH THIS DESSERT!

CHILL:
3 to 4 hours

YIELD:
8 servings

- *1 10-inch baked pie shell*
- *1 cup whipping cream*
- *1 (8-ounce) package cream cheese, room temperature*
- *1 1/2 cups granulated sugar, divided*
- *1 teaspoon vanilla extract*
- *3 tablespoons cornstarch*
- *1/2 cup water*
- *1 cup fresh strawberries, mashed*
- *4 cups whole strawberries for garnish*

In a small mixing bowl, whip cream. Set aside. In a medium bowl, beat cream cheese, 1/2 cup sugar, and vanilla. Fold in whipped cream and beat lightly by hand. Spoon into baked pie shell.

In a medium saucepan, combine remaining 1 cup sugar and cornstarch. Mix in water and mashed berries. Over high heat, bring to a boil, stirring constantly until mixture begins to thicken, about 1 minute. Let cool.

Arrange whole berries on top of cheese mixture, then spoon on berry topping.

Refrigerate 3 to 4 hours. Garnish with additional strawberries.

FRESH OREGON BLUEBERRY PIE

- 1 *9-inch pie shell, baked and cooled (See note.)*
- 1 *cup water*
- 2/3 *cup granulated sugar*
- 1 *tablespoon freshly-squeezed lemon juice*
- 4 *cups fresh or frozen blueberries (if frozen, do not thaw), divided*
- 3 *tablespoons cornstarch*
- 3 *tablespoons water*

TOPPING:

- 1 1/2 *cups sour cream*
- 1/2 *teaspoon vanilla extract*
- 2 *tablespoons granulated sugar*

Preheat oven to 250 degrees.

In a saucepan over medium heat, combine 1 cup water, sugar and lemon juice. Add 1 cup blueberries. Bring to a boil.

In a small bowl, combine cornstarch with the 3 tablespoons water and stir until well dissolved. Stir into saucepan and cook over medium heat, stirring frequently, until mixture thickens. Add remaining blueberries and cook until just warm.

Pour mixture into pie shell.

TOPPING:

In a small bowl, combine sour cream, vanilla and sugar. Pour over top of berries, spreading evenly and covering completely. Be careful not to swirl into berry mixture.

Bake at 250 degrees for 15 minutes. Cool, then chill for 2 to 4 hours.

A LIGHT AND FRESH SUMMER DESSERT.

CHILL:
2 to 4 hours

TEMPERATURE:
Preheat 250 degrees

BAKE:
15 minutes

YIELD:
8 to 10 servings

NOTES:
Use our BASIC PIE CRUST, page 246.

MARIONBERRY PIE

Marionberries are indigenous to Oregon's Willamette Valley. If unavailable, try mixing boysenberries and blackberries.

Temperature:
Preheat 425 degrees

Bake:
30 to 40 minutes

Yield:
8 servings

Notes:
Use our Basic Pie Crust, page 246. For a health-conscious alternative, substitute 3/4 to 1 cup fruit juice concentrate for sugar.

	Pastry for two 9-inch crusts (See note.)
3/4 to 1	*cup granulated sugar, depending on sweetness of berries (See note.)*
3	*tablespoons all-purpose flour*
	Dash of cinnamon
1/8	*teaspoon salt*
4 to 5	*cups fresh or frozen marionberries*
1	*tablespoon freshly-squeezed lemon juice*
2	*tablespoons butter*

Preheat oven to 425 degrees.

In a small bowl, combine sugar, flour, cinnamon and salt. Sprinkle half of this mixture over pastry-lined pan.

Add berries and sprinkle remainder of sugar mixture over berries. Sprinkle with lemon juice and dot with butter.

Cover with top crust; seal and flute edges. Sprinkle top with sugar.

Bake at 425 degrees for 30 to 40 minutes on lower shelf of oven.

APPLE-CINNAMON CUSTARD PIE

TEMPERATURE:
450 degrees/lower 350 degrees

BAKE:
10 minutes/35 minutes/15 minutes

YIELD:
8 to 10 servings

NOTES:
Paring and slicing apples directly into the cream mixture helps retard browning.

CRUST:

- 1¾ *cups all-purpose flour, sifted*
- ¼ *cup granulated sugar*
- 1 *teaspoon cinnamon*
- ⅔ *cup butter*
- ¼ *cup water*

FILLING:

- 1 *egg*
- 1½ *cups sour cream*
- 1 *cup granulated sugar*
- ¼ *cup all-purpose flour*
- 2 *teaspoons vanilla extract*
- ½ *teaspoon salt*
- 2½ *pounds Macintosh apples, pared, quartered, cored and sliced*

TOPPING:

- ½ *cup butter, room temperature*
- ½ *cup all-purpose flour*
- ⅓ *cup granulated sugar*
- ⅓ *cup brown sugar, firmly packed*
- 3 *teaspoons cinnamon*
- 1 *cup walnuts, coarsely chopped*

CRUST:

In a large bowl, combine flour, sugar and cinnamon. Cut in butter with a pastry blender until mixture has the consistency of coarse meal. Sprinkle in just enough water to moisten dough. May add additional water if necessary to form ball.

Preheat oven to 450 degrees.

Roll out dough on a lightly floured surface to a 12-inch diameter circle. Fit into a 10-inch pie plate. Fold under overhanging pastry flush with rim. Flute to make a stand-up edge. Chill until ready to fill.

FILLING:

In a large mixing bowl, beat egg slightly. Stir in sour cream, sugar, flour, vanilla and salt until mixture is smooth. Add sliced apples, stirring gently just to coat apples. Spoon filling into shell.

Bake at 450 degrees for 10 minutes, lower heat to 350 degrees and bake 35 minutes longer. While pie bakes, prepare topping.

TOPPING:

In a small bowl, combine butter, flour, sugar, brown sugar, cinnamon, and walnuts and blend well.

Remove pie from oven and sprinkle topping evenly over filling. Return to oven.

Bake for 15 minutes longer or until topping is lightly browned. Cool pie on wire rack.

SAUTÉED APPLES WITH RUM SAUCE

Letha served 1/94. Delicious.

A great dessert for fall and winter. Try this as the finale to a pork roast dinner.

Cook:
40 minutes

Chill:
Several hours

Yield:
8 servings

SAUCE:

- *6 egg yolks*
- *1 cup whipping cream*
- *1 cup milk*
- *1/2 cup granulated sugar*
- *3 tablespoons dark rum*
- *2 teaspoons vanilla extract*

APPLES:

- *3 tablespoons butter*
- *8 Golden Delicious apples, peeled and sliced*
- *3/4 cup raisins*
- *1/3 cup granulated sugar*
- *1 teaspoon lemon rind*
- *1/4 teaspoon cinnamon*
- *1/4 teaspoon nutmeg*

SAUCE:

In the top of a double boiler over simmering water, combine egg yolks, cream, milk and sugar. Cook, stirring frequently, until sauce thickens and coats spoon, about 30 minutes. Remove from heat, stir in rum and vanilla. Chill.

APPLES:

In a sauté pan over medium heat, melt butter. Add remaining ingredients except nutmeg and sauté over medium heat until apples are soft but not falling apart, about 10 minutes. Add nutmeg. Transfer to a bowl or individual dishes and serve warmed apples with chilled sauce.

GREEN APPLE TORTE

- 1 1/4 *cups zwieback crackers, crushed*
- 1 *cup plus 2 tablespoons granulated sugar, divided*
- 3 3/4 *teaspoons cinnamon, divided*
- 1/4 *cup (1/2 cube) plus 2 tablespoons butter, divided*
- 6 *cups Granny Smith apples (4 large), peeled and thinly sliced*
- 1 *pint sour cream*
- 7 *eggs, well beaten*
- 1 *teaspoon vanilla extract*

Temperature:
Preheat 325 degrees

Bake:
1 hour

Chill:
Several hours

Yield:
10 to 12 servings

Preheat oven to 325 degrees.

In a medium bowl, combine crumbs, 6 tablespoons sugar, 3/4 teaspoon cinnamon and 1/4 cup butter. Mix into fine crumbs. Set aside.

In a large sauté pan over medium heat, melt the remaining 2 tablespoons butter. Add apple slices and 2 tablespoons sugar. Cover pan and cook over medium heat until apples are just tender, about 10 to 15 minutes.

Meanwhile, generously butter the bottom and about 2 inches up the sides of a 9-inch springform pan. Cover bottom and sides of pan with about 2/3 of the crust mixture and press into bottom of prepared pan. Chill.

Add sour cream and eggs to hot apple mixture and stir over medium heat until just thickened, about 3 minutes. Add vanilla.

Pour apple mixture into crust-lined pan and sprinkle remaining crumb mixture over the top.

Bake at 325 degrees for 1 hour. Cool completely and remove pan sides. In a small bowl, mix remaining 2 tablespoons sugar and 3 teaspoons cinnamon together and dust over top of finished cake. Chill.

BLACKBERRY-APPLE CRUNCH

SERVE THIS WARM DESSERT WITH FROZEN VANILLA YOGURT.

TEMPERATURE:
Preheat 350 degrees

BAKE:
1 hour

YIELD:
12 to 15 servings

4 cups sliced tart apples, such as Granny Smiths
2 cups fresh or frozen blackberries (If using frozen berries, do not thaw)
3/4 cup granulated sugar

TOPPING:

1/2 to 3/4 cup brown sugar, firmly packed
3/4 cup all-purpose flour
3/4 cup rolled oats
1/2 cup walnuts, chopped
1/2 cup butter (1 cube)
1/2 teaspoon cinnamon or allspice

Preheat oven to 350 degrees.

In a large bowl, combine apples, berries and sugar. Place into a 9 x 13-inch pan.

In a large bowl, combine brown sugar, flour, oats, walnuts, butter and cinnamon and blend together. Sprinkle over top of fruit.

Bake at 350 degrees for approximately 1 hour, or until top is brown.

SUNDAE BEST

Showcase one of Oregon's finest products, hazelnuts!

Yield: *8 servings*

Chill or freeze: *2 to 4 hours or overnight*

Notes: *Hazelnuts are also known as filberts.*

CHOCOLATE COOKIE CRUMB CRUST:

- *1 1/4 cups chocolate wafers, crushed*
- *1/4 cup hazelnuts, finely chopped and lightly toasted (See note.)*
- *3 tablespoons granulated sugar*
- *6 tablespoons butter, melted*

SAUCE:

- *1 cup granulated sugar*
- *3/4 cup unsweetened cocoa, sifted*
- *1 teaspoon instant coffee powder*
- *1 cup whipping cream, divided*
- *1/4 cup butter, melted*

FILLING:

- *1 to 1 1/2 quarts vanilla ice cream, softened, divided*
- *1 quart mocha fudge ice cream, softened*
- *1/2 cup whipping cream, whipped*
- *Hazelnuts, toasted and coarsely chopped, for garnish*
- *Maraschino cherries with stems, rinsed and drained, for garnish*

CRUST:

In a medium bowl, combine crushed wafers, nuts and sugar. Add melted butter and mix thoroughly. Press evenly into bottom and sides of a 9-inch pie plate. Cover and chill 30 minutes.

SAUCE:

In a medium saucepan over medium heat, combine sugar, cocoa and instant coffee. Add 1/2 cup of whipping cream and blend to smooth paste. Add remaining cream and blend well.

Cook over medium heat, stirring constantly until sugar is completely dissolved. Add butter and cook until mixture is smooth and thickened, 5 to 8 minutes. Let it cool, but keep warm so it can be spread over ice cream.

FILLING:

Spread half of vanilla ice cream evenly over crust and freeze. Drizzle half of warm (not hot) sauce over top. Spread remaining vanilla ice cream over sauce. Return to freezer to firm.

Scoop balls of mocha fudge ice cream and arrange over vanilla layer. Drizzle with remaining sauce. Freeze until firm, 2 to 4 hours or overnight.

When ready to serve, spoon whipped cream into pastry bag fitted with star tip and pipe rosettes around scoops. Decorate with toasted hazelnuts and cherries. Serve immediately.

CHOCOLATE-RASPBERRY TRUFFLES

THE OVEN METHOD OF MELTING CHOCOLATE IS THE VERY BEST WE'VE FOUND! REMEMBER THIS METHOD FOR ALL OF YOUR FAVORITE CHOCOLATE RECIPES.

CHILL:
Several hours

YIELD:
80 truffles

NOTES:
As an alternative to cocoa, roll truffles in 3/4 cup powdered sugar or 3/4 cup chopped almonds. Do not double this recipe.

- 1 *pound good-quality, semi-sweet chocolate chips or Belgian chocolate, chopped into pieces*
- 1 *cup unsalted butter (2 cubes), room temperature*
- 4 *egg yolks*
- 1/2 *cup raspberry jam or jelly; must be seedless*
- 3/4 *cup powdered cocoa*

Preheat oven to 200 degrees.

In a heavy 4 x 6-inch enamel or ceramic ovenproof dish, heat chocolate in oven. Watch carefully and remove from oven just as soon as chocolate has softened, about 5 minutes.

With a wire whisk, immediately beat in butter and egg yolks. When chocolate mixture is smooth and well-mixed, add raspberry jam and stir until thoroughly combined.

Refrigerate for 2 hours or until slightly firm when you put a spoon in the middle of the chocolate. If it's too hard, it will be too difficult to work with.

Roll chocolate between the palms of your hands, into round balls about 1-inch in diameter, working quickly so chocolate does not become too warm. If necessary, roll on a cold surface. Be patient; do not rush the process. Roll truffles in powdered cocoa. Arrange on a rack. Store in an airtight container and keep in refrigerator.

Bring to room temperature to serve. Can be kept in refrigerator up to a week or frozen up to a month.

KAHLUA TRUFFLES

THESE EASY-TO-PREPARE NUGGETS WILL HAVE YOUR GUESTS EATING RIGHT OUT OF YOUR HANDS!

CHILL:
24 hours

YIELD:
Approximately 18 to 20 truffles

- 1 *cup vanilla wafers, finely crushed*
- 1/2 *cup powdered sugar*
- 3/4 *cup pecans, finely chopped*
- 1 *tablespoon instant coffee*
- 3 *tablespoons butter, melted*
- 1 1/2 *tablespoons light corn syrup*
- 1/4 *cup Kahlua*
- *Additional powdered sugar for coating truffles.*

In a medium bowl, combine all ingredients and mix well.

Roll into bite-size balls. Place in an airtight container. Chill for 24 hours.

Roll balls in powdered sugar and serve.

HOT FUDGE SAUCE

YIELD:
2 cups

- 1 *cup granulated sugar*
- 4 *tablespoons butter (1/2 cube)*
- *Dash of salt*
- 1 *(5-ounce) can evaporated milk*
- 1 1/2 *squares of unsweetened chocolate*
- 1 *teaspoon vanilla extract*
- 3 *tablespoons Grand Marnier (optional)*

In a saucepan over high heat, combine sugar, butter, salt and milk and bring to a boil, stirring constantly. Let sauce boil 3 minutes without stirring. Add chocolate and vanilla and Grand Marnier, if desired.

Stir until smooth. Serve at once over ice cream or sponge cake.

GRANDMOTHER'S LEMON CURD

This a favorite from NO REGRETS, an earlier Junior League of Portland cookbook.

Chill:
8 hours

Yield:
2 1/2 cups

Notes:
Use as a topping for Lemon Chiffon Cake, page 227, or as a cake filling, tart filling, or topping on gingerbread. Lighten the consistency by folding in 1 cup of whipped cream.

- 6 *eggs, slightly beaten*
- 2 *cups granulated sugar*
- 1/2 *cup butter (1 cube), cut into small pieces*
- *Rind of 2 lemons, finely grated*
- 3/4 *cup freshly-squeezed lemon juice*

In the top of a double boiler, whisk eggs, sugar, lemon rind and lemon juice until well-blended and slightly thickened. Add butter and stir over hot water until curd thickens, about 25 minutes, stirring frequently. Immediately transfer mixture to a bowl or individual glass jars.

Refrigerate until well chilled, about 8 hours. (Lemon curd keeps for weeks in the refrigerator.)

BLUEBERRY SAUCE

Excellent served over cheesecake.

Cook:
5 to 10 minutes

Yield:
1 cup

Notes:
Sauce may also be served warm on top of pancakes and waffles.

- 2 *cups blueberries (frozen or fresh)*
- 1/3 *cup water*
- 1/4 *cup granulated sugar*
- 1 *tablespoon cornstarch*
- 2 *teaspoons freshly-squeezed lemon juice*
- *Dash of cinnamon*

In a saucepan over medium heat, combine all ingredients and bring to a boil.

Cook 5 to 10 minutes while stirring constantly, or until berries burst and sauce has a rich blueberry color.

Serve hot, or cool the sauce and use as a topping on cheesecake.

Junior League Presidents

Sally Wolcott
1987-88

Chris Tomlinson
1988-89

Patty Brandt
1989-90

Carolee Kolve
1990-91

Corinne Gentner
1991-92

Beth Warner
1992-93

Committee Chairmen

Beth Warner
(Development Director)
1987-88

Corinne Gentner
1988-89

Anne Mangan
1989-90

Lynda Vulles Gebhardt
1990-91

Jane Fisher
1991-92

Holly Rodway
1992-93

Acknowledgements

The Junior League of Portland thanks its members, families and friends who have contributed to this cookbook. It is our sincere hope that no one has been inadvertently overlooked.

Contributors

Stacy Abena
Barbara Acee
Linda Adams
Peggy Alamano
Marla Albrigo
Judy Allen
Cathy Allen
Sue Alstadt
Suzy Andersen
Marti Anderson
Linda Andrews
Jayne Arnold
Darlene Atiyeh
Sydney Baer
Pam Baker
Sidney Bakkan
Lynne Bangsund
Katy Barman
Ann Barta
Judy Beah
Candi Beber
Ellen Belesiu
E. Susan Belknap
Dottie Belknap
Pat Bell
Margaret Benoit
Gwen Berg
Bobette Bird
Heather Black
Helen Bledsoe
Kathyellen Blovits
Ann Blume
Parke Blundon
Kristi Kvistad Blundon
Debbie Boone
Denise Bouhasin
Heather Boyd
Patty Brandt
Carol Bray
Kaki Brenneman
Sharon Brenner
Gretchen Brevig
Janet Brewer
Lorelei Bredle
Mary Brophy
Julie Brown
Mary Brown
Anne Brown
Wendy Brown
Sharley Bryce
Gayle Cable
Margaret Cameron
Katharine Campbell
Jean Carlson
Hugh Carpenter
Cindy Carrier
Ann Carter
Judy Carter
Jude Case
Mari Connolly
Jean Coon
Jaimie Coshow
Margot Cougill
Nancy Cranston
Dana Cress
Jan Crites
Liz Cronin
Helen Curtis
Cathy Cutrera
Cathy Darby
Megan Davis
Barbara Day
Teri Dehaan
Mary DeLaurenta
Frances Diack
Mari Lou Diamond
Raylene Dion
Carol Dixon
Marty Dixon
Susan Dodd
Brenda Doktor
Renee Dominguez
Dawn Doss
Donna Dougherty
Suzanne Dragon
Elizabeth Duffett
Donna Dunlap
Debbie Dutton
Terri Dwyer
Trink Easterday
Judie Eaton
Elsie Edge
Ann Edler
Kris Elliott
Denise Emmerling
Ann Engvall
Elizabeth Etter
Jan Everall
Rorie Ferguson
Janet Ferguson
Jane Fisher
Ruth Fisher
Lori Fletcher
Lori Flexer
Teresa Forni
Linda Frank
Cindi Fraser
Diane Fraser
Amy Frease
Marci Freed
Debbie Fucile
Kathy Graham Gadler
Erin Gamble
Martha Gazeley
Lynda Vulles Gebhardt
Rob, Paige & Blake Gebhardt
Susan Gehr
Carol Gentner
Corinne Gentner
Doug Gentner
Isabelle Gerhart
Kathleen Gianotti
Sharon Gilbert
Anne Goldsmith
Gail Gombos
Alix Goodman
Kathy Gradler
Helen Graeper
Gina Grandmaison
Dorothy Green
Eldon Green
Linda Greenman
Terri Griffiths
Tina Grim
Anne Grimwood
Judy Grodahl
Susan Guyton
Karen Haas
Melissa Haglund
Tammy Hald
Pamela Hallvik
Patsy Halverson
Judy Hamilton
Caren Hardin
Sara Harding
Mary Hartung
Susan Hartwell
Ginger Hausler
Sharon Hayes
Beverly Healy
Karen Henkhaus
Evelyn Henkhaus
Helen Herman
Jan Hill
Jan Hillyer
Kathy Hoffman-Grotting
Susan Holman
Sara Holman
Lisa Holzgang
Betsy Holzgraf
Chris Holzgraf
Ivone Howard
Erica Howe
Sharon Hudspeth
Jill Inskeep
Ann Irving
Becky Jackson
Gay Jacobsen
Helen Jessup
Louise Jones
Sharon Jones
Michele Kehoe
Ginger Kelley
Linda Kerl
Kris Kern
Judy Killen
Judy Klor
Cheryl Kofman
Carolee Kolve
Anna Kooning
Lori Kositch
Mike Kositch
Kristi Kuchs
Eunice Kvistad
Jon Kvistad
Madeline Kvistad
Mary Laird
Daria LaMashley
Wanda Lambert
Danielle Larson
Amy Laurick
Suzanne Lauridsen
Debbie Lawrence
Pam Lawrence
Mary Lou Laybourn
Connie Leiken
Kirsten Leonard
Joan Leonetti
Vicki Linnman
Carole Long
Susan Long
Sheila Loomis
Diane Lowe
Teri Lund
Noelle Lussier
Emily Luthauser
Kathleen Mackey
Maryann MacKinnon

Patricia Madden
Kathy Malet
Cyndy Maletis
Anne Mangan
Carol Mangan
Jennifer Mark
Amy Marks
Maggie Martin
Jane Mayhugh
Jeanne McAlpin
Merrill & Steve McCarthy
Anita McClain
Kathleen McCormick
Denise McDonald
Anne McDowell
Ruby McKernan
Alice McKillop
Janelle McLeod
Carolyn McMurchie
Armine Megurian
Marisa Megurian
Sue Menashe
Peggy Merchant
Laura Bergdoff Merrill
Marcie Merritt
Terry Mettler
Joe Meyer
Diane Meyers
Sally Miller
Leslie Milliken
Karen Mills
Kathy Moller
Becky Moore
Melanie Morris
Susan Moshofsky
Megan Muessle
Anne Munch
Mary Murphy
Suzanne Myhra
Nemyre Family
Darlene Nichols
Debi Nicholson
Keri Nicolaison
Susan Nicoletti
Deborah Novack
Linda O'Keefe
Sharon Odman
Carla Olson
Beverly Ormseth
Nancy Palmer
Paula Palmer
Marilyn Pamplin
Mary Parr
Sandy Patchin
Charmaine Peck
Germaine Peterson
Patricia Peterson
Leslie Petroff
Laurie Pickett
Sandy Pittenger
Carla Pope
Alex Powers
Debby Prentice
Marjorie Putman
Kristin Quinlan
Lee Ragen
Wendy Reddick
Cory Reese
Claudia Reid
Debby Rhoades
Julie Richard
Mary Roberts
Holly Rodway
Kathy Roos
Dru Rosenthal
Carol Roseta
Mary Ross
Michele Roussell

Adrienne Salomon
Kieley Santana
Ellen Sather
Joan Schaub
Susan Schaubel
Sarah Schaubel
Patricia Schleuning
Juliet Schlesser
Michelle Schmidt Leipzig
Deena Semler
Kathy Shea
Rebecca Shellan
Tish Shinn
Maureen Showalter
Cindy Simon
Pam Smith
Julie Sorenson
Cathie Sorenson
Rebecca Specht
Molly Spencer
Trayce Sprouse
Sally Stadum
Maria Stanley
Anne Stein
Midge Sterling
Sandy Stetson
Karen Stevenson
Debra Stickel
Heather, Tom & Madeline Stilley
Monique Stillgar
Christine Stillger
Janet Strader
Shauna Stroble
Ann Stussi
Gale Swanson
Carol Tager
Pam Tainer
Darla Tamasney
Lori Tarlow
Madeline Taylor
Cynthia Thayer
Margie Thies
Carol Thornburgh
Chris Tomlinson
Michelle Tonkin
Jaime Tonneson
Denise Treadaway
Lisa Tromley
Linda Turina
Priscilla Turner
Donna Tyner
Barbara Ueltschi
Debbie Underwood
Liza Van Horn
Leann Vigna
Shelley Voboril
Sandy Wagner
Nancy Walker
Patty Wathey
Jill Welsh
Judy Westapher
Stacie White
Marily Whiteley
Barbara Whiteley
Leal Whittlesey
Pam Wilcox
Laura Wiley
Theresa Willett
Susan Willis
Peggy Ann Wilson
Sally Wolcott
Kathy Wolfson
Sherri Woods
Jennifer Yoakum
Lynn Zimmerman-Lind
P Zoeller
Karlyn Zografos

COMMITTEE

Ann Albrich
Marla Albrigo
Suzy Andersen
Jayne Arnold
Katy Barman
Ellen Belesiu
Pat Bell
Gwen Berg
Nancy Blalock
Kristi Kvistad Blundon
Teresa Bridges
Mary Brophy
Kathy Campbell
Ann Carter
Liz Cronin
Jill DeGarmo
Mary Dernedde
Susan Dodd
Terri Dwyer
Bernardita Ellis
Rorie Ferguson
Lori Flexer
Susan Gehr
Kathleen Gianotti
Gail Gombos
Judy Grodahl
Melissa Haglund
Tammy Hald
Ginger Hausler
Karen Henkhaus
Susan Holman
Karen Hughes
Sara Hval
Gay Jacobsen
Janelle Jarman
Helen Jessup
Rosalie Karp
Cheryl Kofman
Lori Kositch
Michelle Leipzig
Sue Menashe
Marisa Megurian
Sally Miller
Diane Milleson
Karen Mills
Becky Moore
Melanie Morris
Debi Nicholson
Jane Noyes
Nancy Palmer
Marcy Patton
Laurie Pickett
Pamela Puderbaugh
Mary Ross
Doris Shantz
Becky Shellan
Midge Sterling
Debra Stickel
Ashley Talarico
Mary Ann Tawney
Madeline Taylor
Lisa Tromley
Shelley Voboril
Patty Wathey
Virginia Wheeler
Stacie White
Marily Whiteley
Peggy Ann Wilson
Patti Zika
Ann Zafiratos
Lynn Zimmerman-Lind

ABOUT THE ARTIST

Raised in Wyoming, Jennifer Winship Mark graduated from Colorado College in 1983. Mark is a naturalistic artist whose watercolor paintings emanate from her love and enthusiasm for gardens, forests and lush landscapes of the Pacific Northwest. Mark explains, "Painting a field in bloom is like freeze-framing a moment in time. My work exists simply as an affectionate letter transcribed to nature."

For more information on the artist, contact Gango Galleries (503) 222-3850. The Junior League of Portland thanks Jennifer Mark for donating her time and art to further the impact of this cookbook.

A

B

N

O

T

V

W

The Junior League of Portland, Oregon is the fourth oldest League in The Association of Junior Leagues International, Inc. and was the first League on the west coast. Mrs. Henry L. Corbett began our League in 1910 soon after moving to Portland from New York City where she was a member of the first Junior League. Mrs. Corbett foresaw the many problems arising from the rapidly growing Portland population and convinced her sewing group and other friends that together, as volunteers, they could meet some of the needs of their changing city. Thus began a long record of continued service provided to the community by the Junior League of Portland.

The purpose of the Junior League has not changed dramatically since the first group of women met with Mrs. Corbett in 1910. The League continues to identify projects where financial assistance, administration and volunteers are combined to address a specific community need. As each project is established and successfully implemented, the community can then assume the responsibility for continuation. The League continues to emphasize training for its members, through the Provisional course, membership meetings, community projects, workshops and conferences. The League continues to be an organization of women committed to promoting voluntarism and improving the community through the effective action and leadership of trained volunteers.

The Junior League of Portland reaches out to women of all races, religions and national origins, who demonstrate an interest in and commitment to voluntarism.

Order Form

Name

Address

City State Zip

( )

Phone

Please send_____copies

x $19.95 $_______

Shipping & Handling

($2.50) per book $_______

Total Enclosed $_______

make checks payable to:

Junior League of Portland, Oregon

Or Charge to:

☐ VISA ☐ MASTERCARD

Account No. Exp. Date

Signature of Cardholder

Phone Orders Welcome: (503) 297-1278

Send Order to:
Junior League of Portland
4838 S.W. Scholls Ferry Road
Portland, Oregon 97225-1690
(503) 297-1278

Proceeds from the sale of
From PORTLAND'S PALATE
will be returned to the community through
projects sponsored by the
Junior League of Portland, Oregon

Order Form

Name

Address

City State Zip

( )

Phone

Please send_____copies

x $19.95 $_______

Shipping & Handling

($2.50) per book $_______

Total Enclosed $_______

make checks payable to:

Junior League of Portland, Oregon

Or Charge to:

☐ VISA ☐ MASTERCARD

Account No. Exp. Date

Signature of Cardholder

Phone Orders Welcome: (503) 297-1278

Send Order to:
Junior League of Portland
4838 S.W. Scholls Ferry Road
Portland, Oregon 97225-1690
(503) 297-1278

Proceeds from the sale of
From PORTLAND'S PALATE
will be returned to the community through
projects sponsored by the
Junior League of Portland, Oregon